Mahsa Mohammadikaji

Simulation-based Planning of Machine Vision Inspection Systems with an Application to Laser Triangulation

Schriftenreihe Automatische Sichtprüfung und Bildverarbeitung
Band 17

Herausgeber: Prof. Dr.-Ing. habil. Jürgen Beyerer

Lehrstuhl für Interaktive Echtzeitsysteme
am Karlsruher Institut für Technologie

Fraunhofer-Institut für Optronik, Systemtechnik
und Bildauswertung IOSB

Simulation-based Planning of Machine Vision Inspection Systems with an Application to Laser Triangulation

by
Mahsa Mohammadikaji

KIT Scientific Publishing

Karlsruher Institut für Technologie
Lehrstuhl für Interaktive Echtzeitsysteme

Simulation-based Planning of Machine Vision Inspection Systems with an Application to Laser Triangulation

Zur Erlangung des akademischen Grades eines Doktor-Ingenieurs von der KIT-Fakultät für Informatik des Karlsruher Instituts für Technologie (KIT) genehmigte Dissertation

von M.Sc. Mahsa Mohammadikaji

Tag der mündlichen Prüfung: 19. Juli 2019
Erster Gutachter: Prof. Dr.-Ing. Jürgen Beyerer
Zweiter Gutachter: Prof. Dr.-Ing. Carsten Dachsbacher

Impressum

KIT Scientific Publishing

Karlsruher Institut für Technologie (KIT)
KIT Scientific Publishing
Straße am Forum 2
D-76131 Karlsruhe

www.ksp.kit.edu

Print on Demand 2020 – Gedruckt auf FSC-zertifiziertem Papier

ISSN 1866-5934
ISBN 978-3-7315-0989-9
DOI 10.5445/KSP/1000099225

Preface

The current thesis contains the results of my research as a PhD candidate at the Vision and Fusion laboratory (IES), at Karlsruhe Institute of Technology (KIT), from November 2014 to February 2019. This research was carried out in a close collaboration with the Mess-, Regelungs- und Diagnosesysteme (MRD) department at Fraunhofer Institute of Optronics, System Technologies, and Image Exploitation (IOSB), in Karlsruhe Germany. During this time, I had the honor of collaborations with many people, without whom I wouldn't be writing these lines now. Through these collaborations, not only did I learn numerous interesting topics, but I also learned a new language and opened another window to the world to myself.

First and foremost, I would like to express my deep gratitude to my advisor Prof. Dr.-Ing. Jürgen Beyerer, for the professional supervision, continuous support, his encouraging words, and his trust in me to accomplish this task. I wish to thank him for giving me the chance of working in his research group, and for always dedicating his time to support us despite of his busy schedule.

I am particularly grateful to Prof. Dr.-Ing. Carsten Dachsbacher, head of the computer graphics group at KIT, for the co-supervision of this research and his invaluable contributions throughout numerous meetings.

My deep appreciation goes to my colleague Stephan Bergmann, with whom I worked in close collaboration throughout my PhD time, and benefited greatly from his assistance, in particular regarding computer graphics concepts and tools. He has been very generous with his time, knowledge, and ideas, even when he was not officially working at KIT.

My special thanks are extended to Dr. Alexey Pak, and Professor Michael Heizmann for their valuable and constructive suggestions. Furthermore, I am sincerely grateful to Dr. Jan Burke, my group leader at MRD, who always valued scientific work and allowed me to have more time to work on my thesis, despite of multiple other projects which always needed to be done. I wish to thank my colleagues Mathias Ziebarth, Masoud Roschani, Sebastian Höfer, Christian Kühnert, Petra Gospodnetic, and again Alexey Pak, for proofreading this thesis and for their friendship and support all along. I also thank Zheng Li for his assistance regarding diffraction modeling.

I would also like to acknowledge the German Research Foundation (DFG) for financially supporting this project for 3 years. I further wish to thank my colleague Stephan Irgenfried for proposing the idea for founding this interesting project in the first place, and for his contributions to the work.

I extend my thanks further to Christian Frey, head of the MRD department, and Gaby Groß and Ingrid Mariany Alves da Silva, secretaries of IES and MRD, for their very kind assistance during this time.

I also sincerely thank Md Zahidul Huq, who worked as a dedicated student assistant at IES, and greatly helped me in the experimental works. I have also benefited from the optimization methods he developed for his master thesis. I also thank Max Piochowiak for implementation of the visualization software during his work as a student assistant at KIT.

Last but not least, I thank my husband Ali, for his generosity in his love and support, for accompanying me in every happy or hard moment of these over four years, and for encouraging me to put aside my fears and to be the one I wanted to be. I also thank my mother, my father, and my sister, who were sources of inspiration to me, even from thousands of kilometers away.

Karlsruhe, March 2019 *Mahsa Mohammadikaji*

Kurzfassung

Bildverarbeitende Inspektionssysteme spielen heute eine wichtige Rolle bei der Qualitätskontrolle industrieller Produkte. In der Entwurfsphase von Inspektionsaufbauten werden häufig die Anzahl der Messungen und deren geometrische und optische Konfigurationen empirisch von Experten ausgewählt. Dieser Ansatz von Versuch und Irrtum verursacht der Industrie nicht nur viel Zeit- und Personalkosten, sondern führt auch zu suboptimalen Lösungen für komplexe Oberflächen. Mit den sich ständig weiterentwickelnden Produktionslinien, die immer wieder neu konfiguriert werden müssen, und unter Berücksichtigung der hohen Prüfanforderungen, sind automatische Verfahren erforderlich, um das so genannte Inspektionsplanungsproblem zu lösen.

Um den Designraum eines Bildverarbeitungssystems zu erforschen, kann die Planung von realistisch simulierten Bildern profitieren. Darüber hinaus ist es erforderlich, geeignete Bewertungskennzahlen abzuleiten, um die Oberflächenmessung anhand der Toleranzen zu bewerten. Danach muss die Inspektionsplanung als ein Optimierungsproblem formuliert und automatisch gelöst werden. Diese Arbeit stellt einen simulationsbasierten Ansatz für die Inspektionsplanung vor, indem sie zu allen drei Teilkomponenten dieses Problems beiträgt, nämlich Simulation, Bewertung und Optimierung. Während die meisten diskutierten Konzepte und Methode vielen Sichtprüfsystemen gemeinsam sind, konzentriert sich diese Arbeit auf die Inspektion eines komplizierten Zylinderkopfes durch Lasertriangulation.

Auf der Simulationsseite wird in der Arbeit Anwendung verschiedener Rendering-Techniken diskutiert. Weiterhin wird ein realistischer Simulationsrahmen vorgeschlagen, der Ray-Tracing mit Fourier-Optik-Methoden zur Einbeziehung der Wellenoptikeffekten wie Laserspeckle, und dem EMVA-Standard 1288 zur Modellierung unter anderem der Sensorspektralempfindlichkeit kombiniert. Die simulierten Bilder zeigen eine hohe visuelle Ähnlichkeit mit den realen Bildern. Diese Arbeit bietet darüber hinaus eine quantitative Analyse der Simulationskorrektheit gegenüber realen Bildern, sowohl in Bezug auf die Intensitäten als auch auf die Messergebnisse. Die statistische Analyse zeigt, dass die tatsächliche Messunsicherheit mit den realistischen Simulationen mit nicht mehr als 20 Prozent Fehler im Durchschnitt vorhergesagt werden kann.

Um die Ergebnisse einer Oberflächeninspektion zu beurteilen, definiert diese Arbeit Ansätze zur analytischen Bewertung der Oberflächenabdeckung sowie der Messunsicherheit. Zu diesem Zweck wird ein analytischer Rahmen für die Fortpflanzung der Unsicherheiten durch eine Approximation zweiter Ordnung des Messmodells vorgeschlagen. Darüber hinaus wird das Konzept der probabilistischen Oberflächeninferenz vorgestellt, das die Gaußsche Prozessregression an die Oberflächenrekonstruktion mit verrauschten Messungen anpasst.

Diese Arbeit vergleicht weiterhin die Leistung mehrerer Optimierungsalgorithmen mit dem Stand der Technik zur Optimierung der Oberflächenabdeckung, und kommt zu dem Schluss, dass der Partikelschwarm-Optimierungsalgorithmus das effizienteste Ergebnis liefert, indem er über 90 Prozent der Zylinderkopfoberfläche mit 10 Messungen abdeckt. Diese Ergebnisse bedeuten eine signifikante Verbesserung der empirischen menschlichen Planung. Neben der Oberflächenabdeckung wird die Inspektionsplanung um die Optimierung der Messunsicherheiten sowie der optischen Parameter wie Blendenzahl und Belichtungszeit erweitert, mit dem Zweck eine optimale Bildverarbeitungsleistung zu erzielen.

Schlagwörter: Inspektionsplanung, Lasertriangulation, physikalisch basierte Simulation, Sensor-realistische Simulation, Fourier-Optik, Oberflächeninferenz, Propagierung der Unsicherheit, Optimierung, geometrische Planung, optische Planung

Abstract

Nowadays, machine vision systems play a central role in quality inspection of manufactured products. During the design phase of inspection setups, decisions about the number of measurements and their geometrical and optical configurations are typically made by machine vision experts in an empirical way. This trial and error approach not only costs industries a lot of time and human resources, but may also lead to suboptimal solutions for complex surfaces. With the ever-evolving production lines that require constant reconfiguration, and considering the demanding inspection requirements, automatic methods are required to tackle the so-called inspection planning problem.

To explore the design space of a machine vision system, inspection planning can greatly benefit from realistic simulated images. Furthermore, one requires to derive proper metrological metrics to evaluate the surface measurement against the tolerances. Having done so, inspection planning must be formulated as an optimization problem and automatically solved. This thesis proposes a simulation-based approach towards inspection planning by contributing to all three subcomponents of this problem, namely, simulation, evaluation, and optimization. While most of the discussed concepts and methods are common to many visual inspection systems, as an application, this thesis focuses on inspection of a complex cylinder head object by laser triangulation.

On the simulation side, this thesis discusses the application of different rendering techniques to inspection planning. Within this concept, a realistic simulation framework is proposed that combines computer graphics ray tracing with Fourier optics methods for introducing wave optics effects, such as laser speckle, and the EMVA standard 1288 for modeling, among other things, the sensor spectral response. The simulated images exhibit a high visual similarity to the real images. This thesis, moreover, provides a quantitative analysis of the simulation correctness against real images in terms of both the intensities and the measurement results. Statistical analysis indicates that the actual measurement uncertainty can be predicted with no more than 20 percent error on average using the realistic simulations.

To assess the results of a dimensional surface inspection, this thesis defines approaches for analytically evaluating the surface coverage, as well as the measurement uncertainty. To this end, an analytical framework for propagation of uncertainties through a second order approximation of the measurement model is proposed. Furthermore, the notion of probabilistic surface inference is introduced, which adapts Gaussian process regression to surface reconstruction with noisy measurements.

This thesis further compares the performance of several optimization algorithms against the state of the art for optimizing the surface coverage, and concludes that the particle swarm optimization algorithm yields the most efficient result, by covering over 90 percent of the cylinder head surface within 10 measurements. These results indicate a significant improvement over the performance of an empirical human planning. In addition to surface coverage, inspection planning is extended to optimizing the measurement uncertainties, as well as the optical parameters, such as f-number and exposure time, to yield the optimal image processing performance.

Key words: inspection planning, laser triangulation, physically-based simulation, sensor-realistic simulation, Fourier optics, surface inference, uncertainty propagation, optimization, geometrical planning, optical planning

Glossary

Conventions

a, A	Function, scalar, and other quantities
$\boldsymbol{a}$	Vector quantity
A	Matrix quantity

Indices

x, y	2D image coordinates
f_x, f_y	2D spatial frequencies
$x_\mathrm{W}, y_\mathrm{W}, z_\mathrm{W}$	3D worlds coordinates

List of Sets

$\mathbb{N}$	Set of natural numbers
$\mathbb{R}$	Set of real numbers

List of Functions

$\mathscr{F}$	Fourier transform operator
ρ_r	Bidirectional Reflectance Distribution Function (BRDF)
ρ_s	Bidirectional Scattering Distribution Function (BSDF)
ρ_t	Bidirectional Transmittance Distribution Function (BTDF)
c_e	Cost function associated with measurement execution
c_g	Gaussian process covariance function
c_t	Cost function associated with measurement transition
f^cov	Coverage gain function
f_g	A generic planning gain function
f^opt	Cost function for optimization of the optical parameters
f^RA	Relaxed admissibility gain function
f^TU	Total uncertainty gain function
f^u	Uncertainty gain function
$\mathcal{H}^\mathrm{A}$	Amplitude Transfer Function (ATF)
h^coh	Coherent point spread function of an imaging system
h^inc	Incoherent point spread function of an imaging system
$\mathcal{H}^\mathrm{O}$	Optical Transfer Function (OTF)
I^cov	Coverage function
l	Planning constraint function
g	Measurement function
μ_g	Gaussian process mean function
P	Pupil function
$\mathcal{P}$	Generalized pupil function
p	A generic probability density function

P_s	Function to set negative vales to zero in sensitivity planning
$\mathscr{S}$	Surface spectral density function
U	Phasor function of a wave
U_s	Unit step function
u_w	Oscillating wave function
W	Path-length error function of the wavefront at the exit pupil
z	Surface height function

List of Symbols

α,β	Inclination and azimuthal angles of a ray direction
α_c	Crossover rate in genetic algorithm
α_{cov}	Coverage rate of the laser detection algorithm
α_o	Object rotation angle around x-axis
α_m	Mutation rate in genetic algorithm
A	A 2D surface
A_m	Wavefront amplitude
A_p	Pixel area
b	Distance of an image point to the lens
β_o	Object rotation angle around y-axis
c	Speed of light $\approx 3 \times 10^8$ m/s
$\boldsymbol{c}_p$	Camera projection center
c_l,c_g	Weights of the velocity update rule in PSO
d_c	Distance of camera projection point to origin
d_c^{foc}	Focus distance of the camera
d_e^{def}	Distance of exit pupil to image plane in out-of-focus case

δ	Laser divergence angle
δ_r	Lateral resolution
δ_s	Lateral shift of an image point on the sensor
δ_x	Lateral shift of a surface point
δ_z	Vertical shift of a surface point
d_e	distance of exit pupil to image plane
d_g	Distance of a scene point to the lens
$\boldsymbol{d}$	Input data to a measurement function
d_l	Distance of laser projection point to the surface
d_p	Distance of scene point to entrance pupil
Δy	Object translation along y-axis
Δz	Object translation along z-axis
D	Diameter of the entrance pupil
e_i	Relative simulated intensity error
e_u	Relative simulated uncertainty error
E	Irradiance
E^f	Electrical field of a light wave
f	Focal length
f_c	Cut-off frequency
$f^{\#}$	F-number
f_r	Frequency of a surface power spectrum
ϕ	Phase of a wavefront
Φ	Radiant power, flux
ϕ_c	Camera azimuthal angle
ϕ_d	Azimuthal angle of the outgoing light in a BRDF
G	Solution generation in the genetic algorithm

h	Planck's constant $\approx 6.626 \times 10^{-34}\,\mathrm{J\,s}$
$\mathcal{H}$	Unit hemisphere
I	Intensity image
I	Identity matrix
$\mathcal{I}$	Fourier transform of an intensity image
k_{B}	Boltzmann's constant
$\boldsymbol{k}_{*}$	Covariance matrix of measurements in GP regression
K	System gain of an imaging sensor
K_{c}	Camera intrinsic calibration matrix
K_{g}	Covariance matrix of measurements in GP regression
l	Covariance length scale in GP covariance function
λ	Wavelength of an electromagnetic wave
L	Radiance
L_{l}	Length of a laser line
m	Magnification of an imaging system
$\boldsymbol{m}$	Measurement parameters
μ_{d}	Average dark current
μ_{e}	Number of electrons induced in a sensor pixel
μ_{p}	Number of photons reaching a sensor pixel
μ_{*}	Mean of the a posteriori distribution in GP regression
μ_{y}	Average intensity of a camera pixel
$\mathrm{M}, \boldsymbol{q}$	Linear system components in laser triangulation
$\boldsymbol{n}$	Unit normal vector of a planar surface
η	Wavelength-dependent quantum efficiency
$\boldsymbol{p}$	A point in 3D space
p_{w}	Power

$\mathrm{P_r}$	Camera projection matrix
P_{sw}	Particle swarm
q	Radiation energy
$\boldsymbol{r}$	Ray of light as a unit 3D vector
r	Radial distance
r_0	Neighborhood radius for local inference
R	Rotation matrix
s_{t}	Specification tolerance
s	Scale factor
σ_{d}^2	Variance of the dark current
σ_{e}^2	Number of electrons induced in a sensor pixel
σ_{m}^2	Variance of measurement points in GP regression
σ_{pr}^2	Variance in the a priori distribution in GP regression
σ_{*}^2	Variance of the a posteriori distribution in GP regression
σ_{p}^2	Variance of the shot noise
σ_{q}^2	Quantization variance of a sensor pixel
σ_{y}^2	Variance of the intensity of a camera pixel
$\Sigma_{\boldsymbol{d}}$	Covariance matrix of the input uncertainties
$\Sigma_{\boldsymbol{v}}$	Covariance matrix of the resulting measurement
$\Sigma_{\boldsymbol{x}_{\mathrm{w}}}$	Covariance matrix of the 3D coordinate measurement
t_{exp}	Exposure time
θ_{c}	Camera inclination angle
θ_{d}	Inclination angle of the outgoing light in a BRDF
θ_{inc}	Laser incident angle on the surface
θ_{l}	Inclination angle of the incoming light in a BRDF
$\boldsymbol{\theta}$	Plan parameters

$\boldsymbol{\theta}^{\star}$	Optimal plan parameters
$\boldsymbol{t}$	Translation vector
τ	Triangulation angle
T	Temperature in simulated annealing algorithm
T_{tr}	Transmission efficiency of a lens
u	Standard uncertainty
u_{h}	Uncertainty of height measurement
u_{px}	Uncertainty of laser line detection in pixel unit
u_{rel}	Relaxed admissibility threshold
$\boldsymbol{v}$	Velocity vector of a particle in PSO
ν	Frequency of an electromagnetic wave
$\boldsymbol{\upsilon}$	Output of a measurement function
ω	A given solid angle
$\boldsymbol{\chi}$	Generic optimization parameter
$\boldsymbol{\chi}_{\mathrm{g}}$	Globally best position of a particle in PSO
$\boldsymbol{\chi}_{\mathrm{l}}$	Locally best position of a particle in PSO
$\boldsymbol{x}_{\boldsymbol{p}}$	Image of a point $\boldsymbol{p}$ on the image plane
$\boldsymbol{x}_{\mathrm{w}}$	3D world coordinates in laser triangulation
$\tilde{\mathrm{X}}$	Matrix containing measurement points
γ_{o}	Object rotation angle around z-axis
$\tilde{\boldsymbol{z}}$	Vector containing measurement height values

Acronyms

1D	One Dimensional
2D	Two Dimensional
3D	Three Dimensional
ADC	Analog to Digital Converter
API	Application Programming Interface
ATF	Amplitude Transfer Function
BRDF	Bidirectional Reflectance Distribution Function
BSDF	Bidirectional Scattering Distribution Function
BTDF	Bidirectional Transmittance Distribution Function
CAD	Computer-Aided Design
CAIP	Computer-Aided Inspection Planning
DN	Digital Number
EMVA	European Machine Vision Association
GA	Genetic Algorithm
GD&T	Geometrical Dimensioning and Tolerancing
GP	Gaussian Process
GPU	Graphical Processing Unit
ISO	International Organization for Internationalization
LIDAR	Light Detection and Ranging
LTE	Light Transport Equation
MC	Monte Carlo
MCMC	Markov Chain Monte Carlo
MM	Measurability Matrix
NIGP	Noisy Input Gaussian Process

OTF	Optical Transfer Function
PDF	Probability Density Function
PSF	Point Spread Function
PSO	Particle Swarm Optimization
RA	Relaxed Admissibility
SA	Simulated Annealing
SE	Squared Exponential
TU	Total Uncertainty

Contents

1 Introduction

With the widespread deployment of industrial manufacturing processes, industries compete more than ever on providing high-quality products, with lower costs and higher production rates. To assure an acceptable quality, products must be intensively inspected. Although high costs associated with inspection seem as extra costs not directly related to manufacturing, a precise inspection eventually adds value to the product [Kun05]. Therefore, more and more companies thrive for deploying high speed and accurate inspection systems.

The desired features for an industrial inspection can be broadly classified into four main categories [Mal03]:

1. **Dimensional inspection**: measuring coordinates and geometrical features of the products.
2. **Surface inspection**: detection of scratches, pits, and unwanted stains, which degrade the function or appearance of the surface.
3. **Structural inspection**: verification of correct assembly in the products (screws, slots, clamps), or completeness of components.
4. **Operational inspection**: verifying a flawless functionality according to specifications.

Formerly, an inspection was carried out by personnel who visually examined the products [Bey15], or compared them against standards. Human verification, however, could by no means catch up with the evolving production demands. This was partly because of the low human inspection speed as well as factors such as tiredness and lack of attention. In addition, the required production precision necessitated the development of automated inspection systems delivering exact objective measurements.

For dimensional inspection, first automated tools were developed during the 60s, which are still being used in some industrial inspections. In these measuring systems, touch probes mounted on Coordinate Measuring Machines (CMM) mechanically contact the products at predefined points, or along a profile, and acquire precise touch-point coordinates with micrometer to nanometer reproducibility [Wec06]. Nevertheless, the low scan rate of CMMs does not allow them to verify all individual products of a mass production. Therefore, only random samples can be inspected using this approach.

With the advent of vision systems, machine vision provided innovative solutions for much faster and contact-less inspections, even with lower hardware costs. Thus, the majority of industrial inspections tasks are nowadays fulfilled by means of *Automated Visual Inspection (AVI)* systems [Bey15].

1.1 Inspection Planning, A Short Review

In order for a visual inspection system to verify the desired features thoroughly and with acceptable accuracy, the measurement system must be carefully planned. This is especially important for products with critical functionalities which must be possibly completely scanned and verified. Complex surfaces require several measurements from different viewpoints using different optical parameters. Design and configuration of these measurements to achieve an acceptable inspection quality within the allowed time, space, and inspection requirements is not a trivial task, especially for geometrically or optically complex surfaces. This design phase, which is also known as *inspection planning*, is an indispensable part of designing every inspection system.

Inspection planning essentially consists of two main steps [Mor18]:

1. Choosing a measurement strategy, in terms of the type and number of sensors, as well as the number of measurements.
2. Configuring the setup degrees of freedom for each measurement.

An important requirement of inspection planning is to propose an efficient inspection plan, in terms of minimizing the inspection time, number of measurements, or the inspection costs.

To automate inspection planning for mechanical probes, several works [Col08][Mor10][Mar14] have been published under the title of *computer-aided inspection planning (CAIP)*, in which different strategies for sampling points on a surface are studied. For vision systems, however, inspection planning is more challenging, mainly because the physical process of image formation is much more complex.

1.1.1 Design Parameters

Interesting design parameters for a visual inspection system include both the optical and geometrical degrees of freedom, as well as the number of measurements. The optical parameters may include aperture size, shutter time, type of lenses, light source profile, and etc. All degrees of freedom corresponding to the positioning and orientation of the camera(s) and light source(s) with respect to the inspection object count as the geometrical parameters.

1.1.2 Conventional Approach

In the conventional workflow of planning a vision system, sample physical products are first produced and used in a feasibility study [Irg17d] in order to empirically propose potentially good inspection solutions. With the design space of such systems, experts need to resort to some "good practices" [Mor18], which are not only very expensive for industries in terms of time and human resources, but also often lead to compromising solutions between different requirements. This is especially the case for inspection planning of geometrically or optically complex surfaces. Moreover, by changes in the product design or the manufacturing process, the empirical planning needs to be done all over again.

First attempts for proposing automatic inspection planning methods for vision systems date back to late 80s. Although a topic of interest for about three decades [Cow88][Gro16][Sco09], there is still no universally acceptable inspection planning tool for industrial machine vision systems [Irg17c]. Consequently, most visual inspection setups are either being configured by trial and error or are based on evaluation models which are also results of many experimental image acquisitions [Mah11].

1.1.3 Taxonomy of Automatic Planning Methods

The problem of planning machine vision systems can be coarsely divided into *model-based* and *non-model-based* [Sco03]. In the non-model based version, the inspection object is completely unknown at the beginning and the goal of inspection planning is to build a proper model of the object surface by several measurements. Digitalization of ancient statues or unknown objects are examples of this approach. To this end, usually an online planning approach will be applied, where each planned measurement is executed in real world, evaluated, and based on the results further measurements are planned [Kri15]. Model-based approaches rely on an available digital model of the product, and assume the variations of real physical models to be small compared to the ideal model. With this assumption, the planning can be applied offline for all measurements. As digital product models are often available in industries, industrial inspection planning belongs to model-based planning problems.

1.1.4 Inspection Planning and Industry 4.0

Being currently in the era of smart factories, inspection systems must keep satisfying the ever-evolving industrial needs. This means, not only fast automated inspection systems are required, but also they must automatically adapt themselves to any changes in the products or the manufacturing processes. For this to work, we require a new perspective towards inspection planning, in which planning not only happens after the manufacturing process is realized but it can already start alongside the design process as soon as digital product models are produced and the verification requirements are recognized.

Towards this goal, figure 1.1 proposes a workflow for an automatic inspection planning process, which will be briefly introduced in the next section. In case of any changes in the manufacturing process or product specifications, the planning workflow can be utilized to automatically readjust the inspection plan.

1.1.5 Components of Automatic Inspection Planning

- **Inspection specification**: Every inspection starts with a set of specifications, including the product Computer-Aided Design (CAD) model and the requirements for the inspection. For dimensional inspection, requirements often include regions of interest of the nominal geometry, with the corresponding allowed tolerances, in the form of standardized engineering notations. These notations are also known as the Geometrical Dimensioning and Tolerancing (GD&T). The GD&T requirements are often already embedded in the CAD product model, which can be the direct input to an automatic planning process. In addition, the description of the measurement scene and potential setup constraints must be provided at this point.
- **Automatic Planning**: The automatic planning step is the core of inspection planning, which internally relies on three subcomponents:
    1. **Optimization**: Central to inspection planning is an optimization algorithm, which guides the planning towards choosing setup parameters for an improved inspection quality.
    2. **Simulation**: To explore the huge design space of a machine vision inspection system, evaluation of different solutions must rely on simulations, where synthetic images from the viewpoints of virtual cameras are rendered by computers. Relying on simulations instead of experimental work not only avoids the tedious trial and error process but also prevents extra costs of testing different devices. Difficulty in achieving realistic simulations is one of the main reasons for the delayed deployment of automatic inspection planning in industry. Recent advances in the field of computer graphics can be indeed a turning point for the development of automatic planning methods.
    3. **Evaluation**: The simulation results are in the form of images. For metrologically evaluating the images for the comparison against the tolerances, proper evaluation metrics must be extracted, according to the requirements of the inspection.

- **Verification**: No matter how accurate a simulation is, there is always room for some effects not fully reproduced in the simulated images. That is because it is extremely difficult, if not impossible, to perfectly reproduce the reality at all of its levels of detail. Thus, suggested plans must be preferably verified against real experiments, which can be either automatic, if the corresponding configurations can be realized by a robotic system, for example, or manual. If verification does not confirm the proposed plan, inspection planning can be repeated by defining new constraints or providing the planing with more information regarding the imaging scene.
- **Inspection plan**: The final result of an inspection planning is the inspection plan, which includes all the parameters required for configuring the measurement setup, including an optimized set of measurements with their corresponding optical and geometrical design parameters.

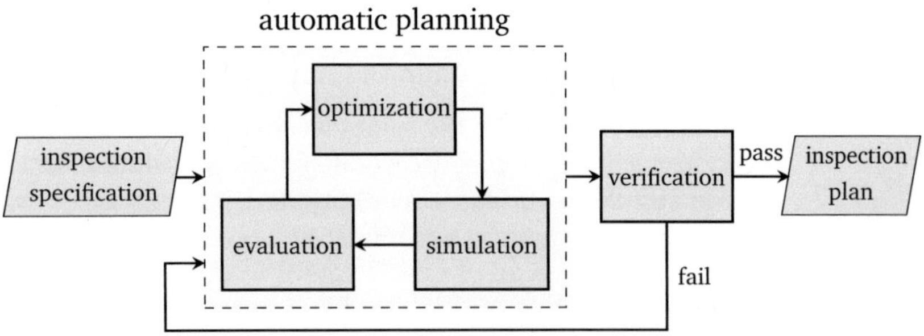

Figure 1.1: Workflow of automatic inspection planning

1.2 Dimensional Inspection with Machine Vision

Before delving into the main planning problem, this section provides a brief insight into the approaches for dimensional measurements using machine vision techniques.

Even before machine vision gained popularity for inspection and 3D measurements, different principles for optical metrology were already introduced. The deployment of the principles in the form of fast industrial sensors happened later on, when technology was ready to transfer them to practice. Chen et al. [Che00] have given an overview of the existing optical solutions for measuring 3D shapes. A more detailed introduction of the methods can be found in the book by Beyerer et al. [Bey15].

A large number of vision systems for 3D measurement fall in the category of *triangulation*. These methods measure an object in terms of 3D points. For measuring each point, a triangle is constructed in which one vertex is the target point and two more vertices are two viewpoints from which the point is seen or illuminated. Stereo or multi-view acquisition methods, also known as passive triangulation, utilize two or more cameras to measure the depth of the image points that can be matched in at least another camera viewpoint [Ack08]. To achieve a better accuracy, as well as a denser measurement, often one viewpoint is replaced by a light source with a particular structure, to code the scene points. In laser triangulation, laser beams or laser planes, and in fringe projection, coded binary or sinusoidal light profiles are used to illuminate the object. These methods can achieve a measurement uncertainty in micrometer range [Fis17][Ish11].

Another group of measurement methods, called *light detection and ranging (LIDAR)*, rely on the time light takes to travel from the light source to the surface, and back to the sensor, in order to measure the distance. These methods can measure much longer distances (tens of meters) with an uncertainty of a few centimeters [Reu03].

Sensors which operate based on the principle of *interferometry*, analyze interference patterns formed by superposition of a reference coherent light with its reflection from a surface. These methods require wave optics modeling of light and can result in measurements with uncertainties comparable to the wavelength.

In recent years, machine vision technology has provided many solutions for non-contact 3D measurements. The methods briefly reviewed here, and many more, such as shape from shading, shape from focus, Deflectometry, and Moiré, to name a few, all tackle the same problem in different scenarios and for different requirements.

In this thesis, inspection planning is exemplified on an application of laser triangulation to measuring complex industrial products. Considering this application, the principle of laser triangulation measurement is introduced in more detail in the next section.

1.2.1 Laser Triangulation Principle

Laser triangulation is a cost-efficient and flexible measurement method, which is widely used for measuring diffuse surfaces in industries. In its simplest form, triangulation is derived for a laser beam illuminating a spot on the surface, whose image would be acquired by a sensor. As illustrated in figure 1.2, a vertical shift of $\delta_z \in \mathbb{R}$ in the height of the surface, leads to a lateral displacement of the image point by $\delta_s \in \mathbb{R}$. By calculating δ_s on the sensor, the point coordinates can be given as

$$\delta_x = \frac{\delta_s}{m}, \tag{1.1}$$

$$\delta_z = \frac{\delta_s}{\tan(\tau)m}, \tag{1.2}$$

in which $\tau \in (-\frac{\pi}{2},0) \cup (0, \frac{\pi}{2})$ is the *triangulation angle* and $m \in \mathbb{R}^+$ refers to the magnification of the imaging system.

In order to avoid a point-wise measurement of a large surface, laser line projectors can be utilized to scan a 2D profile of the surface in a single image. As shown in figure 1.3, the laser plane creates an intersection curve on the surface and the camera records images as the object is moved along a given scan direction. This method allows the products to be inspected as they are moving between the production stations, and there is no need to keep them still during the inspection.

For the reconstruction of the illuminated profile, image locations corresponding to the laser profile are first detected, using peak or ridge detection algorithms [Ste98]. Each detected 2D point on the image provides 2 constraints for the location of the corresponding 3D point in the scene. In both triangulation scenarios, the geometry of the beam or the laser plane provides the third constraint for uniquely determining the 3D coordinates.

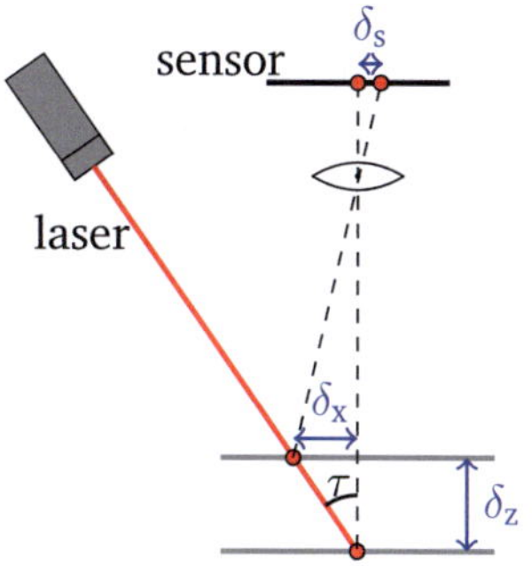

Figure 1.2: Triangulation with a laser beam

By modeling the camera as a *pin-hole camera* [Ma12], the relation between the 3D world coordinates of the measurement point $\boldsymbol{x}_\mathrm{w} = (x_\mathrm{w}, y_\mathrm{w}, z_\mathrm{w})$, and the 2D coordinates (x, y) of its projection on the image plane is given as below [Ma12]. In this equation all parameters except for $(x_\mathrm{w}, y_\mathrm{w}, z_\mathrm{w})$ and s are known. x and y are acquired by detecting the center of the laser line profile on the image.

$$s \begin{bmatrix} x \\ y \\ 1 \end{bmatrix} = \mathrm{K_c}\,\mathrm{P_r} \begin{bmatrix} x_w \\ y_w \\ z_w \\ 1 \end{bmatrix} = \begin{bmatrix} f & 0 & c_x \\ 0 & f & c_y \\ 0 & 0 & 1 \end{bmatrix} \begin{bmatrix} R & \boldsymbol{t} \end{bmatrix} \begin{bmatrix} x_w \\ y_w \\ z_w \\ 1 \end{bmatrix}. \tag{1.3}$$

Here, $\mathrm{P_r} \in \mathbb{R}^{3\times4}$ is the *camera projection matrix*, which brings the 3D measurement point to the camera coordinate frame. By knowing the relative rotation matrix $\mathrm{R} \in \mathrm{SO}(3)$ [1] and translation vector $\boldsymbol{t} \in \mathbb{R}^3$ of the camera with respect to the origin, the projection matrix can be built as $\mathrm{P_r} = [\mathrm{R}\ \boldsymbol{t}]$. Matrix $\mathrm{K_c} \in \mathbb{R}^{3\times3}$ is called the *intrinsic calibration matrix* and is composed of the focal length f and camera projection center (c_x, c_y), expressed in pixels. This matrix transforms the metric coordinates into pixel unit [Ma12]. The result of the matrix multiplications is the image point coordinates scaled by $s \in \mathbb{R}^+$, where s corresponds to the unknown depth of the measurement point. The camera projection equation results in two independent equations for determining the 3D coordinates.

[1] $\mathrm{SO}(3)$ denotes the group of all rotation matrices. These matrices are called "special orthonormal matrices" with the properties $\mathrm{R}^{-1} = \mathrm{R}$ and $\det(\mathrm{R}) = 1$

The third equation is provided by the laser plane equation, as illuminated points also lie on the laser plane with the equation $\boldsymbol{x}_{\mathrm{w}}^{\mathrm{T}}\boldsymbol{n} = d$. Here, $\boldsymbol{n} \in \mathbb{R}^3$ refers to the normal vector of the laser plane and $d \in \mathbb{R}$ is a distance value. Using equation 1.3 and the laser plane equation, the reconstruction of the 3D points can be achieved by solving a system of linear equations [Moh16]

$$\begin{bmatrix} \boldsymbol{v}_3^{\mathrm{T}} - \boldsymbol{v}_1^{\mathrm{T}}\frac{(x-c_x)}{f} \\ \boldsymbol{v}_2^{\mathrm{T}} - \boldsymbol{v}_1^{\mathrm{T}}\frac{(y-c_y)}{f} \\ \boldsymbol{n}^{\mathrm{T}} \end{bmatrix} \begin{bmatrix} x_w \\ y_w \\ z_w \end{bmatrix} = \begin{bmatrix} \frac{(x-c_x)}{f}t_3 - t_1 \\ \frac{(y-c_y)}{f}t_3 - t_2 \\ d \end{bmatrix}. \tag{1.4}$$

The vectors $\boldsymbol{v}_i \in \mathbb{R}^3$ in this equation refer to the row vectors of the camera rotation matrix. Geometrically, these vectors are also visualized in figure 1.3. t_i refers to an element of the camera translation vector $\boldsymbol{t} = [t_1, t_2, t_3]^{\mathrm{T}}$.

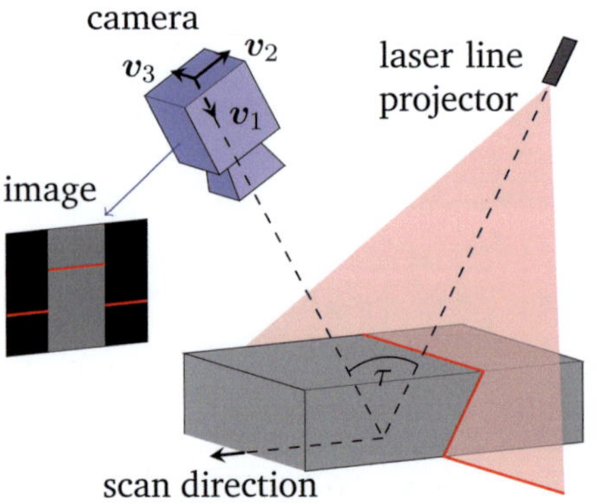

Figure 1.3: Schematic of inspection with a laser line projector.

To keep the notation concise, the expression $\mathrm{M}(\boldsymbol{d})\boldsymbol{x}_{\mathrm{w}} = \boldsymbol{q}(\boldsymbol{d})$ is used to refer to the system of linear equations in equation 1.4, where $\boldsymbol{d}$ is a vector containing all the calibration and image processing results which are required to build the system of equations. Consequently, to obtain the desired measurement point, one can build the M matrix and vector $\boldsymbol{q}$ for each detected laser position on the image and then compute

$$\boldsymbol{x}_{\mathrm{w}} = \mathrm{M}(\boldsymbol{d})^{-1}\boldsymbol{q}(\boldsymbol{d}). \tag{1.5}$$

Figure 1.4 displays a sample point cloud generated by scanning a cylinder head by triangulation of laser lines. Such a point cloud is the result of processing several hundreds of frames captured during the inspection. Considering the speed of the object or the sensor movement during the scan, the reconstructed profiles in each image frame can be shifted accordingly and put together to create such a point cloud.

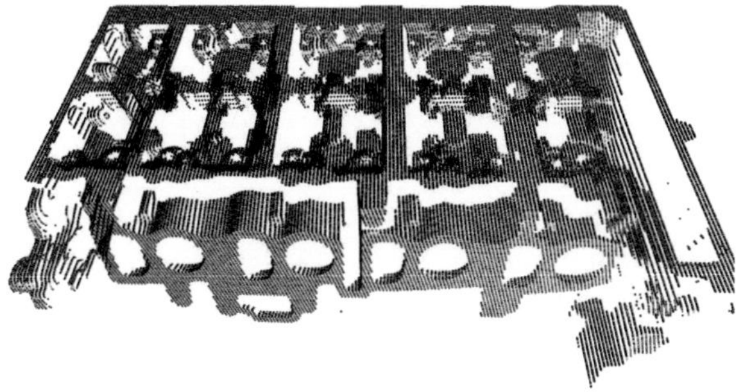

Figure 1.4: Sample point cloud of a cylinder head generated in a linear scan by using laser triangulation.

1.3 Scope & Application of this Thesis

This thesis focuses on different aspects of automatic model-based planning for dimensional inspection of industrial products. The inspection application of this thesis is dedicated to 3D surface measurement by means of laser triangulation. As the inspection object, a real-world cylinder head model with a complicated geometry is chosen. This focuses the application of this thesis to complex surfaces whose manual inspection planning is not trivial.

The three subcomponents of the automatic planning workflow, including simulation, evaluation, and optimization, constitute the core contributions of this thesis. Throughout the upcoming chapters, proposed methods and discussions are oriented towards the application of a cylinder head inspection. Many concepts and methods discussed throughout the thesis are also in common with many other inspection methods.

Figure 1.5 displays the cylinder head CAD model and figure 1.6 shows a real sample of this product, illuminated with a laser line projector. The cylinder head is in the size range of 45 cm×28 cm×10 cm, with 8 intake and 8 exhaust manifolds, and a typical inspection tolerance of ±0.1 mm. The complexity of the object geometry, with many hard-to-reach areas, makes it an interesting task for covering the whole surface as well as satisfying the required measurement uncertainty.

The cylinder head is manufactured using the aluminum casting method. This method typically leads to creating diffusely reflective surfaces which are suitable for measurement with laser triangulation. Due to this reason, and considering the cost-efficiency and flexibility of inspecting objects in motion (e.g. objects on conveyor belts) using laser triangulation, this inspection technique is widely used for inspection of aluminum products.

In spite of the simplicity of the measurement technique, inspection planning with realistic simulation of the laser light on a rough surface is a challenging task, due to the occurrence of certain optical effects (i.e. speckles) caused by the laser coherence.

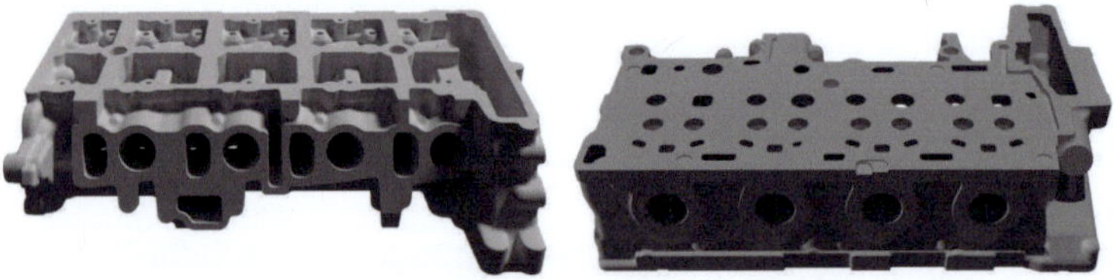

Figure 1.5: Cylinder head CAD model from two viewpoints.

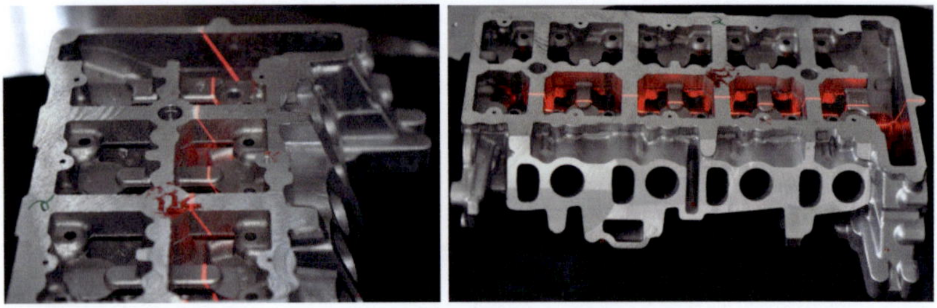

Figure 1.6: Cylinder head under laser line.

1.4 Contributions

Focusing on the application of a cylinder head inspection, this thesis contributes to all three subcomponents of the automatic planning workflow, including optimization, evaluation, and the simulation steps. The main contributions are summarized as follows:

- Planning and Optimization
  - Providing a formal definition of the inspection planning problem, its complexity analysis, and discussion on possible heuristic approaches for solving this problem.
  - Comparison of the performance of different state-of-the-art optimization algorithms for the inspection planning problem.
  - Discussion on the significance of automated inspection planning by comparing the planning results against the performance of a human expert in an empirical planning.
  - Inspection planning for a highly complex geometrical object.
  - Deriving results for inspection planning in terms of “coverage planning”, “uncertainty planning”, and “planning the optical parameters”.
- Evaluation
  - Proposing metrological evaluation criteria for quantitatively assessing the results of a surface inspection. The derived and implemented evaluation criteria focus on the coverage of the surface with a predefined resolution as well as the measurement uncertainty.
  - Introduction of an analytical framework for the propagation of uncertainties (in image processing results and calibration parameters) to the final 3D measurement.
  - Analysis of the problem of reconstructing a 3D surface using noisy measurement points. As a result, the notion of “probabilistic surface inference” is introduced which adapts Gaussian process regression to the problem of surface reconstruction.

- Simulation
  - A complete analysis of the image formation chain in optical measurement systems, starting from the light sources, to the surfaces, further through the optic, up to the formation of digital intensities on the camera sensor. This analysis includes both coherent and incoherent imaging systems.
  - Utilization of methods from the field of computer graphics in combination with Fourier optics techniques for proposing a “sensor-realistic simulation framework” for machine vision inspection systems.
  - Design and implementation of experiments for a thorough verification of the simulation framework against real images. Simulation verifications are carried out qualitatively as well as quantitatively, at both the pixel intensity level and the application level.

1.5 Content Overview

Starting with the problem definition, **chapter 2** formally defines inspection planning as an optimization problem and reviews previous research works for solving this problem. This chapter also provides an introduction to several state-of-the-art continuous optimization algorithms in the literature, and closes with studying the design space and components of the planning problem for the intended application.

Chapter 3 exclusively studies the problem of defining metrological evaluation criteria for assessing the results of a dimensional inspection. Evaluation of the surface coverage, measurement uncertainties, and surface inference given noisy measurements are the main topics of this chapter.

Chapter 4 begins with the concept of image formation simulation by providing sufficient background in radiometry and conventional computer graphics rendering. Fourier optics techniques for modeling optical effects and simulation of the sensor spectral response are also included. This chapter introduces the sensor-realistic simulation framework for synthesizing images of a machine vision inspection system and concludes with a discussion on sample simulation results.

In contrast to the convention of verifying simulated images by visual comparison, **chapter 5**, provides a quantitative analysis of the simulation results compared to real calibrated images, in terms of both the intensity values as well as the corresponding measurement results. Experiments for measurements of the scene elements (surface, light source, optic) as well as the verification process with extensive discussion on the results are provided in this chapter.

Finally, **chapter 6** demonstrates and discusses several achieved inspection planning results for the intended application. In this chapter, the performance of several state-of-the-art optimization algorithms will be compared in terms of the optimality of their proposed plans for measuring the complex cylinder head surface. The results of coverage planning will also be compared against manual human planning with significant improvement.

As the content of this thesis touches several fields of research, a literature review section has been separately provided in each chapter.

2 Planning Problem

The previous chapter gave an overview on the automatic inspection planning problem and its subcomponents. Among these elements, optimization constitutes the core of the planning problem. The main focus of this chapter is on planning as an optimization problem, by providing an explicit problem definition, complexity analysis, design space parametrization, and an overview on potential approaches towards the solution.

2.1 Definition and Complexity

Regardless of the differences between inspection systems and their requirements, the inspection planning optimization problem can be described in a common way. In order to define this problem, some terms and notations will be introduced below.

An *inspection plan* $\boldsymbol{\theta}$ is generally composed of $n \in \mathbb{N}$ measurements, where the parameters of the ith measurement is given by the vector $\boldsymbol{m}_i$. Thus $\boldsymbol{\theta}$ is given by

$$\boldsymbol{\theta} = [\boldsymbol{m}_1, \boldsymbol{m}_2, \ldots, \boldsymbol{m}_n],$$

in which n can take different values, which means the dimensionality of the plan depends on the number and the parameter size of each measurement.

In reality, the execution of an arbitrary measurement is always associated with some non-negative financial or timing overhead $c_{\text{e}}(\boldsymbol{m}) > 0$, such as the duration of the measurement or the costs of the required devices. In addition, there can also be transition costs when switching from one measurement to the next one $c_t(\boldsymbol{m}_i, \boldsymbol{m}_{i+1}) > 0$. For instance, the overhead of changing the sensor, or simply the time a robot arm takes to move to its new location.

Central to the definition of the optimization problem, is the *plan gain function* $f_g(\boldsymbol{\theta})$. This function associates a quantitative metric to a plan $\boldsymbol{\theta}$, indicating the information gain of the given sequence of measurements. f_g can represent different metrological criteria, based on the inspection goals and the features of interest. Chapter 3 exclusively studies different choices for f_g. In this chapter, f_g is supposed to be provided, and without loss of generality, we assume the gain function reaches its optimal value when it is maximized. In addition, there are constraints for the realization of different measurements, including limitations in time and space, or collision situations between the sensor, robot arms, and the inspection objects. All such limitations can be formulated as a function $l(\boldsymbol{\theta})$ which takes a positive value if all the constraints are met.

The proposed inspection plan is desired to obtain some required amount of information about the inspection object (i.e. $f_g(\boldsymbol{\theta}^\star) > f_g^{\min}$) and meet the constraints. Among potentially many plans with these properties, the optimal plan $\boldsymbol{\theta}^\star$ is the one which also induces the minimum cost, i.e.

$$\begin{aligned} \boldsymbol{\theta}^\star = & \operatorname*{arg\,min}_{n,[\boldsymbol{m}_1,\ldots,\boldsymbol{m}_n]} \left(\sum_{i=1}^{n} c_e(\boldsymbol{m}_i) + \sum_{i=1}^{n-1} c_t(\boldsymbol{m}_i, \boldsymbol{m}_{i+1}) \right), \\ \text{subject to} \quad f_g(\boldsymbol{\theta}^\star) > & f_g^{\min}, \\ l(\boldsymbol{\theta}^\star) > & 0. \end{aligned} \tag{2.1}$$

To clarify why minimizing the cost term is crucial, we have to note that in general adding more measurements is in favor of the gain function f_g, as the information gain (let it be surface coverage or measurement precision) will never get worse by adding more measurements. Thus, without considering the cost term, the optimization problem will be an ill-posed problem, with most of its solutions being very long or even never-ending plans.

2.1.1 Design Space

The inspection planning design space corresponds to the degrees of freedom of single measurements m. The most commonly considered design space in this regard is the viewpoint space of the sensor [Sco09] [Mav15], including the sensor position and orientation. That is why inspection planning has been also called *view planning*. Some previous works which are known under the title of *sensor planning* also allow different sensors to be planned at the same time [Gro16]. Tarabanis et al. [Tar95a] first used the term *generalized view points*, in which not only the viewpoints of the sensor, but also some optical parameters were taken into account as the degrees of freedom.

2.1.2 Analogy to the Set Covering Problem

It can be easily verified that a simplified version of the inspection planning problem can be reduced to the well-known *set covering problem* in computer science. The set-covering problem is known to belong to the NP[1]-hard computational complexity class [Cor07], and thus, there is no known algorithm to solve it in polynomial time. This implies that the search space exponentially grows with the problem dimension. The set covering problem is defined as below [Cor07].

Set Covering Problem

An instance of the set covering problem consists of a set X with a finite number of elements, and another set $\mathscr{X}$ containing a collection of subsets of X, such that every element of X belongs to at least one subset in $\mathscr{X}$. In other words, $\mathscr{X}$ covers X because

$$X = \bigcup_{S \in \mathscr{X}} S. \tag{2.2}$$

The problem is to find a minimum-sized subset of $\mathscr{X}$ whose elements still cover the main set X.

To reduce the planning problem to the set covering problem, we consider a scenario in which the space of all possible measurements and the space

[1]NP stands for nondeterministic polynomial complexity in an algorithm, whereas P refers to deterministic polynomial complexity. More information is provided in [Cor07].

of all surface points are both discrete and finite, and the gain function corresponds to the number of covered surface points in the measurements. By neglecting constraints and transition costs, and considering a common execution cost for all measurements, i.e. $\forall \boldsymbol{m}\, c_\text{e}(\boldsymbol{m}) = 1$, the planning problem will be equivalent to the set covering problem. In this case, each measurement covers a subset of the surface points (analogue to a subset S in $\mathscr{X}$) and inspection planning looks for the minimum number of measurements which cover all the surface points (elements in X).

In the general case, however, the problem is more complex. Often the number of valid measurements are not finite and the gain function is based on complex quantities such as the measurement uncertainty. The best practically achievable fitness value is also often unknown. For typical inspection planning problems, one is not able to search the whole parameter space and needs to resort to approximations.

Solutions to the Set Covering Problem

The set covering problem is a discrete optimization problem. If the number of elements in the set is small, one may apply a full combinatorial search, similar to the pseudo-code provided in algorithm 1.

Algorithm 1: Full combinatorial search for set-covering

```
Result: 𝒳_sub
n ← 0
while X ≠ ⋃_{S ∈ 𝒳_sub} S do
    n ← n + 1                          /* increase number of subsets */
    𝒳_sub ← getBestSubsetsOfSizeN(n, 𝒳)
end
```

In this algorithm, the function getBestSubsetsOfSizeN(n,$\mathscr{X}$) searches through all combinations of n subsets which cover the most number of elements. If X is covered, the algorithm stops, otherwise the number of subsets is increased and the search is repeated for $n+1$ subsets.

Most practical approaches for solving the set covering problem are, however, approximative, unless the problem space is small enough to apply a brute-force search. One of the well-known approximations is the *iterative greedy algorithm*, which has been shown to be the best known polynomial approximation to this problem [Fei98]. In this approach, one repeatedly picks a subset that covers the largest number of uncovered elements, and continues adding more subsets to the previous ones until all elements are covered. The greedy algorithm can overestimate the optimal number of covering subsets maximally by the factor $(\ln |X| + 1)$ [Sla97]. This approach is presented in algorithm 2.

Algorithm 2: Iterative greedy algorithm for set covering

Result: $\mathscr{X}_{\text{sub}}$
$\mathscr{X}_{\text{sub}} \leftarrow \emptyset$
while $X \neq \bigcup_{S \in \mathscr{X}_{\text{sub}}} S$ **do**
    $S \leftarrow$ getNextBestSubset($\mathscr{X}_{\text{sub}}, \mathscr{X}$)
    $\mathscr{X}_{\text{sub}} \leftarrow \mathscr{X}_{\text{sub}} \bigcup S$ `/* add to subsets */`
end

In addition to the greedy approach, relaxation of the problem to linear programming and randomization are two other alternatives for tackling this problem [Cor07].

2.1.3 Solution Approaches to Inspection Planning

The ideas behind the approaches towards solving the set covering problem can be borrowed for solving the inspection planning problem. A noticeable difference of inspection planning with the set covering problem is that the design parameters for inspection planning are often continuous. Thus, we can differentiate between the approaches that discretize the design space and those applied in the continuous space.

In both continuous and discrete planning cases, an optimization problem must be solved in each iteration of the algorithms 1 or 2. The significant advantage of the greedy approach is that the optimization overhead remains constant. Even for moderate number of measurements, e.g. 10 to 20, the complexity of the full search will be so high that one cannot search the whole space. Heuristic search algorithms are good alternatives for cleverly searching the space, without going through all possible solutions. The performance of such algorithms also depend on the dimensionality and complexity of the search space. With higher complexity, the chances of converging to a locally optimum solution (instead of the global optimum) significantly increases [Moh18b].

Inspired by the solutions to the set covering problem, a greedy approximation to inspection planning is given in algorithm 3. This algorithm iteratively adds measurements to the plan, which inspect the unmeasured surface area with minimal cost. The complexity of the optimization step “getNextBestMeasurement” remains constant in each iteration and is determined by the dimensionality of the measurement space.

Algorithm 3: Iterative greedy algorithm for inspection planning

Result: $\boldsymbol{\theta}^{\star}$
$\boldsymbol{\theta}^{\star} \leftarrow [\,]$
while $f_{\mathrm{g}}(\boldsymbol{\theta}^{\star}) \leq f_{\mathrm{g}}^{\min}$ **do**
  $\boldsymbol{m}_{\text{next}} \leftarrow$ getNextBestMeasurement$(\boldsymbol{\theta}^{\star}, f_{\mathrm{g}}, c_{\mathrm{t}}, c_{\mathrm{e}}, l)$
  $\boldsymbol{\theta}^{\star} \leftarrow [\boldsymbol{\theta}^{\star}, \boldsymbol{m}_{\text{next}}]$ `/* append measurement to plan */`
end

2.2 State of the Art in Inspection Planning

This section gives a closer look on different aspects of the proposed approaches in the literature towards formulating and solving the inspection planning problem.

2.2.1 Discrete Planning with Measurability Matrix

A prevailing approach towards solving the planning problem is to discretize the space of both the measurements and the surface points, so as to map the problem to the set covering problem, or in general an integer programming problem. This is the main approach in the publications by Scott [Sco09] and Gronle et al. [Gro16]. In this method, the discretized space is stored in a so-called *measurability matrix (MM)*, where the columns span the surface space (patches or sampled points) and the rows span the measurement space. As visualized in figure 2.1, element m_{ij} in this matrix refers to a metrological criteria, such as a binary visibility flag, resolution, or the measurement uncertainty, which can be determined by simulating the measurement i and evaluating the surface measurement at point j. The goal here is to find the minimum number of measurements (rows) which decently measure all surface points (columns). For solving the optimization problem, both works apply the iterative greedy approximation and argue that it yields a good balance between computation time and result optimality.

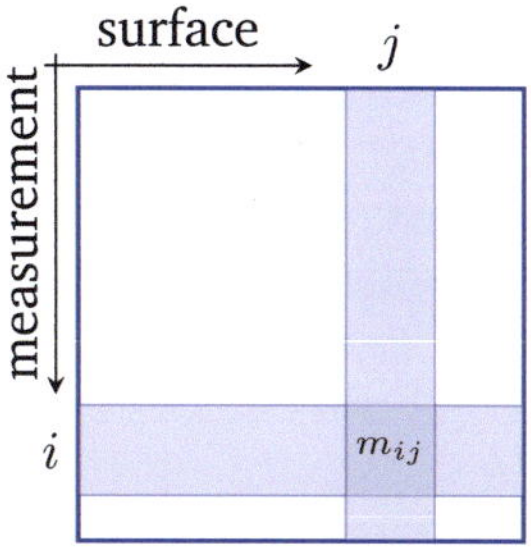

Figure 2.1: Measurability matrix.

The measurement space in these works is specifically concerned with the viewpoints of the sensor. To discretize this space, a viewpoint generation strategy is applied. Gronle et al. [Gro16] and Scott [Sco09] both choose the sensor viewpoints mainly considering the local surface normals. This approach can be beneficial for simple surfaces. For complex geometries, such as the cylinder head presented in the previous chapter, local surface geometry cannot provide enough clue to preselect the viewpoints without considering the extensive occlusion of the surrounding geometry.

For a sufficient sampling of the parameter space, one requires dense samples leading to matrices of high dimensions (e.g. millions to billions of viewpoints). In addition, potentially good viewpoints might be missing from the sampled points. Planning in a continuous design space, on the other hand, allows one to arbitrarily fine-tune the parameters.

2.2.2 Continuous Planning

Continuous planning has the advantage of avoiding the space discretization. In a number of previous works, the optimization gain function has been explicitly derived [Mav15][Tar95a][Pri03], based on mathematical formulations of the inspection requirements, such as resolution, focus, measurement uncertainty, etc. These formulations are mostly similar to those proposed much earlier by Cowan [Cow88] for formalizing the inspection requirements, or rely on experimental analysis [Pri03]. They further apply continuous optimization methods for a previously given number of cameras [Mav15], and some without the constraint to minimize the number of measurements [Pri03][Tar95a].

Without minimizing the number of measurements (or the costs in general) these methods do not attempt to solve the full inspection planing problem. In addition, many optical and geometrical effects appearing in image formation are too complex to be modeled as closed-form formulas. Consequently, the image formation effects which are more difficult to model analytically must be approximated or totally neglected. In the best case, all desired effects can be taken into account when the entire image formation chain in the optical system is realistically simulated. This approach, does not lead to closed-form gain functions, rather it requires evaluating simulation results as a black box function. This is the main approach of this thesis.

In the planning method proposed by Roschani et al. [Ros13], the sensor configuration parameters are partially discretized and partially continuously optimized. This planning method focuses on deflectometric measurement applications.

2.3 Continuous Optimization Methods

Any strategy for solving the inspection planning problem requires an optimization algorithm. This section provides an introduction to some important concepts and algorithms regarding continuous optimization. Generally, the approaches towards continuous optimizations can be categorized into **deterministic** and **probabilistic** methods.

Deterministic methods either rely on function gradients, such as the gradient descent [Sny18] optimization, or follow deterministic steps to converge to the solution, such as the Nelder-Mead optimization [Nel65]. These methods are best suited for convex optimization problems, in which each local optimum is also a global optimum. For general problems, such approaches may be trapped in local optima depending on their starting points.

Probabilistic methods, on the contrary, treat the optimization function as a black box without deriving any derivatives. Instead, these methods utilize probabilistic and randomized approaches for heuristically searching the design space, which can often escape local optima and be applied to non-convex non-differentiable functions [Lob17].

Inspection planning gain functions which are based on simulations can be, in general, best evaluated as black boxes, by scoring or verifying the fulfillment of the requirements based on the simulation results. Therefore, such gain functions can indeed turn out to be complex and in general, non-convex and non-differentiable. Consequently, the probabilistic approaches are the suitable choice for the optimization in this case.

Weise in his book [Wei09] provides an interesting overview on different global optimization algorithms. According to him, the majority of the probabilistic optimization methods are variants of Monte Carlo (MC) simulations, such as stochastic hill climbing and Simulated Annealing (SA). More advanced methods improve the pure MC simulations by using intelligent biologically inspired optimization strategies, such as the Genetic Algorithm (GA), the Particle Swarm Optimization (PSO), and the ant colony optimization. In all such algorithms with a random nature, a *random restart* of the algorithm after convergence can potentially improve the performance by allowing it to start a new random search.

In what follows, *SA*, *GA*, and *PSO*, which are widely applied algorithms in research and technology, will be briefly introduced. In this section, optimization corresponds to the maximization of a given function f_g. A more detailed consideration of the algorithms can be found in the book by Weise [Wei09]. These algorithms will later be compared in terms of their results on inspection planning of the cylinder head in chapter 6.

Simulated Annealing (SA)

Simulated Annealing is inspired by the natural process of annealing metals. As a piece of metal melts, the metal particles spread in random ways and slow down as it is gradually cooled. This idea has been applied to numerical optimizations, in which one starts with a parameter and randomly modifies the solution by moving towards different directions. Algorithm 4 contains the pseudo-code of this algorithm.

Algorithm 4: Pseudo-code for simulated annealing optimization

```
Result: χ*
χ_curr ← randomCreate( )                    /* random initialization */
χ* ← χ_curr
T ← T_start                                 /* initial temperature */
k ← 1                                       /* iteration number */
while not termination( ) do
    T ← reduceTemperature(k, T)
    χ_temp ← mutate(χ_curr)                 /* temporal solution */
    Δf_g ← f_g(χ_curr) − f_g(χ_temp)

    if Δf_g < 0 then
        χ_curr ← χ_temp                     /* solution accepted */

        if f_g(χ*) < f_g(χ_curr) then
            χ* ← χ_curr                     /* global solution improved */
        end
    else
        if random( ) < exp(−Δf_g / (k_B T)) then
            χ_curr ← χ_temp                 /* worse solution accepted */
        end
    end
    k ← k + 1
end
```

In each iteration of this algorithm, the temperature is reduced and a new solution candidate is generated by slightly modifying the current solution (mutate(χ_{curr})). If the new parameter improves the function value, the algorithm moves to this new parameter. If not, the worse movement is accepted with a probability indicated by the temperature parameter and the amount of solution deterioration. To this end, a random number with uniform distribution in the interval [0,1] is generated and the solution is accepted only if the random number is smaller than the probability threshold. This helps the algorithm to explore more at the beginning when the temperature is higher. The probability threshold is typically determined by the *Boltzmann probability factor* indicated by

$$p(T,\Delta f_{\mathrm{g}}) = \exp\left(-\frac{\Delta f_{\mathrm{g}}}{k_{\mathrm{B}}T}\right), \tag{2.3}$$

in which T determines the temperature in Kelvin, Δf_{g} is the amount of deterioration in the function values, and k_{B} is the Boltzmann's constant $\approx 1.38 \times 10^{-23}\,\mathrm{J\,K^{-1}}$. For algorithmic purposes, the actual physical values may be dismissed and the quantities are often set to heuristic values.

Increasing the number of iterations, the temperature decreases and the probability of accepting worsening solutions declines. The random behavior and allowance of initially worse solutions enables the search to escape local optima and better explore the space. At termination, the best visited solution parameter is returned as the optimization result.

Genetic Algorithm (GA)

Inspired by the Darwinian evolution principle, the Genetic algorithm is a variant of population-based evolutionary optimizations. The pseudo-code of this algorithm is provided in algorithm 5. This optimization starts with a set of random solution candidates, also known as chromosomes. As in Darwinian evolution, in every iteration a set of better solutions G_{mate} are selected and used as a mating pool for reproduction of further solutions. The offspring solutions are produced using *crossover* and *mutation* of the selected chromosomes in the mating pool. Crossover combines two candidate chromosomes to get an offspring, whereas mutation induces small random changes to a single chromosome. The mutation and crossover rates, α_{c} and α_{m}, indicate the proportion of newly generated solutions using each of the two techniques. After reproduction, both the current generation and the newly generated solutions are sorted and the best candidates are chosen for the next generation.

The population size, mutation and crossover rates, and selection strategies are the main parameters, governing the convergence speed and global optimality of the algorithm. In multiple evolution iterations, the population fitness values tend to increase, and at termination, the best produced individual solution is returned as the optimization result.

Algorithm 5: Pseudo-code for genetic algorithm

```
Result: χ*
G ← createPopulation( )                          /* initial generation */
χ* ← getBestSolution(G)                             /* initial solution */

while not termination( ) do
    G_mate ← select(G)                           /* select mating pool */
    G_co ← crossover(G_mate, α_c)
    G_mu ← mutate(G_mate, α_m)
    G ← nextGeneration(G, G_co, G_mu)              /* sort and select */
    χ_curr ← getBestSolution(G)

    if f_g(χ*) < f_g(χ_curr) then
        χ* ← χ_curr                        /* global solution improved */
    end
end
```

Particle Swarm Optimization (PSO)

Swarm intelligence refers to the phenomenon of the collective intelligent behavior that emerges from the communication and actions of individuals in a group [Yan13]. Most of the biological systems with social living habits such as ants, bees, and birds often exhibit this kind of intelligence, although individually they exhibit simple acts. The PSO algorithm is especially inspired by flocks of birds when they search a field for food. Individual birds can randomly search in different directions and when a promising region is found, they communicate this with the surrounding birds. This way, any bird can receive multiple information about the field and together with its own experience, it can decide on where to search next. Similar to this, PSO searches a design space with a number of particles, the so-called particle swarm P_{sw}, which are randomly chosen at the beginning. These particles are not only individual searchers (like many parallel simulated annealing optimizers), but they also communicate.

Algorithm 6 gives an overview of this algorithm. Every particle is composed of three vectors: its current position in the search space χ, its best individually found position so far χ_l, and its velocity $\boldsymbol{v}$. The particle is also aware of the best visited position of the other particles χ_g which have so far communicated with it.

Algorithm 6: Pseudo-code for particle swarm optimization

```
Result: χ*
P_sw ← createSwarm(N)                        /* initial particle swarm */
χ* ← getBestSolution(P_sw)                          /* initial solution */

while not termination( ) do
    for i ← 1 to N                               /* for N particles do */
    do
        /* information exchange                                        */
        P_sw[i].χ_g ← getBestFromNeighborParticles( )

        /* update particle velocity and position                       */
        P_sw[i].updateVelocity( )
        P_sw[i].updatePosition( )

        if f_g(P_sw[i].χ) > f_g(P_sw[i].χ_l) then
            P_sw[i].χ_l ← P_sw[i].χ                 /* particle improved */
        end
    end

    χ_curr = getBestSolution(P_sw)

    if f_g(χ*) < f_g(χ_curr) then
        χ* ← χ_curr                          /* global solution improved */
    end

end
```

Every iteration of this algorithm updates the velocity vector $\boldsymbol{v}$ according to the following equation:

$$\boldsymbol{v} \leftarrow \boldsymbol{v} + c_l \begin{bmatrix} \varepsilon_1 & & \\ & \ddots & \\ & & \varepsilon_d \end{bmatrix} (\chi_l - \chi) + c_g \begin{bmatrix} \delta_1 & & \\ & \ddots & \\ & & \delta_d \end{bmatrix} (\chi_g - \chi).$$

The parameters ε_1 to ε_d and δ_i to δ_d are independent uniform random variables in [1,0], which are being regenerated in each iteration. The diagonal matrices in these update rules are meant to randomly weight individual dimensions of the vectors. Here, d refers to the dimension of the position vector. c_l and c_g are further constant weighting factors that balance the tendencies of the particle to search towards the local and global optimum. A particle also has a preference to keep its previous direction, therefore the term $\boldsymbol{v}$ is added to the velocity update rule. The updated particle position vector is simply computed as moving from the previous position along the updated velocity:

$$\chi \leftarrow \chi + \boldsymbol{v}.$$

If an iteration improves the best visited parameter for a particle, the particle remembers this, and in the next iteration, the neighboring particles will also inquire this information. Based on the standard approaches for configuring PSO [Bra07], the neighbors of a particle must be randomly selected (not necessarily based on Euclidean distances) and dynamically changed to get the best performance. At termination, the best visited parameter point during the whole search is reported as the optimization final result.

2.3.1 Handling Constraints

The previous content of this section discussed the generic problem of continuous optimization. Most real-world optimization problems including inspection planning also include constraints. A solution is feasible, if and only if all the constraints are met. Based on the book by Weise [Wei09], strategies for handling constraints can be summarized as follows.

- **Death Penalty**: This approach is probably the easiest way for handling the constraints, in which each solution candidate which is not consistent with the constraints will be rejected, and totally removed from the optimization process. This method can be useful for problems in which the feasible region is large enough, so that the search algorithm can still find enough feasible solutions when the infeasible ones are being thrown away.
- **Penalty Function**: In this method, the constraints are combined with the gain function to yield a new function. This combination is done in a way that the new function always returns a worse value for an infeasible solution compared to a feasible one.
- **Additional Objectives**: Another way of dealing with constraints is to express them as new objective functions, which will be additionally optimized besides the main function. For instance, if $g(x) \geq 0$ must be fulfilled, an equivalent objective function of the form $f(x) = \max\{-g(x),0\}$ can be defined, subject to minimization. The minimum value of $f(x)$ is zero and is achieved for all solutions for which $g(x) \geq 0$ holds. This way, the constraint is transformed to an additional optimization function.
- **Method of Inequalities**: This method builds a framework of preference between the solution candidates, in order to generate more solutions which are feasible, but keeps some infeasible solutions as well, hoping that they can be improved in further iterations. Following this approach, the solutions which fulfill all the constraints are preferred to all the other solutions. Solutions which satisfy some but not all the constraints are preferred to those that do not satisfy any constraint. Using the concept of dominance from multi-objective optimization, a Pareto-front of such solutions will be generated. The idea of this method is to guide the optimization process into feasible regions, without investing lots of effort in generating and evaluating infeasible solutions.

2.4 Components of the Planning Application

At the beginning of this chapter, the inspection planning problem was generically formulated in equation 2.1, and general concepts for solving or approximating the solutions were proposed. In this section, the components of this problem will be mapped to the planning application of this thesis, which includes inspection planning for an industrial product in a laser triangulation inspection system. The proposed approaches for planning can be applied to any other object whose CAD model and surface properties are known. The next section introduces the geometrical and optical design space of the inspection application.

2.4.1 Design Space of the Planning Application

Geometry

The laser and the camera can theoretically follow arbitrary trajectories around the object to capture several image frames. Each positioning of the camera and the laser as two rigid bodies has a maximum of 12 degrees of freedom. To cover an object with an area comparable with the cylinder head and considering that the laser line only covers a 2D profile in each frame, one needs thousands of frames. Obviously, for the inspection planning problem this leads to a very large plan and an enormous optimization complexity.

One can, however, make meaningful simplifications to reduce the complexity. For instance, the scan trajectory can be constrained to a linear motion along a particular axis instead of an arbitrary trajectory, but the object may be freely positioned under the sensor. A single measurement in this scenario is then defined as completely scanning the object along the predefined scan direction. Therefore, instead of planning for single frames, the plan $\boldsymbol{\theta}$ contains a sequence of such linear scans, with each measurement covering a portion of the surface. To further reduce uninteresting setup configurations, the laser and the camera can be parametrized so as to look at a common point, considered as the origin, to keep the laser always in the field of view. Fig. 2.2 illustrates the 9-dimensional degrees of freedom for the laser triangulation measurement. In this design space, 4 parameters are dedicated to sensor placement (θ_c,ϕ_c,τ,d_c) and 5 parameters to the object placement (α_o, β_o,γ_o,Δy,Δz).

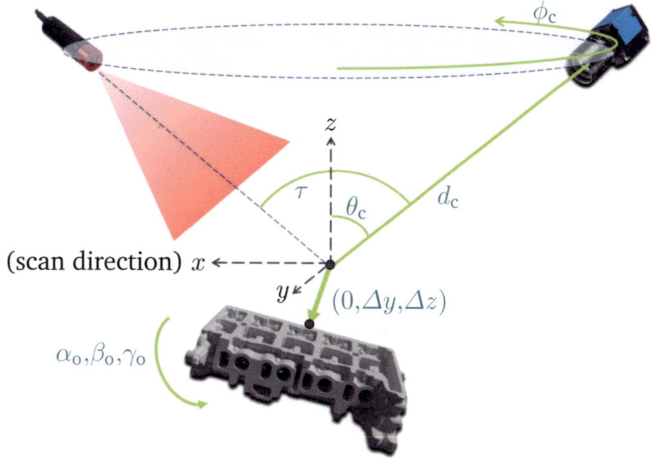

Figure 2.2: Proposed 9-dimensional geometrical parameter space for the inspection planning application.

The camera view point is determined by the polar angle θ_c, an azimuthal angle ϕ_c, and the distance d_c. The laser holds a triangulation angle τ to the camera, with positive values corresponding to bright field illumination and negative values for dark field illumination. The camera azimuthal angle ϕ_c rotates both the camera and the laser to always keep the laser line aligned with the image rows. The object can be freely positioned under the sensor by a 3D rotation using the Euler angles α_o, β_o,γ_o, and a translational vector determined by Δy and Δz. The translation has only 2 degrees of freedom because the object is completely scanned in one direction and the translational components parallel to this direction do not introduce new constellations. In the proposed parametrization, the x-axis is considered as the constant scan direction. Due to rotational degrees of freedom of the sensor and the object, variations of the scan direction within the xy-plane will be redundant and do not count as extra degrees of freedom. Therefore, the scan direction can be kept constant.

In this parametrization, the effect of the laser distance has been neglected. Laser distance can cause laser focusing issues, which can be adjusted once one knows the operating distance. In addition, it can also slightly influence the coverage of the laser line on the surface, because the actual angle of laser light rays reaching a point vary with laser distance. These effects can only slightly influence the measurement and thus they were not included in the modeling.

Optical Parameters

The adjustable optical parameters generally include the choice of lens, its focal length, aperture diameter, as well as the choice of the digital sensor and its exposure time. It is often not possible to optimize some optical parameters, such as the focal length, to an arbitrary value. In this thesis, the lens and the digital sensor are assumed to be given, and the aperture diameter (i.e. the f-number), and the exposure time are subject to optimizations.

Due to the complexity of simulating the effect of these parameters on the measurements, optimization of the optical parameters will be applied separately from the geometrical parameters. This will be elaborated in more detail in chapter 6.

2.4.2 Summary of the Planning Approach

Design Space

As discussed previously, a plan $\boldsymbol{\theta}$ is a sequence of measurements. Each measurement for a laser triangulation inspection can be parameterized based on the design space introduced in section 2.4.1.

Gain Function

For the gain function $f_{\mathrm{g}}(\boldsymbol{\theta})$, different metrological criteria such as surface coverage and measurement uncertainty will be applied. Definition and derivation of these evaluation criteria are the main subject of the next chapter. Later in chapter 6 another criteria for optimization of the feature detection performance at the image level will be proposed and optimized, to further fine-tune the planning results.

Constraints

To avoid proposing geometrically infeasible constellations, the measurements in which the camera, laser, or the object collide during the scan are banned for inclusion in the plan. In addition, a minimum value of 10° is considered for the triangulation angle τ, so as to provide some necessary triangulation angle for the measurement principle to work. The maximum allowed distance of measurement points to the camera is limited to 1.5 m. Simulated measurement points lying further away will be dismissed to ensure all planned measurements happen within a given distance to the camera. Every parameter is also subject to an upper bound and a lower bound, given in table 2.1. The constraint function $l(\boldsymbol{\theta})$ returns a positive value, if all the mentioned conditions are met. For handling the constraints during the planning, the "death penalty" strategy described in section 2.3.1 is integrated with the optimizations.

Planning Method

The inspection planning algorithm follows a greedy approach, in which each optimization step adds one optimized measurement to the plan. It continues adding further measurements until the inspection result is satisfactory. To benefit from intelligent search algorithms, this thesis applies and analyzes the performance of several continuous optimization algorithms as well as the discrete optimization of the measurability matrix method. The analysis of inspection planning results will be delayed until chapter 6, in which the performance of different methods will be demonstrated and compared.

Table 2.1: Assumed constraints for the geometrical parameters

Parameter	Constraint
d_c	$[0.1\,\text{m}, 0.8\,\text{m}]$
τ	$[-80°, -10°] \cup [10°, 80°]$
ϕ_c	$[0°, 360°)$
θ_c	$[0°, 90°]$
α_o	$[0°, 360°)$
β_o	$[0°, 360°)$
γ_o	$[0°, 360°)$
Δy	$[-0.5\,\text{m}, 0.5\,\text{m}]$
Δz	$[-0.4\,\text{m}, 0.4\,\text{m}]$

Assumptions

In this thesis, and similar to most previous works, the measurement transition costs are considered to be negligible and the execution costs of the measurements are assumed to be the same, i.e. $\forall \boldsymbol{m}\, c_{\mathrm{e}}(\boldsymbol{m}) = 1$. This essentially conveys that the planning aims at minimizing the number of measurements which best inspect the surface.

3 Metrological Evaluation

As discussed previously in chapter 1, evaluation is an essential part of the inspection planning workflow, which must be in accordance with the goals and requirements of the inspection task. To link this with the content of chapter 2, metrological evaluation of an inspection plan $\boldsymbol{\theta}$ corresponds to the quantitative value returned by the gain function $f_g(\boldsymbol{\theta})$, which evaluates the quality of a plan. In dimensional inspection, the quality of the plan corresponds to the amount of geometrical information delivered about the surface. This chapter exclusively discusses relevant metrological evaluation criteria for measuring a 3D surface by point-wise measurements.

The content of this chapter begins with an overview on commonly used evaluation criteria for inspection planning in the next section, and continues with the definition of the metrological criteria considered in this thesis. Later on, the concept of *surface inference* will be introduced, which fuses different metrological criteria into a single gain function, encoding the amount of information an inspection delivers about the surface.

3.1 Introduction to Commonly Used Criteria

In all kinds of inspection planning, either model-based or non-model-based, achieving a maximum coverage on the surface or features of interest is a central goal [Tar95b][Cow88][Pit99]. For a surface point to be measured, it must be firstly illuminated by the light source and further lie inside the camera field of view without being occluded by any other scene component. This measurability check leads to a binary coverage flag for each surface point.

Another important metric associated to each measurable point is the *lateral resolution* of the optical system. Lateral resolution corresponds to the distance of adjacent measured points in the locality of a surface point and can vary across the surface based on surface geometry relative to the sensor. Scott [Sco09] incorporated a similar metric called the *scan density* into his planning method.

The paper by Cowan et al. [Cow88] is one of the early works which mathematically describes four constraints for admissibility of sensor viewpoints. Adaptations of his work have been further applied by other planning methods [Tar95a][Ell05][Mav15]. In addition to the criteria discussed above, Cowan considered the focus as a constraint for the measurability of a surface point.

Each quantitative measurement is always concerned with some level of uncertainty [Joi08]. The *measurement uncertainty* is the result of many different factors during image formation, such as optical effects, aberrations, sensor noise and digitalization effects, as well as calibration inaccuracies, and errors in image processing algorithms. Incorporation of measurement uncertainty in inspection planning is very beneficial as it can result in a plan robust against disturbing factors.

Recent planning works have also taken the measurement uncertainty into account [Gro16][Pri03][Sco09], all using experimental models. Prieto et al. [Pri03], for instance, use a measurement uncertainty model depending quadratically on the distance of the sensor to the measured point and exponentially on the angle of the sensor viewpoint. The model proposed by Scott [Sco09] also grows quadratically with distance but has an inverse cosine relation with the laser incident angle. The model used by Mahmud et al. [Mah11] is only a variable of the laser incident angle. The considerable differences between the uncertainty models indicate that these models are device dependent, which implies the experiments for fitting uncertainty models must be repeated for each individual sensor.

One of the main contributions of this thesis is the analytical approach towards propagating the uncertainties in the measurement, which together with using sensor-realistic simulations, can fully automate the uncertainty planning and avoid the experimental work. This approach attempts to estimate the uncertainty factors, and further propagate them through the measurement to predict the final measurement uncertainties.

The rest of this chapter discusses different criteria for evaluating a 3D surface measurement, including surface coverage, measurement uncertainty, and probabilistic surface inference. These criteria can be beneficial to many other point-based measurement methods as well, such as all structured-light techniques.

3.2 Surface Coverage

For measuring the surface geometry using touch probes, there are some strategies [Lee97][Nam99] which are traditionally being used in order to sample the measurement points on the surface. These strategies can be adopted to vision-based inspection systems to define a set of *target points* on the surface to be covered during the inspection. For different resolution requirements along the surface, target points can be generated with varying resolution. The coverage gain function $f^{\mathrm{cov}}(\boldsymbol{\theta})$ will be then defined as the number of target points which are covered by the inspection plan as

$$f^{\mathrm{cov}}(\boldsymbol{\theta}) = \sum_{j=1}^{k} I^{\mathrm{cov}}(\boldsymbol{p}_j,\boldsymbol{\theta}) \tag{3.1}$$

In this equation, I^{cov} is a binary function which returns 1 if target point $\boldsymbol{p}_i$ is covered by plan $\boldsymbol{\theta}$. We have to note that it is very unlikely that a measurement scenario measures the surface in the exact coordinates of a target point. Therefore, it is important to consider the target points as covered if the surface is measured in a vicinity of this points smaller than the required lateral resolution. The calculation of I^{cov} actually depends on processing simulated measurement images, which we discuss in the next chapter.

If standard target points are available for a product, they can be directly used to define the coverage gain function. Otherwise, there are well-known point sampling algorithms, which can sample a CAD model with adequate discrete points. An interesting example is the *Poisson disk sampling* algorithm [Cor12] which can sample a polygonal mesh with a number of points which are mutually not closer than a given distance. This algorithm can generate sample points which uniformly cover the area of the product surface, providing a consistent target point density all over the surface. Figure. 3.1 illustrates the target points sampled for the cylinder head model with a distance of 5 mm between the points.

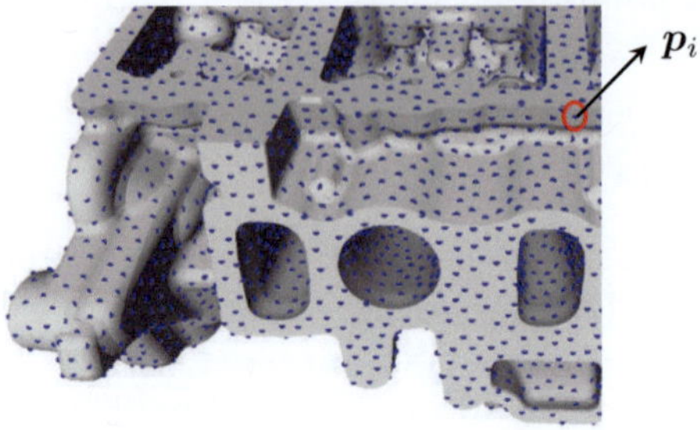

Figure 3.1: Target points sampled on the cylinder head CAD model, using Poisson disk sampling as proposed by Corsini et al. [Cor12], and a distance of 5 mm between the points.

3.3 Measurement Uncertainty

Due to the presence of random effects and imperfections in a real world measurement, every measurement device essentially reports an estimate of the value of its measurand. Inaccuracies in a measurement can either be caused by a systematic error or a stochastic uncertainty. A systematic error can be studied and accounted for, however, the stochastic uncertainty is an important characteristic of a measurement which indicates its reliability. According to the "Guide to the Expression of Uncertainty in Measurement (GUM)" [Joi08] methodologies for evaluating the uncertainties in a measurement can be either based on statistics of repeated measurements (type A), or they are based on analytical methods for propagating the uncertainties through the measurement (type B).

In both type A or B uncertainty estimation approaches, the *standard uncertainty* u is considered to be the estimated standard deviation of the measurement result, regardless of the actual distribution.

Given the specification tolerance zone for the acceptance of a product dimension as an interval of length s_t, the measurement uncertainty limits the acceptance zone by $2u$ from the upper and the lower decision limits (corresponding to 95% probability of coverage in a Gaussian distribution), as recommended by the International Organization for Internationalization (ISO) [ISO17]. Figure 3.2 visualizes the specification and acceptance zones in an uncertain measurement. An admissible uncertainty u for inspecting a dimension with tolerance s_t must therefore satisfy $u < s_\mathrm{t}/4$. Consequently, the gain function for uncertainty planning can be given as

$$f^u(\boldsymbol{\theta}) = \sum_{j=1}^{k} U_\mathrm{s}\left(\frac{s_\mathrm{t}(\boldsymbol{p}_j)}{4} - u(\boldsymbol{p}_j,\boldsymbol{\theta})\right), \tag{3.2}$$

in which U_s is the unit step function which assigns negative and zero values to zero and positive values to one. In this function, $u(\boldsymbol{p}_i,\boldsymbol{\theta})$ refers to the a posteriori uncertainty at a target point $\boldsymbol{p}_i$ after measuring the surface by plan $\boldsymbol{\theta}$. The a posteriori uncertainty results from an information fusion step, which combines both the uncertainty of several measurements as well as the prior knowledge about this point, i.e. the a priori uncertainty. This will be more elaborated in section 3.4. $f^u(\boldsymbol{\theta})$ then calculates the number of target points which can be measured within the admissible uncertainty by applying plan $\boldsymbol{\theta}$.

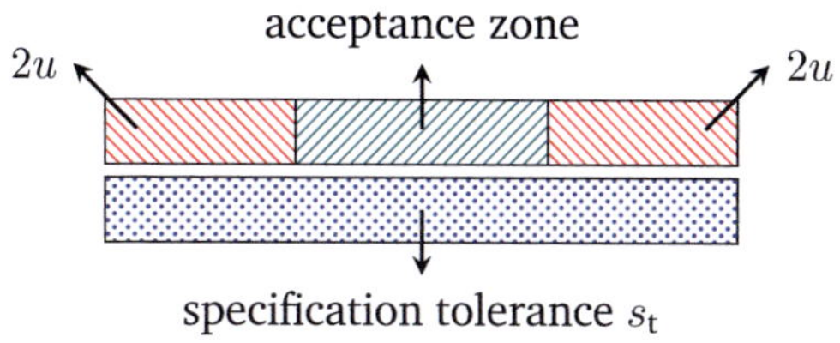

Figure 3.2: Effect of standard uncertainty u on the acceptance zone of a dimensional inspection, according to ISO standard 14253-1 [ISO17].

An automatic planning for minimizing the uncertainty requires evaluating the term $u(\boldsymbol{p}_i,\boldsymbol{\theta})$ for each target point and every desired plan. Thus, it is essential to analytically estimate this term. To this end, first of all, it is required to analytically derive the measurement standard uncertainty based on propagating the sources of uncertainty through the measurement (type B uncertainty evaluation). And furthermore, an information fusion step is necessary to fuse the uncertainties of several measurements and the prior knowledge to derive the a posteriori uncertainty.

3.3.1 Analytical Propagation of Uncertainties

The sources of uncertainty in a typical optical measurement can be generally grouped into two categories:

1. **Feature detection uncertainty**: the uncertainty in detecting or measuring relevant features on the image, which is influenced by both the signal to noise ratio of the image and the image processing algorithm.
2. **Calibration uncertainty**: uncertainties associated with the geometrical positioning of the sensors (extrinsic calibration), as well as inaccuracies in optical parameters which are involved in the measurement (e.g. focal length, center of projection, etc.).

In order to study the effect of these uncertainty factors in the final measurement, one needs to propagate the standard deviation or covariance matrix of the noisy input values through the measurement and obtain an estimate of the resulting standard deviation for the measurement result.

Standard Approach

Supposing a measurement function g is available, this function maps the input data to some output measurement vector $\boldsymbol{v}$ as given by

$$\boldsymbol{v} = g(\boldsymbol{d}). \tag{3.3}$$

The input data $\boldsymbol{d}$ consists of all what the measurement needs to estimate the measurand, such as the result of the image processing algorithms and the calibration data. In an uncertain measurement, $\boldsymbol{d}$ is subject to unwanted noise $\boldsymbol{\delta d}$, which in turn induces an error to the output result

$$\boldsymbol{v} + \boldsymbol{\delta v} = g(\boldsymbol{d} + \boldsymbol{\delta d}). \tag{3.4}$$

For quantities of more than one dimension, standard uncertainty is expressed in terms of covariance matrices (here $\Sigma_{\boldsymbol{d}}$, $\Sigma_{\boldsymbol{v}}$), which contain the variances as well as covariances between the noisy vector elements. The standard way of analytically propagating the input uncertainties to the output measurement is to use a first order approximation of the measurement model [Joi08], by the following equation. Here, the partial derivatives result in Jacobian matrices, and the symbol T stands for transposition. More exact approximations are also possible, by including higher order terms in the Taylor series of the measurement function g.

$$\Sigma_{\boldsymbol{v}} \approx \frac{\partial g}{\partial \boldsymbol{d}} \Sigma_{\boldsymbol{d}} \left(\frac{\partial g}{\partial \boldsymbol{d}}\right)^{\mathrm{T}}. \tag{3.5}$$

Implicit Functions

The standard way of propagating the covariance matrix through a model requires an explicit function which maps the input to the output. It is, however, very common that some parameter is not obtained through an explicit function, but rather through an optimization of the form

$$\boldsymbol{v} = \arg\min_{\boldsymbol{v}'} g'(\boldsymbol{d}, \boldsymbol{v}'). \tag{3.6}$$

This formulation is very familiar in image processing algorithms for detecting features (lines, edges, etc.) in which the desired parameter is estimated using least squares regression. Haralick in 1998 proposed an interesting mathematical framework entitled "propagating covariance in computer vision" [Har96], where he exactly studied uncertainty propagation through optimizations in the form of equation 3.6. According to the derivations in this work, the covariance of the model output in this case can be estimated as

$$\Sigma_{\boldsymbol{v}} \approx \left(\frac{\partial^2 g'}{\partial \boldsymbol{v}'^2}\right)^{-1} \frac{\partial^2 g'^{\mathrm{T}}}{\partial \boldsymbol{v}' \, \partial \boldsymbol{d}} \Sigma_{\boldsymbol{d}} \frac{\partial^2 g'}{\partial \boldsymbol{v}' \, \partial \boldsymbol{d}} \left(\left(\frac{\partial^2 g'}{\partial \boldsymbol{v}'^2}\right)^{-1}\right)^{\mathrm{T}}. \tag{3.7}$$

This yields a second order approximation of the output covariance matrix. The second order partial derivatives result in Hessian matrices.

Interestingly, every explicit function $\boldsymbol{v} = g(\boldsymbol{d})$ can be also written in the form of equation 3.6 by setting $g'(\boldsymbol{d}, \boldsymbol{v}') = |\boldsymbol{v}' - g(\boldsymbol{d}))|$. This formulation can be used to derive the measurand by $\boldsymbol{v} = \arg\min_{\boldsymbol{v}'} |\boldsymbol{v}' - g(\boldsymbol{d}))|$.

Therefore, Haralick's formulation can be used for both cases, to give a compact second order uncertainty propagation. As we will see later on, in some cases it is more straightforward to use the implicit method for uncertainty propagation than deriving the explicit function.

3.3.2 Measurement Sensitivity

Given a covariance matrix Σ_d for the input measurement parameters, two different inspection setups may respond differently to the same source of uncertainty and result in different uncertainties in the final measurement. This is referred to as the *measurement sensitivity* and its analysis is very similar to uncertainty analysis. The only difference is that for sensitivity analysis, the response of the system to a constant input covariance matrix will be studied; whereas for uncertainty analysis the absolute input uncertainties for each system configuration must be given, which do not necessarily remain constant by changing the system parameters.

3.3.3 Uncertainty Propagation for Laser Triangulation

To apply an uncertainty propagation technique to the application of laser triangulation, the first step is to model the sources of uncertainty. The underlying measurement function and its input parameters for laser line scanning were studied earlier in section 1.2.1. All these parameters constitute the input data $\boldsymbol{d}$, thus without considering noise $\boldsymbol{d} = [x, y, \mathrm{R}, \boldsymbol{t}, \boldsymbol{n}, d, f, c_x, c_y]$.

The input parameters for the laser triangulation measurement are summarized in table 3.1. This table also contains the uncertain form of the parameters, where they have been perturbed by different random variables. In the following section, the modeled uncertainties will be briefly reviewed. A more detailed consideration can be found in the author's publication [Moh16].

Laser Detection Uncertainties

The image coordinates (x,y) of a detected laser profile are subject to random noise, caused by the signal to noise ratio of the image and the image processing algorithm. Figure 3.3 displays the fluctuations of detected laser centers along a profile. The uncertainty in a laser detection is approximated as an additive Gaussian noise $(x + e_x, y + e_y)$.

Table 3.1: Summary of uncertainty modeling for a laser line scanner

Type	Parameter	Error-Free	Uncertain Form	Random Factors
laser detection	pixel coordinates	x, y	$x + e_x, y + e_y$	e_x, e_y
geometrical calibration	camera rotation	R	$\mathrm{R_e R}$	$e_\alpha, e_\beta, e_\gamma$
	camera position	$\boldsymbol{t}$	$\mathrm{R_e}\boldsymbol{t} + \boldsymbol{e}_\mathrm{o}$	$e_{\mathrm{o}_x}, e_{\mathrm{o}_y}, e_{\mathrm{o}_z}$
	laser equation	d	$d + e_d$	e_d
		$\boldsymbol{n}$	see [Moh16]	e_θ, e_ϕ
intrinsic calibration	focal length	f	$f + e_f$	e_f
	projection center	c_x, c_y	$c_x + e_{c_x}$ $c_y + e_{c_y}$	e_{c_x}, e_{c_y}

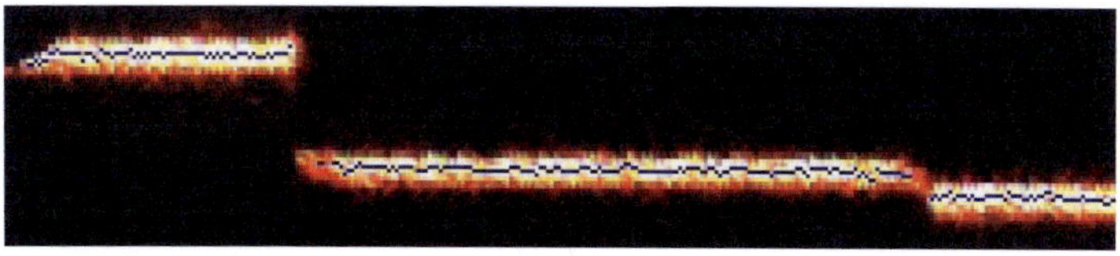

Figure 3.3: Result of a laser detection algorithm on a real image.

Geometrical Calibration Uncertainties

The placement and angular uncertainties of positioning systems or robot arms are usually reported by the manufacturer or they need to be estimated by experiments. As depicted in figure 3.4, positioning uncertainties can lead to a transformation of the camera coordinate frame by a vector $\boldsymbol{e}_\mathrm{o}$ and some rotation matrix $\mathrm{R_e}$. The vector $\boldsymbol{e}_\mathrm{o}$ is modeled by three independent zero-mean Gaussian random variables $(e_{\mathrm{o}_x}, e_{\mathrm{o}_y}, e_{\mathrm{o}_z})$ for each direction. The rotation matrix $\mathrm{R_e}$ has three degrees of freedom which must be parameterized according to the degrees of freedom of the positioning system. Here, rotation uncertainties are modeled using 3 zero-mean Gaussian Euler angles $(e_\alpha, e_\beta, e_\gamma)$. These angles describe unwanted rotations around the x-, y-, and z-axis. If the angular errors are small enough, one can make a linear approximation in the Euler rotation formula and approximate the rotation error as

$$R_e = \begin{bmatrix} 1 & e_\gamma & -e_\alpha \\ -e_\gamma & 1 & e_\beta \\ e_\alpha & -e_\beta & 1 \end{bmatrix} \tag{3.8}$$

This way, the error-free geometry of the camera $[\mathrm{R}, \boldsymbol{t}]$ will be perturbed as $[\mathrm{R_e R}, \mathrm{R_e}\boldsymbol{t} + \boldsymbol{e}_\mathrm{o}]$ according to the method of combining two rigid transformations [Ma12] (transformations which only contain rotation and translation components). Figure 3.4, illustrates the geometrical uncertainties in positioning the laser line projector with equation $\boldsymbol{x}_\mathrm{w}^\mathrm{T}\boldsymbol{n} = d$. The uncertainties can deviate the laser plane normal direction as well as displace the plane. Although there are three degrees of freedom for the laser displacement, only the component parallel to the normal vector is taken into account (i.e. e_d), since the other directions cause no changes in the geometrical equation of the plane. Here, e_d is modeled as a zero-mean Gaussian random variable. Deviations of the normal direction are modeled by a cone parameterized by two independent random variables e_ϕ and e_θ. Variable e_θ is distributed by a zero-mean Gaussian distribution whose standard deviation defines the cone half-angle. Given this angle, the normal vector is assumed to equiprobably point to anywhere on the perimeter of the cone base. This is modeled by a uniform variable e_ϕ in the interval $[-\pi, \pi]$. The perturbed normal vector can be then geometrically calculated using these two random variables [Moh16].

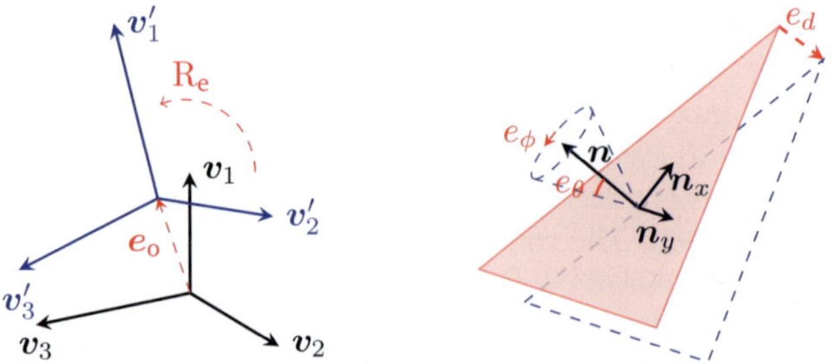

Figure 3.4: Geometrical uncertainty models for the camera coordinate frame (left) and the laser plane (right).

Intrinsic Calibration Uncertainties

By taking care of the inaccuracies during the intrinsic calibration process, the intrinsic parameters can be associated with an estimate of their standard deviations. The calibration method proposed by Di Leo and Paolillo [Di 11] is an example of such calibration methods. Although different calibration approaches may model the optical projection by numerous parameters, here only two major parameters for the pin-hole camera model have been considered which include the focal length f (to determine the distance of projection center to the image plane) and the center of projection (c_x, c_y). It has been assumed that these parameters are subject to a zero-mean Gaussian additive noise.

Based on the uncertainty modeling discussed in this section, the measurement parameters will be perturbed by a total number of 14 random variables and thus the covariance matrix Σ_d is of size 14×14, whose diagonal elements are the variances of the random variables and the non-diagonal elements denote the covariances of each pair of them. It has been assumed that all pairs of variables that are not in the same group (e.g. feature detection and geometrical calibration noise) are uncorrelated. In case of correlations between the random variables, especially in the calibration parameters, they can be estimated from the calibration process or the setup parameters. Table 3.2 defines the standard deviation of the defined random variables used for the uncertainty propagation in this chapter. These variables are assumed to be uncorrelated.

Uncertainty Propagation through Measurement

As previously discussed about triangulation of laser lines in equation 1.5 of chapter 1, the 3D coordinates of a measurement point $\boldsymbol{x}_{\mathrm{W}}$ are obtained by solving a system of linear equations of the form $\boldsymbol{x}_{\mathrm{W}} = \mathrm{M}(\boldsymbol{d})^{-1}\boldsymbol{q}(\boldsymbol{d})$, where M and $\boldsymbol{q}$ are both dependent on the noisy input parameters in $\boldsymbol{d}$.

To propagate the uncertainties using the standard approach, one needs to linearly approximate this function in terms of the noisy input parameters. As this function is highly non-linear with respect to the random variables in $\boldsymbol{d}$, even considering higher order terms can lead to an improper function approximation with cumbersome derivations.

By borrowing the ideas from Haralick's uncertainty propagation framework [Har96], the measurement function can be reformulated as

$$\boldsymbol{x}_{\mathrm{w}} = \arg\min_{\boldsymbol{x}'_{\mathrm{w}}} |\mathrm{M}(\boldsymbol{d})\, \boldsymbol{x}'_{\mathrm{w}} - \boldsymbol{q}(\boldsymbol{d})|. \tag{3.9}$$

Using Haralick's second order uncertainty propagation framework, the derivatives are directly derived from this function, which avoids the matrix inversion term. Therefore, by computing the partial derivatives and building the input covariance matrix $\Sigma_{\boldsymbol{d}}$, the desired covariance matrix $\Sigma_{\boldsymbol{x}_{\mathrm{w}}} \in \mathbb{R}^{3\times 3}$ results from equation 3.7. $\Sigma_{\boldsymbol{x}_{\mathrm{w}}}$ describes a 3D ellipsoid, which can be evaluated to estimate the measurement standard deviation along each direction.

Figure 3.5 illustrates the result of uncertainty propagation for a sample laser triangulation measurement. In this example, the uncertainties are calculated in the direction pointing out of the page. The assumed standard deviations for the random variables are summarized in table 3.2.

To calculate the uncertainties, first the measurement point cloud is extracted from simulations and then the uncertainty propagation method is separately applied to each measured point. Based on the relative position of a 3D point to the sensor, the measurement exhibits different sensitivities to the parameter uncertainties. This figure shows the sensitivity map of 2 measurements to constant uncertainties of table 3.2, with each measurement covering one side of the cylinder head object.

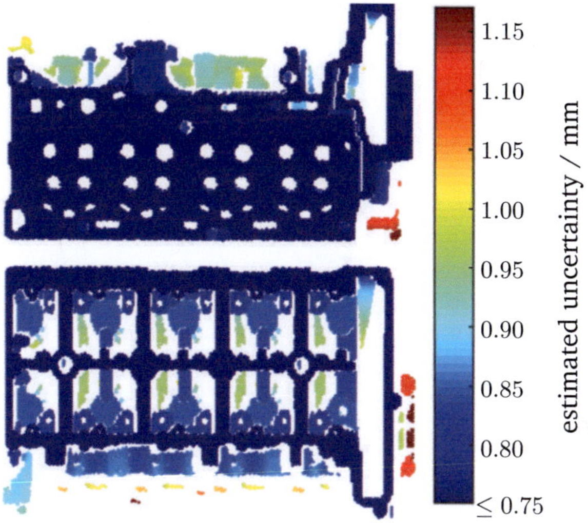

Figure 3.5: Sensitivity map of a laser triangulation measurement to parameter uncertainties given in table 3.2. The resulting point cloud is simulated for two measurements, in which the camera looks perpendicularly on the surface with a distance of 0.2 m and a triangulation angle of 30°.

Table 3.2: Assumed standard deviations for parameters

Type of uncertainty	Standard deviation
positioning of laser and camera along each axis	0.5 mm
rotation of camera and laser along each axis	0.01°
laser detection uncertainty on the image, in both vertical and horizontal directions	0.2 px
focal length calibration	2 px
projection center calibration	0.5 px

3.4 Probabilistic Surface Inference

Optical inspection of a surface results in a point cloud with varying resolution and measurement uncertainty along the surface. The concept of uncertainty propagation discussed previously focuses on calculating the resulting 3D uncertainty of measurement points. The term $u(\boldsymbol{p}_i,\boldsymbol{\theta})$ in the uncertainty gain function of equation 3.2, however, corresponds to the uncertainty of measuring the target point and not the measurement points. It is, therefore, crucial to merge the information of several measurements in the inspection plan and determine a probability distribution for the height of the target point $\boldsymbol{p}_i$ on the surface. In this thesis, this process is called *surface inference*. Figure 3.6 visualizes this concept where each ellipse represents the uncertainty of a measurement point, and p refers to an arbitrary target point to be inferred.

The Bayesian information fusion framework allows us to derive the contribution of the measured points to the uncertainty of the surface value at $\boldsymbol{p}$. In such a framework, one always has some prior knowledge about the subject under study in the form of an a priori distribution [Ber94]. In this case, the a priori distribution can be given based on the typical variations in the manufactured products. As new measurements are made, the prior belief is updated, and an a posteriori distribution is calculated based on the Bayes' law. The a posteriori standard deviation $u(\boldsymbol{p})$ indicates the remaining uncertainty at an arbitrarily chosen point $\boldsymbol{p}$, after the surface has been measured. Here, $u(\boldsymbol{p})$ will be referred to as the *inference uncertainty*.

Modeling each surface point as a random variable turns the whole surface into a stochastic process. To model the surface as a function, let us consider a generic function $z(\boldsymbol{x})$.

In a 3D inspection, the surface is measured in a number of points $\boldsymbol{x}_{\mathrm{w}}$, where each measurement is approximated by a Gaussian distribution with covariance matrix $\Sigma_{\boldsymbol{x}_{\mathrm{w}}}$, depicted as red ellipses in figure 3.6. As a compact notation, let us assume the matrix $\tilde{\mathrm{X}} \in \mathbb{R}^{n\times 2}$ contains the x_w and y_w coordinates of n measurement points, and $\tilde{\boldsymbol{z}} \in \mathbb{R}^{n\times 1}$, is the vector corresponding to their height values.

Inferring the surface at a desired point $z_* = z(\boldsymbol{x}_*)$, corresponds to computing the probability distribution $p(z_*|\tilde{\mathrm{X}}, \tilde{\boldsymbol{z}})$ [Ras06], based on the Bayes' law given by the equation 3.10. In this equation $p(z_*)$ is the a priori distribution for the surface height.

$$p(z_*|\tilde{\mathrm{X}}, \tilde{\boldsymbol{z}}) = \frac{p(\tilde{\mathrm{X}}, \tilde{\boldsymbol{z}}|z_*)\, p(z_*)}{p(\tilde{\mathrm{X}}, \tilde{\boldsymbol{z}})} \tag{3.10}$$

Applying the Bayes' law for each inference point is computationally very expensive. With the assumption of a *Gaussian process*, there exists a closed-form solution for the a posteriori distribution, which makes the inference very efficient. A classical Gaussian process, however, does not fully represent the complex inference process required for industrial surface inspection. In the rest of this chapter, firstly the classical regression with Gaussian processes is introduced in section 3.4.1. The adaptation of the regression method to the inference of industrial surfaces will be later discussed in section 3.4.2.

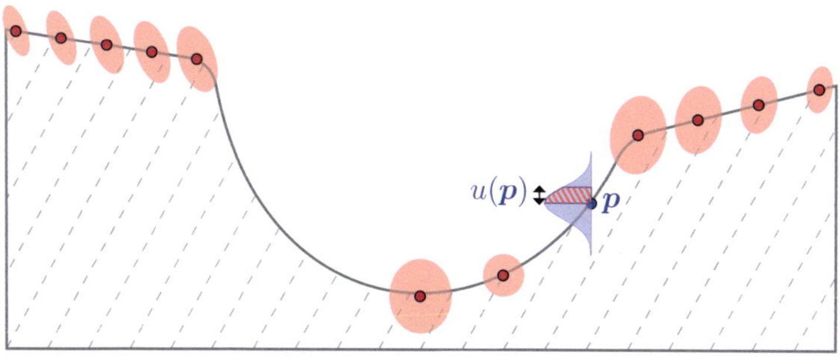

Figure 3.6: Surface inference with noisy measurements. Red ellipses denote uncertain measurement points, and $\boldsymbol{p}$ is a target point to be inferred.

3.4.1 Gaussian Process Regression

A Gaussian Process (GP) [Ras06] is a special variant of a stochastic process, in which the joint distribution between each subset of function values $\{z_1,...,z_k\}$ is a multivariate Gaussian distribution. This property leads to a closed-form solution for the desired conditional probability $p(z_*|\tilde{\mathrm{X}}, \tilde{\boldsymbol{z}})$. This is why GPs are widely used in many problems dealing with non-parametric function regression. In the classical GP, $\{\tilde{\mathrm{X}},\tilde{\boldsymbol{z}}\}$ are referred to as the training data and it is allowed for the measured function values $\tilde{\boldsymbol{z}}$ to be subject to some uncorrelated noise with variance σ_{m}^2. This variance is constant and does not correspond to $\tilde{\mathrm{X}}$.

A GP can be fully specified by its mean function μ_{g} and a covariance function c_{g}, as below. E refers to the expectation operator here.

$$\mu_{\mathrm{g}}(\boldsymbol{x}) = E\left[z(\boldsymbol{x})\right], \tag{3.11}$$

$$c_{\mathrm{g}}\left(\boldsymbol{x}, \boldsymbol{x}'\right) = E\left[\left(z(\boldsymbol{x}) - \mu_{\mathrm{g}}(\boldsymbol{x})\right)\left(z(\boldsymbol{x}') - \mu_{\mathrm{g}}(\boldsymbol{x}')\right)\right] \tag{3.12}$$

The choice of the covariance function and its free parameters determines important properties of the underlying surface function, such as smoothness and correlation length. It is common to consider many processes as isotropic stationary in which the covariance function is a function of the distance between two points $c_{\mathrm{g}}\left(\boldsymbol{x}, \boldsymbol{x}'\right) = c_{\mathrm{g}}\left(r\right) = c(|\boldsymbol{x} - \boldsymbol{x}'|)$. A comprehensive study of covariance functions is given by Rasmussen and Williams [Ras06]. In section 3.4.2, meaningful choices of covariance functions for surface inference will be discussed.

For a GP, the desired a posteriori distribution $p(z_*|\tilde{\mathrm{X}}, \tilde{\boldsymbol{z}})$ is another Gaussian distribution, with mean μ_* and variance σ_*^2 defined as [Ras06]

$$\mu_* = \mu_{\mathrm{g}}(\boldsymbol{x}_*) + \boldsymbol{k}_*^{\mathrm{T}}\left[\mathrm{K}_{\mathrm{g}} + \sigma_{\mathrm{m}}^2\,\mathrm{I}\right]^{-1}(\tilde{\boldsymbol{z}} - \mu(\tilde{\mathrm{X}})), \tag{3.13}$$

$${\sigma_*}^2 = \sigma_{\mathrm{pr}}^2 - \boldsymbol{k}_*^{\mathrm{T}}\left[\mathrm{K}_{\mathrm{g}} + \sigma_{\mathrm{m}}^2\,\mathrm{I}\right]^{-1}\boldsymbol{k}_*. \tag{3.14}$$

Here, $\mathrm{K}_{\mathrm{g}} \in \mathbb{R}^{n\times n}$ is a square matrix containing the pairwise covariances between n measurement data and the vector $\boldsymbol{k}_* \in \mathbb{R}^{n\times 1}$ contains the covariances of the inference point $\boldsymbol{x}_*$ with the measurement data, all calculated based on the covariance function. In these equations, $\mathrm{I} \in \mathbb{R}^{n\times n}$ is the identity matrix and σ_{pr}^2 is the variance of the prior distribution $p(z_*)$.

As an intuition to the role of equations 3.13 and 3.14, we can consider the following interpretation: Assuming there is no data to update our belief about $z(\boldsymbol{x}_*)$, we can get an expected value for the mean and variance of this point by using the GP mean function $\mu_{\mathrm{g}}(\boldsymbol{x}_*)$ and the prior variance σ_{pr}^2. As soon as there is some data available, these initial estimations can be further updated. This is essentially what equations 3.13 and 3.14 deliver. Especially about the variance, it can be noticed that having some correlated measurement data reduces the inference variance.

As mentioned earlier, σ_{m}^2 is a constant variance corresponding to the height values of the measurement data. To take the variable uncertainties of the measurements into account, there exists a number of related works in the field of *heteroscedastic GP* [Gol97], in which the noise of the function values are a function of the position, i.e. $\sigma_{\mathrm{m}}^2(\boldsymbol{x})$. In this case, the constant term $\sigma_{\mathrm{m}}^2 \mathrm{I}$ in equations 3.13 and 3.14 will be replaced by $\mathrm{diag}(\sigma_{\mathrm{m}}^2(\tilde{\mathrm{X}}))$ [Gol97], which is again a diagonal matrix but with specific variance values for each training point.

In the application of surface inspection, the CAD product model can be directly used as the mean function $\mu_{\mathrm{g}}(\boldsymbol{x})$. The a priori distribution for an inference point can be chosen based on the expert knowledge about the production variations. Despite of this analogy, the classical GP version cannot be directly applied to the problem of industrial surface inference yet, because of some inherent limitations listed below.

Smoothness

For function regression using GP, some degree of smoothness is assumed for the underlying function, in order to calculate the correlation of the surface points. This is defined by the covariance function c_{g}. Typical industrial products can have complex geometries, with sharp edges and corners. In addition, different parts of the product might be independently manufactured which means their surface points are uncorrelated to each other.

Inference Variance Axis

Classically, the function to infer is defined in a single coordinate system. This means the function values and their variances are given along a particular axis, e.g. the z-axis. For evaluation of an industrial inspection, it makes sense to evaluate the inference uncertainties along the local normal direction of the surface for each point, which better encodes the deviations from the nominal surface. To this end, the function values and their uncertainties must be calculated along a varying local axis.

Measurement Uncertainty

In equation 3.13, the x and y coordinates of the measurements in $\tilde{\mathrm{X}}$ are considered noise-free and only their corresponding function values $\tilde{z}$ are subject to a constant variance. In surface inspection, the measurement data are 3D points which are correlatedly subject to a 3D measurement uncertainty $\Sigma_{\boldsymbol{x}_\mathrm{w}} \in \mathbb{R}^{3\times3}$. Moreover, the measurement uncertainty is not constant along the surface, a feature called heteroscedasticity [Mch14].

Choice of Covariance Parameters

As the term $(\tilde{z} - \mu(\tilde{\mathrm{X}}))$ in equation 3.13 suggests, the mean function (CAD model) will be subtracted from the measured height values which means that what is effectively being modeled is the deviation from the CAD model corresponding to the defects. Therefore, the covariance function and its free parameters should be chosen in a way that suits reconstructing the defects of the surface up to the desired detail. As illustrated in figure 3.7, a surface defect is a non-deterministic and unlimitedly detailed structure, and therefore, one requires a method to determine the covariance function based on the desired amount of details from the surface.

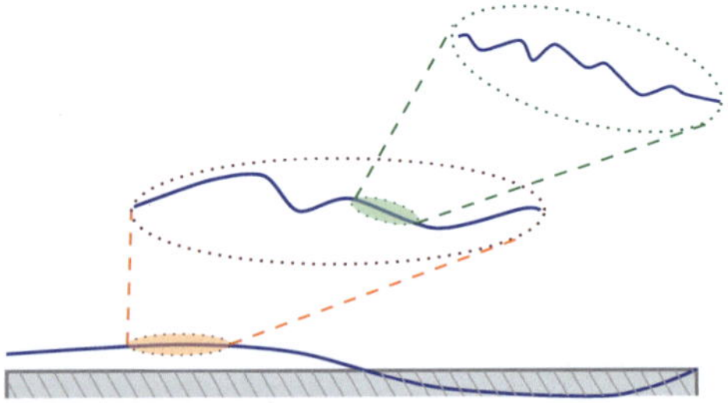

Figure 3.7: Surface defects at several levels of detail.

3.4.2 Adaptation of GP to Surface Inference

To meet the requirements of a surface inference, the conventions in GP inference can be modified in the way to address the previous limitations.

CAD Segments

To avoid the difficulties caused by the unsmooth edges and corners of the model, the CAD model can be segmented into regions which fulfill the requirements of the chosen covariance function (e.g. differentiability).

The inference for each region will be applied separately. This way, the independently manufactured surface parts can be also separated. If a segmented model is not available or is too cumbersome to generate, a useful approach can be to consider only the measurement points whose surface normals do not dramatically differ from that of the inference point. This way, only the points on a potentially smooth region close to the inference position will be utilized for inference.

Local Inference

All covariance functions decay monotonically with distance, except for some special cases like periodic functions which are not of interest here. Therefore, for the inference of a point $\boldsymbol{x}_*$, only the measurement points inside a neighborhood radius r_0 from the point can effectively contribute. The value of r_0 can be directly derived from the covariance function, based on a low threshold. This leads to the idea of a *local inference*, in which for each inference point of interest, only the measurement points inside a neighborhood are used for inference. The local inference significantly improves the runtime, as only a limited set of effective points are considered for each inference. Moreover, it allows one to overcome the previously mentioned "inference variance axis" limitation.

Having selected a set of neighbor points for an inference point, they can be transformed to a new local coordinate frame by a rotation R, so that the transformed heights of the points align with the direction of the local surface normal. An illustration of this transformation is depicted in figure 3.8. The 3D ellipsoids $\Sigma^i_{\boldsymbol{x}_\mathrm{w}}$ corresponding to the measurement uncertainties will be also represented in the new coordinate frame by $\mathrm{R}\Sigma^i_{\boldsymbol{x}_\mathrm{w}}\mathrm{R}^\mathrm{T}$. Consequently, by applying the inference in the new coordinates, the inference uncertainty $u(\boldsymbol{x}_*)$ will be calculated along the z' direction which is parallel to the normal direction. The neighborhood sphere in figure 3.8 moves along the surface and at each point a local transformation and thus a local inference is derived. For those points which are close to edges or corners of the model, the inference only takes the measurement points into account which lie on the same CAD region as of the inference point (e.g. only one side of the edge).

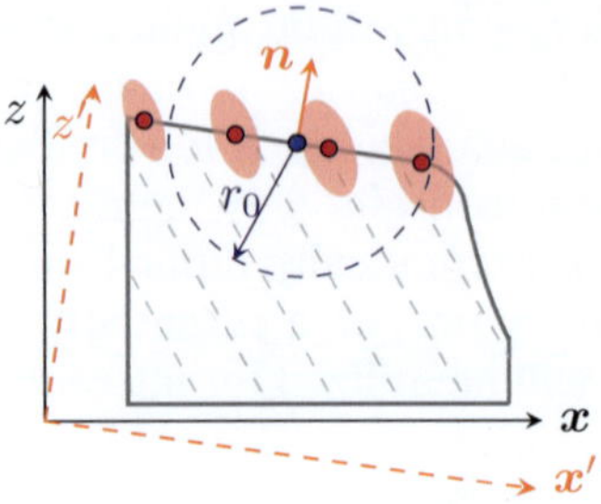

Figure 3.8: Illustration of the local inference with a local rotation of the points along the surface normal, to derive the inference uncertainty along this direction.

Integration of 3D Measurement Uncertainties

As discussed earlier, classical GP only allows the function values to be noisy, and not the x, y positions. For a measurement point $\{\tilde{\boldsymbol{x}}_i,\tilde{z}_i\}$ with $\tilde{\boldsymbol{x}}_i \in \mathbb{R}^2$ and $\tilde{z}_i \in \mathbb{R}$, one can decompose the measurement noise as [Mch14]

$$\tilde{z}_i = z(\tilde{\boldsymbol{x}}_i + \boldsymbol{\varepsilon}_{\tilde{\boldsymbol{x}}_i}) + \varepsilon_{\tilde{z}_i}, \tag{3.15}$$

where $\boldsymbol{\varepsilon}_{\tilde{\boldsymbol{x}}_i}$ and $\varepsilon_{\tilde{z}_i}$ are denoted as the input and the output uncertainties in the literature. The classical GP described in section 3.4.1 only takes $\varepsilon_{\tilde{z}_i}$ into account, modeled as independent identically distributed noise common to all measurements. In this context, the 3D covariance matrix of the measured surface points, which results from the previous uncertainty propagation method, can be written as

$$\Sigma_{\boldsymbol{x}_{\mathrm{w}}} = \mathrm{cov}[\boldsymbol{\varepsilon}_{\tilde{\boldsymbol{x}}_i},\varepsilon_{\tilde{z}_i}]. \tag{3.16}$$

McHutchon in his dissertation in 2014 [Mch14], introduced the method *noisy input Gaussian process (NIGP)* and considered the case where both the input and the output uncertainties are taken into account. As it is intractable to consider each point $(\tilde{\boldsymbol{x}}_i + \boldsymbol{\varepsilon}_{\tilde{\boldsymbol{x}}_i})$ as a distribution in the GP framework [Mch14], he applies an approximation in which he treats the input as deterministic and inflates the corresponding output variance to compensate the input uncertainty. To do so, $\varepsilon_{\tilde{\boldsymbol{x}}_i}$ is propagated through a local linear approximation of the function model

$$\tilde{z}_i \approx z(\tilde{\boldsymbol{x}}_i) + \nabla z(\tilde{\boldsymbol{x}}_i)\boldsymbol{\varepsilon}_{\tilde{\boldsymbol{x}}_i} + \varepsilon_{\tilde{z}_i}, \tag{3.17}$$

which results in a special form of heteroscedasticity, where the new output variance is dependent on the input and is approximated by

$$\sigma_{\mathrm{m}}^2(\boldsymbol{x}) \approx \mathrm{var}\left[\nabla z(\tilde{\boldsymbol{x}}_i)\boldsymbol{\varepsilon}_{\tilde{\boldsymbol{x}}_i} + \varepsilon_{\tilde{z}_i}\right]. \tag{3.18}$$

The interpretation of the NIGP method is that, up to a linear approximation of the function, the input noise $\varepsilon_{\tilde{\boldsymbol{x}}_i}$ affects the function evaluation proportional to the local gradient $\nabla z(\tilde{\boldsymbol{x}}_i)$, and thus has almost no effect if the function is flat [Mch14].

With this intuition, we are interested to approximate the surface at each inference point with a locally linear model to be able to integrate the 3D uncertainties into the inference using the NIGP method. Considering the local inference described previously, the selected local neighborhood will be transformed into a new coordinate frame, so that the gradient of the transformed function $\nabla z'$ becomes zero at the central inference point, because the function height will be aligned to the local normal vector. This means the local inference always infers a locally flat surface. If the neighborhood is also small (as will be seen in the next section), the function gradient will be negligible in the whole region. As the input uncertainties are being multiplied by the surface gradient, neglecting the gradient term turns the problem into the classical GP inference in the transformed coordinates of the local inference, up to a linear approximation. The transformed 3D measurement uncertainties were already computed by $\Sigma'_{\boldsymbol{x}_{\mathrm{w}}} = \mathrm{R}\Sigma^i_{\boldsymbol{x}_{\mathrm{w}}}\mathrm{R}^{\mathrm{T}}$ during the local inference. σ_{m}^2 in the new coordinates will be the last diagonal element of this matrix (i.e. variance along the normal direction), computed separately for each measurement point.

Estimating Covariance Function Parameters

The main intention of a dimensional inspection is to verify a surface for possible defects. As depicted in figure 3.7, the surface defects can be theoretically detected at infinitely many levels of detail. The parameters of the covariance function used for the GP inference determine the smoothness of the surface, and thus control the level up to which the surface variations can be reconstructed in the GP regression. Covariance functions smoothly decaying with distance tend to reconstruct smoother surfaces and rapidly decaying covariance functions let the underlying function contain higher frequencies [Ras06]. To set those parameters, one needs to find a correspondence between the required resolution for inspection and the parameters in the covariance function. In conventional GP applications, these parameters are learned from the training data, however, the levels of detail for a manufactured surface are endless and how detailed one wants the surface to be inspected depends on the requirements.

A conventional choice for the covariance function in GP regression is the Squared Exponential (SE) function, given in equation 3.19. This covariance function can be seen in many natural surfaces and random processes, and is also mathematically straightforward for implementations. Therefore, it has been used for the inference in this thesis. In this function, σ_{pr}^2 is the prior variance of the function values which we had earlier, and l is the *covariance length scale* which determines the decaying behavior of the covariance function. As it can be seen in figure 3.9, larger values of l lead to reconstructing smoother functions, whereas smaller values yield a function with higher variations. Estimating the value of l for a surface corresponding to the required inspection resolution is the main topic of the next section.

$$c_{\mathrm{g}}(r) = \sigma_{\mathrm{pr}}^2 \exp\left(\frac{-r^2}{2l^2}\right) \tag{3.19}$$

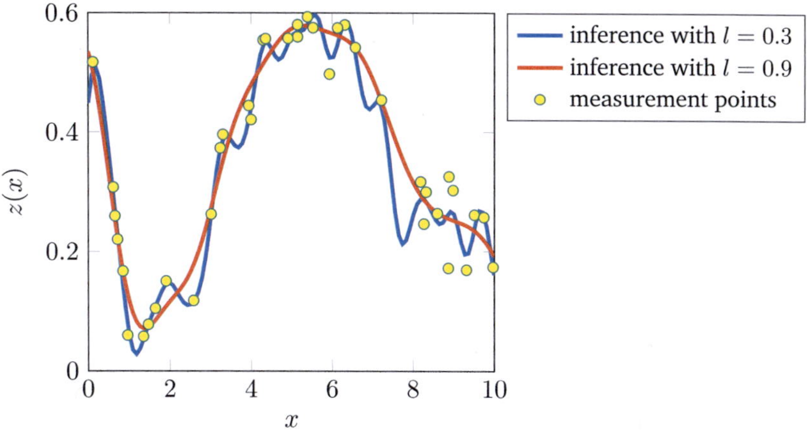

Figure 3.9: Expected functions inferred from noisy sampled points with variance $\sigma_{\mathrm{m}}^2 = 0.03$ using GP regression and different covariance length scales. Here, a squared exponential covariance function is used with $\sigma_{\mathrm{pr}}^2 = 1$.

Estimating Covariance Length Scale

By subtracting the mean function (CAD model) from the surface function, the resulting process is zero-mean stationary. In this case the process covariance function is equivalent to the auto-correlation function of the process, and therefore, the power spectrum $\mathscr{S}(f_{\mathrm{r}})$ of the process can be directly obtained by the Fourier transform of the covariance function [Pap02] as

$$\mathscr{S}(f_{\mathrm{r}}) = \int_{-\infty}^{+\infty} c_{\mathrm{g}}(r) e^{-j2\pi f_{\mathrm{r}} r} \mathrm{d}r, \tag{3.20}$$

where f_{r} indicates the frequency of the power spectrum. Using the Fourier transform of the SE function, the corresponding spectral density function will be derived as

$$\mathscr{S}(f_{\mathrm{r}}) = \sigma_{\mathrm{pr}}^2 \, l \, \sqrt{2\pi} \; e^{-2\pi^2 f_{\mathrm{r}}^2 l^2}. \tag{3.21}$$

Figure 3.10 illustrates a comparison of the SE covariance functions and their corresponding spectral densities for different length scales. As it can be seen, a slowly decaying covariance function contains most of its energies concentrated on lower frequencies. When the covariance decays more rapidly with distance, the power spectrum contains a wider range of frequencies, which means the underlying function is allowed to contain higher frequencies.

The different levels of surface detail in figure 3.7 can be also seen as reconstructing the surface up to different frequencies. The amount of frequencies one can recover from a surface is theoretically limited by the point sampling resolution, based on the Nyquist sampling theorem [Ale16]. There are often lateral resolution requirements given for the inspection, which can be translated into the desired corresponding surface frequency coverage. Thus, one can adjust the covariance function parameters in a way that the process spectrum best covers the given frequency range.

To determine the length scale l, a spectrum-based approach is proposed here. Assuming a given inspection resolution requirement of δ_r, this corresponds to a surface frequency coverage of $[-f_\mathrm{c}, f_\mathrm{c}]$ with the cut-off frequency given by $f_\mathrm{c} = 1/2\delta_\mathrm{r}$. This is equivalent to reconstructing the surface low-pass filtered for the given interval. Thus, this motivates one to set l so that the power spectrum of the corresponding process has the best frequency coverage in this desired interval, and the least power outside. Moreover, the frequency power at the boundary, i.e. $\mathscr{S}(f_\mathrm{c})$, must be non-negligible, otherwise the defects at this scale will not be covered. Therefore, the desired solution corresponds to maximizing the frequency coverage $\int_{-f_\mathrm{c}}^{f_\mathrm{c}} \mathscr{S}(f_\mathrm{c})\mathrm{d}f$ at the same time as maximizing $\mathscr{S}(f_\mathrm{c})$.

For the SE covariance function, these are, however, two conflicting criteria. The frequency coverage is maximized by $l \to \infty$, which makes the power spectrum approach a Dirac delta function, bringing the integral of the whole spectrum to a small interval around $f_\mathrm{c} = 0$. Maximizing $\mathscr{S}(f_\mathrm{c})$ however, tends to flatten the spectrum. Consequently, the optimum solution is a compromise between the two criteria. Defining $\mathscr{S}(f_\mathrm{c}, l)$ as the l-dependent power spectrum, the following concave objective function yields an intermediate solution l^*

$$l^* = \arg\max_{l} \left[\mathscr{S}(f_\mathrm{c}, l) \, \frac{\int_{-f_\mathrm{c}}^{f_\mathrm{c}} \mathscr{S}(f, l)\mathrm{d}f}{2f_\mathrm{c}} \right]. \tag{3.22}$$

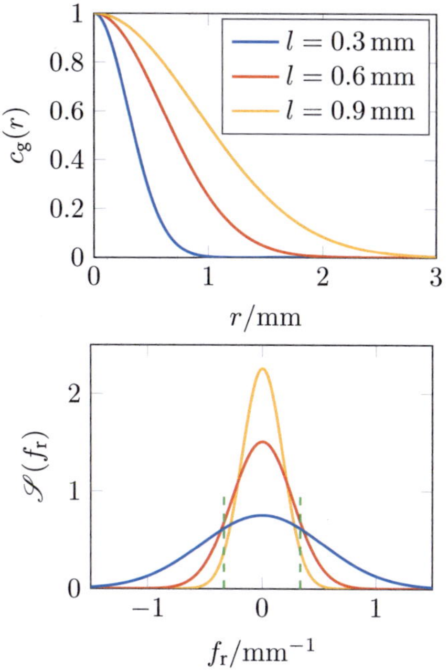

Figure 3.10: (top): SE covariance function with different length scales and $\sigma^2_{\mathrm{pr}} = 1$, (bottom): the corresponding spectral densities. Dashed green lines indicate the frequency interval of interest $[-\frac{1}{3}, \frac{1}{3}]$ corresponding to an inspection resolution of $\delta_{\mathrm{r}} = 1.5\,\mathrm{mm}$.

This objective function is composed of multiplying the average power in the desired interval with the power at the interval boundary. By approximating the integral using the Riemann integral [Shi66] and letting the partitioning approach zero, l^* is estimated by

$$l^* \simeq \frac{1.25\,\delta_{\mathrm{r}}}{\pi}. \tag{3.23}$$

To the best of the author's knowledge, the paper by Wang et al. [Wan14] is the only work with a spectrum-based approach for learning the length-scale of the covariance function. They take a different approach in that they directly use the discrete Fourier transform of the training data. Based on the specific application of this thesis, it is not feasible to access to all types of possible surface defects at several resolution scales to estimate the parameters in that way.

By choosing the parameter l^*, the neighborhood radius r_0 for the local inference can be determined as well. For the SE covariance function, a value of $r_0 = 3 \times l^* = \frac{3.75\,\delta_\mathrm{r}}{\pi}$ is sufficient as the covariance decays down to 1% of the maximum value. This leads to relatively small values of r_0 for typical resolution requirements and, therefore, the assumption of a small neighborhood in section 3.4.2 for the integration of the 3D uncertainties holds. As an example, $\delta_\mathrm{r} = 1.5\,\mathrm{mm}$ yields a neighborhood radius of $r_0 \simeq 1.79\,\mathrm{mm}$.

3.5 Inference of a Cylinder Head Surface

This section demonstrates a sample inference for the intake manifolds of the cylinder head using the methods described in this chapter. For the inference, a sequence of four measurements displayed in figure 3.11 is simulated subsequently, to obtain the measurement points corresponding to each of them. Each scan simulation contains 700 frames in which the cylinder head is moved 1 mm per frame, along the scan direction. The simulated camera captures 512 × 512 px images with a vertical field of view of 45°. Each measurement point is further associated with a 3D covariance matrix using the method for uncertainty propagation described in section 3.3.1. For the measurement uncertainties, a 0.2 px standard deviation for the laser detection on the image and a 0.5 mm standard deviation for positioning the whole setup have been taken into account. Rotational and optical calibration uncertainties were considered negligible in this case.

Figure 3.12 illustrates the results of inferring two intake cavities during the four scans. The top left figure refers to the inference standard deviation after the first scan and the lower right image illustrates the same result after all four scans are done. As it can be seen, the inference uncertainty generally decreases as more measurements are taken into account. This is however, mainly dependent on the coverage of each measurement, how they complement each other, and their corresponding measurement uncertainty. For surface inference, the SE covariance function is used and an a priori standard deviation of 10 mm is considered for the surface. These results correspond to a resolution requirement δ_r of 1.5 mm.

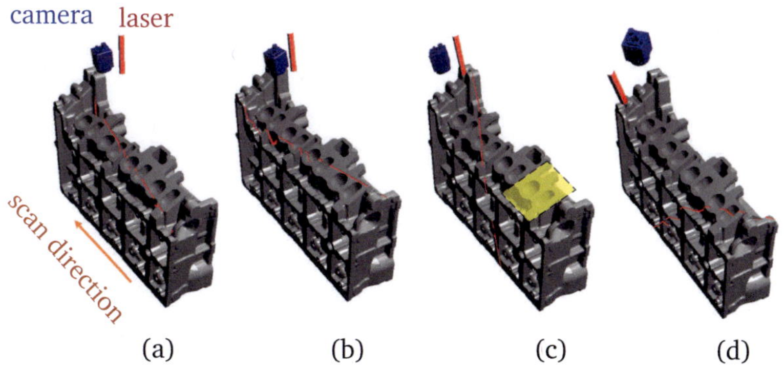

Figure 3.11: Sequence of four simulated measurements for inspecting the intake manifold of the cylinder head. The inference region of figure 3.12 is highlighted in this figure in acquisition (c).

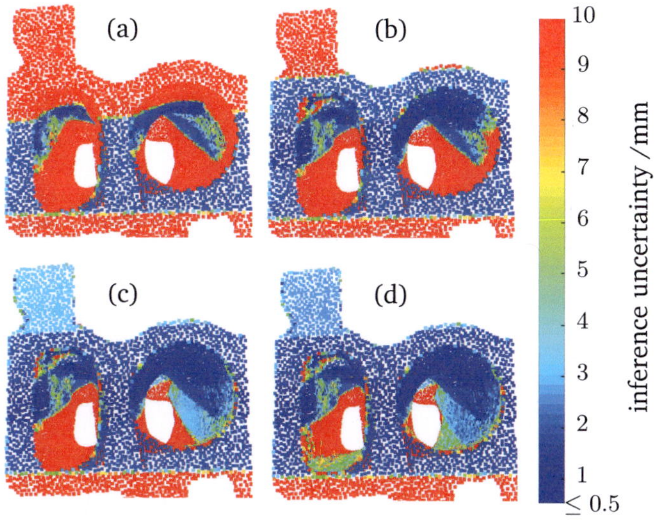

Figure 3.12: Inference uncertainty of a part of the cylinder head intake manifold during four consecutive scans of figure 3.11. Inference points are uniform samples on the surface. Regions with 10 mm uncertainty are uncovered surface parts with their a priori standard deviation.

3.6 Summary

This chapter focused on defining quantitative metrics to evaluate the result of a 3D surface measurement. It began with a simple coverage function, which quantified the surface region covered by the measurement, and further extended the quantifications to evaluate the uncertainties in the measurement. The two important concepts discussed in this chapter include the mathematical framework for "uncertainty propagation", and the "probabilistic surface inference" approach.

Section 3.3.1 discussed the analytical approach towards propagation of uncertainties through the measurement. To use this framework, the sources of uncertainty in the measurement environment or in the measurement process must be approximated and provided to this framework. By doing so, one can associate each 3D measurement point with its corresponding covariance matrix, indicating the expected spread of its values in the 3D space, based on a second order approximation of the measurement model.

Section 3.4 then complemented the uncertainty propagation method by introducing the notion of probabilistic surface inference. In this method, one attempts to reconstruct a 3D surface given noisy measurement points, which can be the results of several uncertain measurements put together. The introduced surface inference method is based on Gaussian process regression with extensive modifications to adapt it to the intended application. The result of surface inference is an a posteriori distribution whose variance is an indicator of the amount of information the measurement has delivered to each part of the surface.

The surface coverage function and the inference variance are the core results of this chapter, which will be used later in chapter 6 for coverage and uncertainty planning.

4 Image Formation Simulation

Solving the inspection planning problem requires searching through many different setup constellations. In the industry machine vision experts often carry out experiments to evaluate the measurement in different geometrical and optical configurations. This approach turns out to be expensive, tedious, and sometimes even unsuitable for nontrivial imaging tasks. To automate this process, realistic synthetic images allow us to evaluate and optimize imaging setups without employing physical parts and sensors. This links the content of this chapter to the concepts of *computer graphics*.

The field of computer graphics addresses the problem of synthesizing digital images, also known as *rendering*, as seen by a virtual camera given the 3D description of an imaging scene. Film production, video game development, and visualizations are only a few of many widespread applications of this field. Considering the huge recent success of rendering techniques in generating highly realistic images, these methods have found rather new use cases, such as generating training data for machine learning tasks [Zha17] or simulating images of an optical measurement system [Ret17].

This chapter focuses on the application of graphical and optical simulation methods for simulating machine vision inspection systems. After an introduction on radiometry in the next section, an overview of the prevailing rendering approaches in computer graphics will be given in section 4.2. Later in section 4.3, a brief review of the state of the art in utilizing rendering techniques for simulation of optical systems will be presented. This chapter further reviews the usage of real-time and photorealistic rendering approaches for inspection planning, and at the end, a simulation framework will be proposed which is the core contribution of this chapter. The image simulation framework introduces the necessary components to supplement typical ray tracing methods in order to synthesize sensor-realistic images in a machine vision inspection system.

4.1 Background on Radiometry

A fundamental part of the image formation chain in vision systems is light transport, to study which, we require to measure light and model its interaction with the objects. Quantification of light is the main subject studied in the field of *radiometry*. This section covers some basic physical concepts and definitions in brief, which are later needed in this chapter. The content mostly follows the definitions from the books by Beyerer et al. [Bey15] and Dutre et al. [Dut06] with some notation modifications.

4.1.1 Light

Light is an interesting phenomenon in physics which has been studied for more than 3000 years. The behavior of light can be studied at different scales. *Wave optics* studies the propagation of light as an electromagnetic wave and provides a framework for describing light at the scales down to the order of magnitude of the wavelength, such as when light scatters at a slit aperture. *Geometric optics* is an approximation of the wave optics suitable for the scenarios where light interacts with objects much larger than its wavelength. In this model, rays of light travel instantly along straight lines. Although wave optics provides an exact framework to study propagation of light, it is not versatile enough to explain why the sensed energy of light is always quantized. In the field of *quantum electrodynamics*, light is modeled as a collection of *photons* carrying quantized amounts of energy proportional to its frequency.

Typical computer graphics simulations only use the geometric modeling of light. This provides a good framework for modeling relevant geometric optic effects; however, the formation of interference and diffraction patterns which are relevant to many optical measurement systems require wave optic modeling.

The Wave-Particle Nature

Light can be described as both an *electromagnetic wave*, and as a collection of *photons*. As a wave, light consists of oscillating electric and magnetic fields traveling at a constant speed of $c \approx 3 \times 10^8$ m/s in vacuum, with a specific frequency ν. The distance light travels in one oscillation cycle is called the *wavelength* λ, calculated as $\lambda = \frac{c}{\nu}$. An electromagnetic radiation may consist of only a single wavelength, called *monochrome*, or cover a range of wavelengths, which may or may not be visible to human eye. The range of visible wavelengths to human are about 380 nm to 780 nm. In the particle perspective to light, light is seen as a large collection of photons traveling with the speed of light on a straight line.

Light Energy

The energy q of a photon with frequency ν is given by $q = h\nu$, where $h \approx 6.626 \times 10^{-34}$ J s is a physical constant known as the Planck's constant. Light with a particular frequency (e.g. particular wavelength) cannot carry an arbitrary amount of energy, rather only a natural multiple of the energy of one photon. This is why the light energy is known to be quantized. Radiation with $n \in \mathbb{N}^+$ photons carries an amount of $q = nh\nu$ energy.

Phasor Model

The electric and magnetic fields of a monochromatic wave are both a function of time t and space $\boldsymbol{x} \in \mathbb{R}^3$, formally described as

$$u_\mathrm{w}(\boldsymbol{x},t) = A_\mathrm{m} \cos(2\pi\nu t - \phi(\boldsymbol{x})), \tag{4.1}$$

where A_m and ϕ are the wave amplitude and phase respectively. Using complex notation, this equation can be also given as [Goo17]

$$u_\mathrm{w}(\boldsymbol{x},t) = \mathrm{Real}\{U(\boldsymbol{x}) \exp(-j2\pi\nu t)\}, \tag{4.2}$$

in which $U(\boldsymbol{x}) = A_\mathrm{m} \exp(j\phi(\boldsymbol{x}))$ is a time-invariant term, also known as a *phasor*. In wave optics modeling, the phasor is used to model the wavefronts independent of their temporal behavior.

4.1.2 Radiometric Quantities

To quantify light transport in an imaging scene, there are a few useful and commonly used quantities, which are covered in this section. Figure 4.1 gives a simplified visualization of these quantities.

Flux

The radiant power or *flux* corresponds to the rate of radiation energy q passing through a two dimensional area, measured in $[\Phi] = \mathrm{W}$. Assuming n photons pass through some given surface A, flux Φ of this surface is calculated as

$$\Phi = \frac{\mathrm{d}q}{\mathrm{d}t} = \frac{\mathrm{d}n}{\mathrm{d}t} h\nu. \tag{4.3}$$

Irradiance

Flux passing through an infinitesimal area dA at position $\boldsymbol{p} \in \mathbb{R}^2$ is referred to as *irradiance* $E(\boldsymbol{p})$, measured in $[E] = \mathrm{W\,m^{-2}}$. Mathematically, irradiance is calculated as

$$E(\boldsymbol{p}) = \frac{\mathrm{d}\Phi}{\mathrm{d}A}. \tag{4.4}$$

In figure 4.1, $\mathrm{d}\Phi$ refers to the part of the whole flux passing through $\mathrm{d}A$. For a uniform radiation power, irradiance is flux per unit area.

Radiance & Solid Angle

Irradiance defined previously does not differentiate between light rays from different directions. *Radiance* further quantifies this radiation power along a particular direction, or along a ray, as often modeled in computer graphics.

Considering a point light source, the irradiance of the light decreases quadratically with distance, because the power is distributed over a larger sphere by going away from the light source. The interesting fact about radiance is that it remains constant along a ray, as long as it propagates in vacuum. The perceived brightness of an object is proportional to the radiance reflected from the object to the camera or the eye. In computer

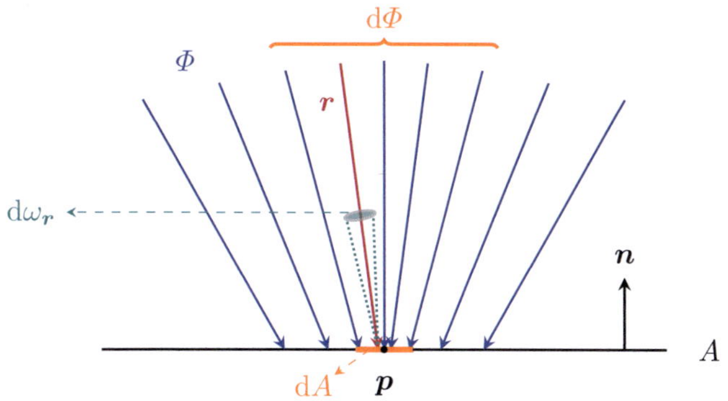

Figure 4.1: Illustration of the relationship between radiometric quantities. Blue rays represent incoming flux to surface A, and $\mathrm{d}A$ refers to an infinitesimal surface element at point $\boldsymbol{p}$. Vector $\boldsymbol{n}$ refers to surface normal, and r represents a particular ray passing through infinitesimal solid angle $\mathrm{d}\omega_{\boldsymbol{r}}$.

graphics, radiance determines the value a ray carries. To formally define radiance, the definition of a *solid angle* is required.

Similar to a 2D angle which is equal to its subtended arc on a unit circle, a solid angle ω in 3D space is defined as an area on the unit sphere [Bär10]. In imaging scenarios, the use case of solid angle is to calculate the field of view through which a point sees a surface. A solid angle is expressed in steradian (sr), which is a dimensionless unit. More details and a formal definition of a solid angle can be found in the book by Beyerer et al. [Bey15]. For defining radiance, a differential solid angle is of interest. Figure 4.1 illustrates an infinitesimal solid angle $\mathrm{d}\omega_{\boldsymbol{r}}$ in direction of ray $\boldsymbol{r}$.

The radiance $L(\boldsymbol{p},\boldsymbol{r})$ of a point $\boldsymbol{p}$ along ray direction $\boldsymbol{r}$ is defined by the equation below and is expressed in $[L] = \mathrm{W\,sr^{-1}\,m^{-2}}$.

$$L(\boldsymbol{p},\boldsymbol{r}) = \frac{\mathrm{d}E(\boldsymbol{p})}{\mathrm{d}\omega_{\boldsymbol{r}}|\cos(\boldsymbol{n},\boldsymbol{r})|}, \tag{4.5}$$

Wavelength Dependency

All radiometric quantities are also dependent on the wavelength of light (e.g. $L(\boldsymbol{p},\boldsymbol{r},\lambda)$). To simplify the formulations in this thesis, the wavelength dependency is implicitly assumed. In graphical simulations, typically only the red, green, and blue channels are simulated. Some *spectral renderers* such as Mitsuba [Wen10], provide the option to sample more wavelengths of the visible spectrum for simulations.

4.1.3 Interaction of Light and Matter

The appearance of objects to our eyes or in an image is mostly dependent on how light interacts with that object. Depending on the light scattering properties of materials, they look different even under the same lighting condition. When matter is exposed to light with some spectral range, a portion of the photons with particular frequencies will be absorbed and dissipated as heat. The rest of the incoming light is reflected or transmitted according to the scattering characteristics of the material, formulated in terms of the *Bidirectional Scattering Distribution Function (BSDF)* [Dut06].

Bidirectional Scattering Distribution Function (BSDF)

The BSDF ρ_{s}, as illustrated in figure 4.2, is a mathematical model to characterize how the incoming light in a direction $\boldsymbol{r}_{\mathrm{i}}$ to a point $\boldsymbol{p}$ scatters in the sphere around $\boldsymbol{p}$. Scattering in the same hemisphere as the incoming light ($\mathcal{H}_+$) determines the reflectance of the surface, while scattering in the other hemisphere characterizes the transmittance, only relevant to transmissive surfaces. Therefore, a BSDF is implicitly composed of a reflectance part ρ_{r} and a transmittance part ρ_{t}

$$\rho_{\mathrm{s}} = \rho_{\mathrm{r}} + \rho_{\mathrm{t}}, \tag{4.6}$$

known as the *Bidirectional Reflectance Distribution Function (BRDF)* and the *Bidirectional Transmittance Distribution Function (BTDF)*, respectively. For opaque surfaces, such as metals, which exhibit almost no transmittance, the BSDF is only composed of the BRDF. In this thesis, only surfaces with negligible transmittance for visible light are considered.

As given in equation 4.7, a BRDF at a point $\boldsymbol{p}$ is formally defined as the ratio of the differential radiance reflected in direction $\boldsymbol{r}_{\mathrm{o}}$, and the differential incident irradiance $\mathrm{d}E(\boldsymbol{p})$ through a differential solid angle $\mathrm{d}\omega_{\boldsymbol{r}_{\mathrm{i}}}$ [Dut06]. Ignoring the wavelength, polarization, and scale dependencies,

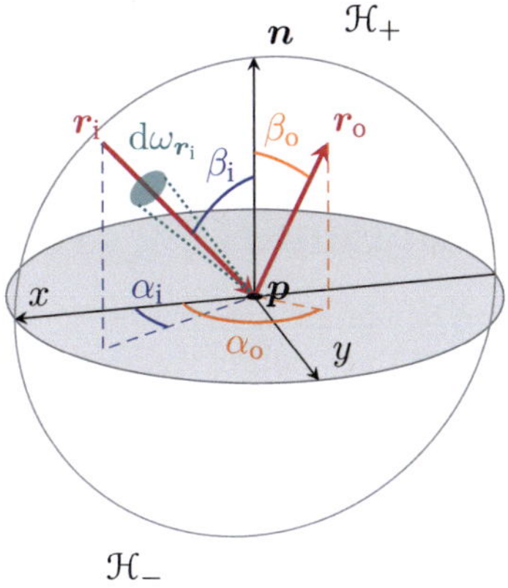

Figure 4.2: Visualization of a surface BSDF. Angles α_i and β_i refer to the azimuthal and polar angles of the incoming light $\boldsymbol{r}_\mathrm{i}$, and angles α_i and β_i refer to the same quantities for definition of the outgoing light $\boldsymbol{r}_\mathrm{o}$. $\mathrm{d}\omega_{\boldsymbol{r}_\mathrm{i}}$ is a differential solid angle in the direction of the incoming light.

the BRDF is 6-dimensional. Four dimensions describe the incoming and outgoing ray directions $(\alpha_\mathrm{i},\beta_\mathrm{i},\alpha_\mathrm{o},\beta_\mathrm{o})$ and two dimensions refer to the position $\boldsymbol{p}$. A BTDF is defined in a similar manner, only the outgoing ray is in the opposite hemisphere.

$$\rho_\mathrm{r}(\boldsymbol{p},\boldsymbol{r}_\mathrm{i},\boldsymbol{r}_\mathrm{o}) = \frac{\mathrm{d}L(\boldsymbol{p},\boldsymbol{r}_\mathrm{o})}{\mathrm{d}E(\boldsymbol{p})} = \frac{\mathrm{d}L(\boldsymbol{p},\boldsymbol{r}_\mathrm{o})}{L(\boldsymbol{p},\boldsymbol{r}_\mathrm{i})|\cos(\boldsymbol{n},\boldsymbol{r}_\mathrm{i})|\mathrm{d}\omega_{\boldsymbol{r}_\mathrm{i}}} \tag{4.7}$$

An implicit assumption in this definition is that light exits the surface at the same point, time, and wavelength, as it arrives at the surface. Therefore, phenomena such as fluorescence, phosphorescence, and subsurface scattering (multiple scattering within the surface and exiting at another point) are not modeled.

Isotropic and Anisotropic Surfaces

The incoming ray in the definition of a BRDF was determined by two separate angles α_i and β_i. For many surfaces which do not have a particular directional micro-structure, such as sand casted metals, only the relative azimuthal angle of the incoming and the outgoing rays $\alpha_\mathrm{i} - \alpha_\mathrm{o}$

is relevant for defining the BRDF. Such surfaces are known as *isotropic surfaces*. Others, such as brushed surfaces, which require all 6 BRDF dimensions to be fully described are called *anisotropic surfaces*.

4.2 Overview on Rendering Methods

After an introduction to the quantities for measuring light, this section provides an overview on the prevailing rendering techniques in the field of computer graphics. Looking from a high level perspective, synthesizing an image consists of two steps: the *visibility* step, which is to determine which object is visible from a sensor point, and the *shading* step, for calculating the color of that point. The term color in this context refers to an intermediate value, usually in radiometric units, generated during rendering which will be later mapped to a digital intensity value. The shading of a sensor point is influenced by the distribution of light in the scene and material of the surfaces.

On the application level, there are two main approaches towards rendering: real-time rasterization and offline ray tracing. The next two sections provide an introduction to these two rendering techniques.

4.2.1 Real-Time Rasterization

3D real-time rendering for interactive media is a very popular area of computer graphics, which aims at generating images typically between 20 up to 200 frames per second [Ake08]. With the speed requirement of applications such as video games and interactive visualizations, the realism must be sacrificed to some extent in order to achieve the rendering rate. Thus, these methods often avoid a rigorous modeling of the light transport.

As shown in figure 4.3, rasterization is a fast rendering technique which creates an image by projecting the objects on the image plane. The real-time rendering model is historically known as the *rendering pipeline*, consisting of three main stages: application, geometry processing, and rasterization [Ake08].

At the application stage, the interaction of the user is captured and a description of the scene is prepared and sent to the Graphical Processing

Unit (GPU), where the next two stages take place. In the traditional rendering pipeline, the geometry stage is responsible for the majority of geometrical operations on the models, including shading the vertices and projecting the objects on the image plane. The rasterizer then fills up the covered pixels with their corresponding colors, based on the data structures provided in the previous stage. In addition to the shading values passed to the rasterizer, another important data structure is the *z-buffer*, indicating the distance of the projected points to the image plane. In case of occlusions, the z-buffer enables the rasterizer to only render objects visible to the camera.

Although rasterization is only a part of the rendering pipeline, mostly addressing the visibility problem, the whole process of real-time rendering is sometimes referred to by this term. In the 80s and 90s, when computational capabilities were far from those of today, rasterization was the method of choice for almost all rendering applications. Within this trend, GPU developments were oriented by the rasterization tasks and therefore, dedicated hardware support was built for parallel geometry processing and rendering. Today, rasterization is highly hardware-accelerated with available application programing interfaces (API), such as OpenGL[1] and DirectX[2], and still accounts for one of the mostly used rendering techniques.

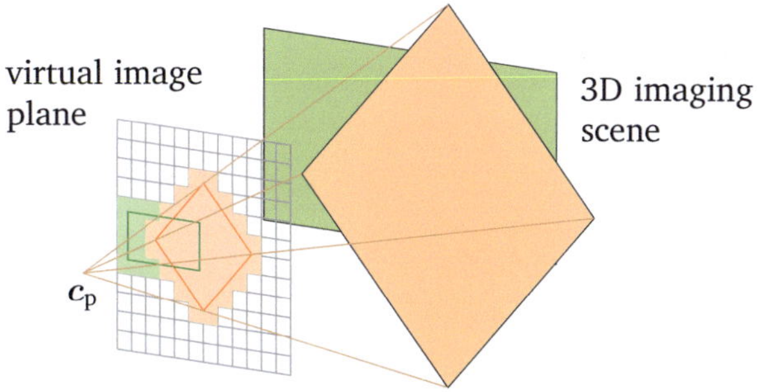

Figure 4.3: Illustration of real-time rendering with rasterization. To determine visibility, scene objects are projected on the image plane of a virtual camera with the projection center c_p.

[1]https://www.opengl.org/

[2]https://docs.microsoft.com/en-us/windows/desktop/directx

Shading

Although rasterization is a very efficient way of determining the visibility of the scene objects, it does not inherently include a method to calculate the pixel colors. Based on the application, the shading step in the rasterization may be based on physical models, similar to what we will discuss about offline rendering in the next section, or it may depend on simplified heuristic models. One famous BRDF model for shading is the *Phong model* [Ake08], which is composed of a diffuse and a specular reflection term

$$\rho_{\mathrm{r}}(\alpha_{\mathrm{o}}) \propto c_{\mathrm{diff}} + c_{\mathrm{spec}} \cos^{k} \alpha_{\mathrm{o}}. \tag{4.8}$$

Here, c_{diff} and c_{spec} are the empirical diffuse and specular coefficients respectively, and α_{o} is the angle between the perfect specular direction and the outgoing ray. BRDFs based on more complicated models, such as those based on the *microfacet theory*, are being commonly used in most rendering systems. As it will go beyond the scope of this thesis, these shading models will not be discussed any further. For more information, the publication by Holzschuch and Pacanowski [Hol15] provides a brief overview on commonly used BRDF models.

4.2.2 Photorealistic Rendering

Photorealistic rendering serves the applications where rendering time is not the critical issue, but the quality and realism matters most. A predominant application of this rendering technique is creating cinematic movies. As its name implies, the ultimate goal in photorealistic rendering is to synthesize images which look very similar to real images. Although this is the goal of almost all rendering techniques, photorealistic rendering which is referred to in this section is different in the sense that it can take more time in calculating better images using more sophisticated models without the need for providing a high frame rate.

Light Transport Equation (LTE)

To realistically simulate the light transport, photorealistic rendering methods attempt to physically simulate multiple interactions of light and matter, which essentially rely on the *Light Transport Equation (LTE)*.

Kajiya et al. in 1986 [Kaj86] introduced this formulation of the light transport which is also known as the rendering equation. In contrast to nonphysical simulations which may only consider direct lighting or use unrealistic light sources, equation 4.9 formulates what is known as *global illumination*, incorporating both direct and indirect light.

$$L(\boldsymbol{p},\boldsymbol{r}_{\mathrm{o}}) = L_e(\boldsymbol{p},\boldsymbol{r}_{\mathrm{o}}) + \int_{\mathcal{H}_+} \rho_{\mathrm{r}}(\boldsymbol{p},\boldsymbol{r}_{\mathrm{i}},\boldsymbol{r}_{\mathrm{o}})\, L(\boldsymbol{p},\boldsymbol{r}_{\mathrm{i}}) \cos(\boldsymbol{r}_{\mathrm{i}},\boldsymbol{n})\, \mathrm{d}\omega_{\boldsymbol{r}_{\mathrm{i}}} \quad (4.9)$$

In this equation, the outgoing radiance $L(\boldsymbol{p},\boldsymbol{r}_{\mathrm{o}})$ from a point $\boldsymbol{p}$ in direction $\boldsymbol{r}_{\mathrm{o}}$ is composed of two components: the emitted radiance L_{e}, if the surface is emissive, and the scattered radiance. The scattered radiance is determined by the integrated contribution of each possible incoming radiance $L(\boldsymbol{p},\boldsymbol{r}_{\mathrm{i}})$ (directly or indirectly) over the whole positive hemisphere $\mathcal{H}_+$, which is scattered by the surface into the desired outgoing direction $\boldsymbol{r}_{\mathrm{o}}$.

The LTE in the above form implicitly assumes that light is propagating in vacuum, or in other words, radiance remains constant along a ray. The propagation of light in dense media, such as water or foggy air, or propagation of light in thin media but over large distances requires further considerations for *volume scattering* which we neglect here.

The LTE gives a compact formulation of light transport, but it is in fact infeasible to be analytically solved for non-trivial imaging scenes. The complexity owes to the fact that, outgoing radiance at a point is dependent on all incoming radiance values to this point, which must be in turn calculated using other LTEs. This gives it a recursive nature, which forms the basis of the algorithms for global illumination rendering.

Numerical Approximation

There are generally two common approaches to numerically approximating the LTE: finite-element solutions known as *radiosity*, and Monte Carlo based *ray tracing*. Radiosity is a scene-based method as opposed to ray tracing, which is image-based [Dut06]. In radiosity, the scene is subdivided to surface elements and the equilibrium of light distribution in the scene is described by a system of linear equations. Once the radiometric values for the scene elements are calculated, an image can be rendered for arbitrary view points, making this method also suitable for real-time interactive applications. Ray tracing on the other hand, sends and traces rays of light in the scene for approximating the light transport. Although both radiosity and ray tracing have received wide attention, the radiosity method has not been as popular as ray tracing [Dut06]. The rest of this section focuses only on ray tracing methods.

Ray Tracing

Ray tracing is based on sampling paths of light, also known as *path integration*. To this end, rays of light are sampled and then sent to the scene, and further traced along multiple paths, as they interact with the surfaces. Figure 4.4 provides a simple illustration of this approach.

In ray tracing, the new direction of a ray after intersection with a material is determined using Monte Carlo (MC) sampling and according to a Probability Density Function (PDF) $p(\boldsymbol{r}_\mathrm{i})$ over possible directions $\boldsymbol{r}_\mathrm{i}$. In this approach, the MC estimation of the LTE will be given as [Vea97]

$$L(\boldsymbol{p},\boldsymbol{r}_\mathrm{o}) \approx L_\mathrm{e}(\boldsymbol{p},\boldsymbol{r}_\mathrm{o}) + \frac{1}{N}\sum_{k=1}^{N}\frac{\rho_\mathrm{r}(\boldsymbol{p},\boldsymbol{r}_k,\boldsymbol{r}_\mathrm{o})\, L(\boldsymbol{p},\boldsymbol{r}_k)\cos(\boldsymbol{r}_k,\boldsymbol{n})}{p(\boldsymbol{r}_k)}. \tag{4.10}$$

As a special case, when N rays are uniformly selected in a hemisphere of 2π solid angle (i.e. $p(\boldsymbol{r}_k) = \frac{1}{2\pi}$), equation 4.10 changes to

$$L(\boldsymbol{p},\boldsymbol{r}_\mathrm{o}) \approx L_\mathrm{e}(\boldsymbol{p},\boldsymbol{r}_\mathrm{o}) + \frac{2\pi}{N}\sum_{k=1}^{N}\rho_\mathrm{r}(\boldsymbol{p},\boldsymbol{r}_k,\boldsymbol{r}_\mathrm{o})\, L(\boldsymbol{p},\boldsymbol{r}_k)\cos(\boldsymbol{r}_k,\boldsymbol{n}).$$

The best numeric approximation results from a PDF which is a scaled variant of the integrand function [Vea97], i.e.

$$p(\boldsymbol{r}_k) \propto \rho_\mathrm{r}(\boldsymbol{p},\boldsymbol{r}_k,\boldsymbol{r}_\mathrm{o})\, L(\boldsymbol{p},\boldsymbol{r}_k)\cos(\boldsymbol{r}_k,\boldsymbol{n}).$$

This choice would yield a minimum variance (i.e. zero) approximation which is impossible to achieve. That is why in general it is not possible to fully determine the PDF in this way. Therefore, often only the cosine term and/or the BRDF function are used to design a PDF close to the optimal one for sampling of rays (importance sampling).

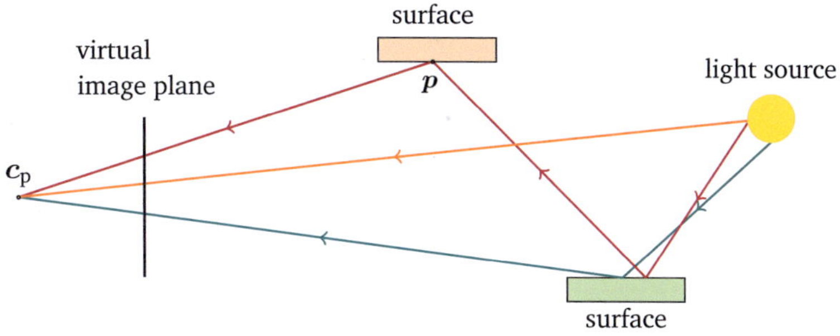

Figure 4.4: Illustration of basic ray tracing. This figure shows sampling paths of light from the light source to the camera projection center c_{p}. For efficiency, rays are typically traced in the reversed way, starting from c_{p}.

Although initial ideas in ray tracing date back to 1979 [Whi79], integration of the complete light transport with a high number of rays was achieved much later. For the sake of efficiency, rays are typically sent from an image point through the camera view point, and further traced to find a potential intersection with an object in the scene. At each intersection point, one or more directions are sampled, weighted based on the surface BRDF, and new rays are generated from that point. To terminate the rays, one approach is to continue until a ray reaches a light source or its radiance falls below some threshold, or it can be done according to a probability function. Strategies for sampling the paths of light between the camera and the light source has been an active area of research in computer graphics and many different rendering approaches have been introduced.

For example, *distributed ray tracing* [Coo84] generates and follows a fixed amount of random rays at each intersection, whereas in *path tracing* [Kaj86] only one ray is sampled to avoid the exponential growth. *Light tracing* [Arv86] follows a reverse ray generation strategy and generates rays starting from the light sources. *Bidirectional path tracing* [Laf93] is a combination of light and path tracing, in which rays generated from both directions will be connected. Each of these algorithms, and a couple of others not mentioned here, essentially differ in their strategy for stochastically generating paths of light, which, depending on the scene geometry and materials, can perform differently in terms of the rendering efficiency and noise. Retzlaff et al. in their paper [Ret17], give a review of different Markov Chain Monte Carlo (MCMC) rendering approaches, with a special focus on their suitability for rendering optical measurement systems.

In theory, ray tracing methods are able to simulate most geometric optic effects in light transport and converge to the correct radiance values, however in practice, the simulation results are limited by, at least, the numerical approximations (i.e. number of samples and the path integration approach), and the deficiencies in the description of the scene (e.g. lacking details in geometry or deviations from real BRDFs). This statement holds the assumption that the geometric optic modeling in calculating light transport is sufficient to describe the light transport, which is typically the case in far field rendering.

4.3 Overview on Previous Work

After an introduction to computer graphics methods for rendering images, this section provides an overview on previous research regarding utilization of simulated images in other application fields, including simulation of optical systems.

Initial ideas for utilization of graphical simulations in other fields of technology date back to the paper by Greenberg et al. [Gre97], where they pose challenging questions to the graphics community such as:

> *Why can't these accurate but artificial scenes be used for algorithmic development in image processing, robotics, and machine vision?*

To this end, they suggested a framework for realistic image synthesis, which appeared as a role model for many future works. The framework consisted of an image simulation chain with three prevailing components: measurement of the scene components, light transport simulation, and perceptually-based visual display. The main concern of Greenberg et al. and many following works [Lon04][Sun07] is oriented towards providing a believable appearance to a human observer. Therefore, they model the perception of human vision based on biological and psychological models.

Simulation of lens systems by ray tracing was first realized by Kolb et al. [Kol95], where they trace rays through lenses and integrate light over the aperture. Some aberrations and diffraction effects were also later included by Steinert et al. [Ste11]. Previous diffraction simulations are typically based on the *geometrical theory of diffraction* introduced in 1962 by Keller [Kel62]. In this work, diffracted rays at the boundaries and edges are modeled as scattering rays, which are normally traced further after being diffracted.

Lens aberrations can indeed be simulated by tracing rays through complex lens systems; however, this extremely reduces the rendering efficiency, as for straightforward ray tracing 95% of all traced rays, or more, might not leave a real-world lens system and get blocked by the lens housing or the aperture [Han14][Ret17]. To improve the performance of ray tracing through lenses, there have been a number works including the paper by Hanika et al. [Han14] which model the lens system using polynomials and avoid direct ray tracing through them.

Although such methods can be useful to simulate an optical imaging system, they typically fail to generate wave optic effects and interference patterns. The recent paper by Retzlaff et al. [Ret17] directly studies simulations for optical measurement systems. They mainly focus on reviewing potentially useful ray tracing methods and neglect the simulation of the imaging optic.

In the sensor-realistic simulation framework which will be introduced later in section 4.7, simulation of the whole imaging chain including light transport, optics, and the digital sensor will be studied, with a special focus on simulation of wave optics effects.

4.4 Image Synthesis for Inspection Planning

In this section, we return to the main goal of this chapter, which is to synthesize images to serve as the input for the metrological evaluations of an inspection planning. The most important aspect in this regard is to generate images which are reliable for evaluating the intended criteria. The next priority is to keep the rendering time as low as possible, to let the optimization process search the design space with enough samples in a practical amount of time.

With the speed priority in mind, hardware-accelerated real-time rendering methods (rasterization) are naturally the first alternative to consider. Although these methods often sacrifice realism to achieve a high frame rate, they are still the right choice for correctly evaluating many important imaging criteria, such as the field of view, geometry of the projected objects on the image, image resolution, visible surface area, and light source reachability to the surface through direct light. In most visual inspection systems, the light sources are designed to illuminate the desired features through direct light and the indirect illumination in the scene is a side-effect often even unwanted. Real-time renderings can be, therefore, the suitable tool for planning the coverage of cameras and direct illuminations, or more specifically, the surface coverage metric discussed earlier in section 3.2.

For metrological evaluations, such as measurement uncertainty (see section 3.3), physically-based renderings with realistic intensity and noise simulations are required. As we will later see, additional building blocks are required to complement off-the-shelf physically-based rendering tools to realistically simulate images for inspection planning.

Sections 4.5 and 4.6 briefly review the application of rasterization and photorealistic rendering to planning machine vision systems.

4.5 Rasterized Images for Visualization and Coverage Planning

With a rendering time within a millisecond, inspection planning can benefit from rasterized images for both visualization of the imaging scene and the coverage planning. As one use case, rasterized images rendered from arbitrary view points, enable the expert to visualize and interactively apply changes to the imaging scene to explore the design space.

In addition, rasterization can be utilized to evaluate surface coverage. For such purposes, simulations do not have to be photorealistic, rather it suffices if the simulated geometry is consistent with reality to correctly visualize the scene and evaluate surface visibility. For instance, figure 4.5(a) visualizes a selected measurement in the laser triangulation setup from a free view, and figure 4.5(b) illustrates the same measurement from the camera view. Both images are rendered using a perfectly diffuse BRDF for shading.

To evaluate surface coverage, the images can be either rendered, saved, and further processed as in a real measurement, or one can benefit from the additional information available in the rendering pipeline (e.g. coordinates of the points projected on the image plane), to speed up the coverage evaluation. For the intended laser triangulation planning application, the calculation of the 3D measurement points in the simulated images is a built-in part of the simulation to avoid the overhead of saving and processing images.

Rasterized images can also be used to visualize quantitative metrics to assist an expert with a better visualization of the measurement results. To this end, the quantitative metrics will be assigned to some color map which is used for shading the surface. Figure 4.6 displays a visualization of the corresponding surface coverage. Although measurement points are discrete points on the surface, the interpolation of surface colors based on the distance to a neighboring measurement point can give a continuous look to the metric visualization, resulting in a better visual impression.

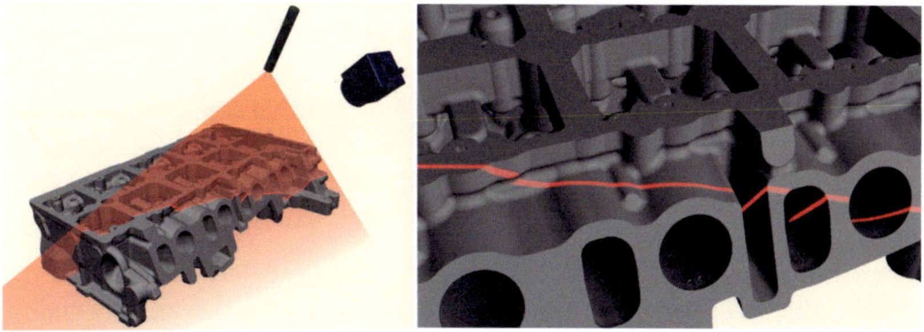

(a) (b)

Figure 4.5: Rasterized images for visualization of (a): the imaging scene from arbitrary viewpoints, and (b): the camera view corresponding to the setup in figure (a).

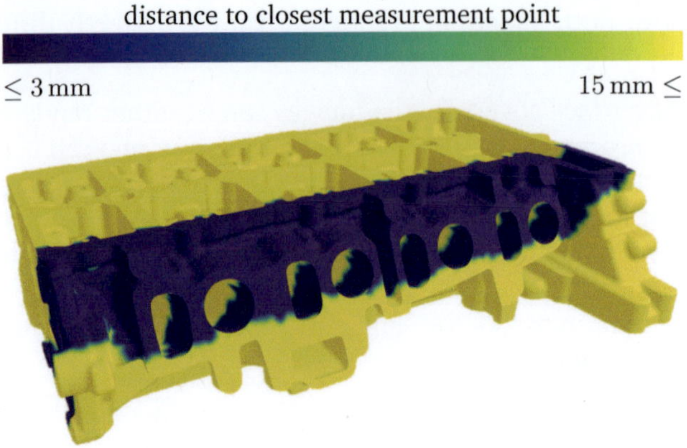

Figure 4.6: Visualization of the measurement coverage corresponding to the measurement of figure 4.5. The surface color is interpolated based on the distance to measurement points with a Gaussian kernel of width 0.5 cm.

4.6 Photorealistic Rendering of Images in a Machine Vision System

Each optical measurement which relies on image processing to extract some features can be subject to an inaccuracy based on the signal to noise ratio of the image. For incorporating such inaccuracies in the inspection planning, the simulations must be reliable in generating both the correct signal values and the noise statistics. The interesting question which arises here is if available photorealistic rendering techniques are already competent enough for simulating image-based measurement systems.

To answer this question, we take a closer look at the components of the photorealistic rendering methods. As briefly discussed earlier, the original realistic image synthesis framework proposed by Greenberg et al. [Gre97] consisted of three components. In what follows, we take a closer look at the components.

1. **Measurement of scene data**: As a first step, all scene components including light sources, surfaces BRDFs, and objects geometries must be measured, to incorporate physically-correct properties in the simulations.

2. **Light transport simulation**: The next step is to apply a numerical method for solving the LTE. The output of this step is the physically-based global illumination solution represented by radiometric values.

3. **Perceptually-based visual display**: The last step focuses on visualizing the physical quantities in a digital image, also known as *tone mapping*. The main concern of Greenberg et al. and many following works [Lon04][Sun07] is to generate an image which is indistinguishable from real photos by a human. Therefore, they model the *perception* of an observer based on models of human vision.

Although Greenberg et al. originally propose using physically-based simulations for other application fields, the final image generation goal in this framework is still oriented towards providing a believable appearance. Utilizing computer graphics in other domains, however, requires an adapted perspective to guarantee the rendering quality for the intended purpose. To physically simulate the image formation process in a machine vision system, especially those delivering measurements, at least two more components need to be physically simulated: the **imaging optics**, including relevant optical effects such as diffraction and aberrations, and the light sensitive **sensor**. Sensor simulation replaces perceptual tone mapping in Greenberg's framework. Although sensor simulation is not a totally new concept in computer graphics, this thesis proposes using a standard model for simulating the sensors and their corresponding intensity noise, which can include a wide range of imaging sensors in the market. Figure 4.7 gives an overview to the simulation framework which will be introduced in the next section.

4.7 Sensor-Realistic Simulation Framework

Similar to the framework presented by Greenberg et al., each realistic simulation framework must begin with proper scene measurements. With enough information to accurately describe a scene, the next step is the *sensor-realistic rendering*. The term sensor-realistic rendering in this framework refers to not only physically-based rendering but also simulating a particular digital imaging sensor. Figure 4.7 shows an overview of the prevailing components of this framework and figure 4.8 illustrates the role of the simulation components in the image formation chain.

Sensor-realistic simulation can be decomposed into three main parts: light transport simulation, optics simulations, and the digital sensor simulation. The first part is in common with all photorealistic rendering approaches and concerns utilizing a proper ray tracing approach for approximately solving the LTE. As the light transport simulation was the focus of this chapter in the previous parts, in this section the other two components will be elaborated.

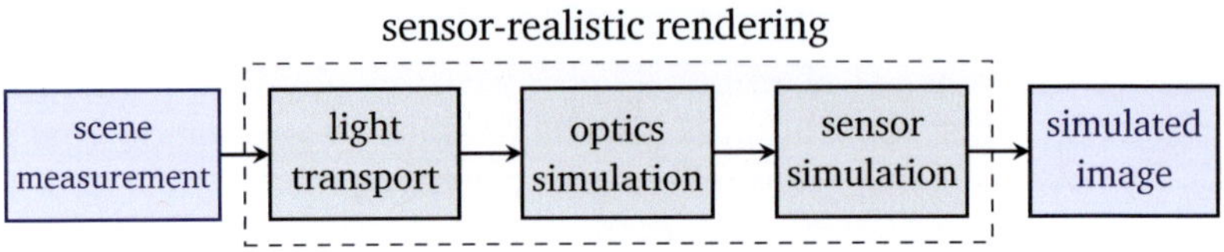

Figure 4.7: Components of the sensor-realistic simulation framework.

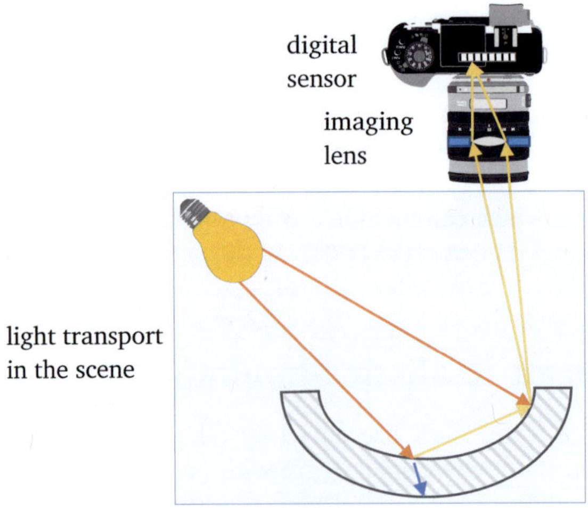

Figure 4.8: Illustration of the sensor-realistic simulation framework.

Although many concepts in the rest of this chapter are dedicated to laser light and its optical effects, the proposed simulation framework can be useful in simulating many machine vision systems with coherent and/or incoherent light sources.

4.7.1 Imaging Optic

The role of the imaging lens is to focus the light coming from one point in the scene space into another point in the image space. Therefore, in the optimal scenario, the lens turns a diverging spherical wave into a converging spherical wave which comes into focus on the image plane, i.e. the sensor. Another functionality of the lens is to control the amount of light reaching the imaging system, by means of an *aperture*. Figure 4.9 illustrates a simplified schematic of a lens.

Aperture Integration

The common goal of ray tracing algorithms is to correctly estimate the scene radiance $L(\boldsymbol{x_p},\boldsymbol{r}_\mathrm{c})$ of a sensor point $\boldsymbol{x_p}$ along the main ray direction $\boldsymbol{r}_\mathrm{c}$ (the ray passing through the center of the optic as in pinhole camera model). This value can be obtained by applying physically-based ray or path tracing methods. As illustrated in Fig. 4.9, the actual incoming irradiance from the scene to the imaged point requires an integration of radiance values received by the aperture over the subtended solid angle ω. In ray tracing, the MC sampling must be extended to sampling not only the main rays, but also rays from the whole light bundle that enters the optical system through the aperture. This generalization is straight forward to be integrated with ray tracing methods, however, with an increase of the rendering time.

In many imaging scenarios, the distance of the object to the entrance pupil (d_p in figure 4.9) is considerably larger than the pupil diameter, and therefore, the solid angle subtended by the lens is small. In such cases, we can approximate the scene radiance to be almost uniform over the solid angle ω. With this assumption, the irradiance collected by the aperture is approximated as [Sin12]

$$E(\boldsymbol{x_p}) = \frac{\pi}{4}\left(\frac{D}{f}\right)^2 \cos^4(\theta)\, L(\boldsymbol{x_p},\boldsymbol{r}_\mathrm{c}), \tag{4.11}$$

where f corresponds to the focal length of the lens, D denotes the diameter of the entrance pupil, and θ is the angle between the main ray $\boldsymbol{r}_\mathrm{c}$ and the optical axis. The ratio of the focal length to the entrance pupil diameter $f^{\#} = \frac{f}{D}$ is also known as the *f-number* of the imaging system. Using the definition of f-number, the irradiance equation 4.11 can be rewritten as:

$$E(\boldsymbol{x_p}) = \frac{\pi}{4}\frac{L(\boldsymbol{x_p},\boldsymbol{r}_\mathrm{c})}{f^{\#^2}}\cos^4(\theta). \tag{4.12}$$

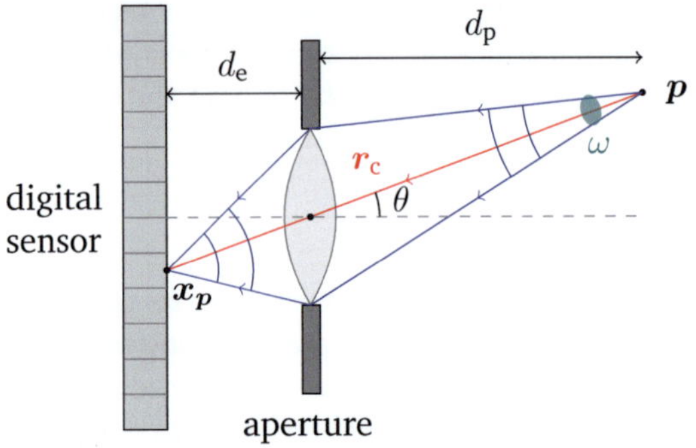

Figure 4.9: Simplified schematic of a lens. The lens collects light over solid angle ω and in the ideal case transforms the diverging incoming spherical wave into a converging one, focused at a sensor point. $\boldsymbol{r}_\mathrm{c}$ is the main ray entering the optical system. In this simplified schematic, exit pupil, entrance pupil, and the physical aperture are the same. General scenarios with multi-lens systems are given in [Bey15].

Transmission Efficiency

One important factor to take into account is the *transmission efficiency* of the optic. The previous equations assume a 100% efficiency in transmitting light through the lens system; however, one must account for some loss of light due to reflection and absorption. The transmission efficiency T_tr is the ratio of the transmitted and incident light intensities, which is dependent on the number of lenses used in the imaging optic as well as the wavelength [Sin12]. T_tr can be either experimentally measured or analytically estimated based on the number of lenses used in the optic and the reflection and absorption coefficients of the optical material.

4.7.2 Optical Effects

Optical imaging from scene space to image space by a lens system is in practice not optimal, but rather associated with optical effects degrading the image formation. Optical effects relevant to the focus of this thesis fall into two categories: *diffraction* and lens *aberrations*.

Diffraction

Sommerfeld [Som54], one the founders of the diffraction theory, defines diffraction as "any deviation of light rays from rectilinear paths which cannot be interpreted as reflection or refraction". When light encounters an obstacle or slit in a size comparable to its wavelength, it scatters at the boundary of the obstacle as the source of a secondary spherical wave, and leads to the formation of a pattern with a particular intensity distribution, known as an *interference pattern* (see figure 4.10). There is no physical difference between interference and diffraction; however, it has been historically common to refer to interference when considering the superposition of a few waves, and diffraction when treating a large number of waves [Hec02].

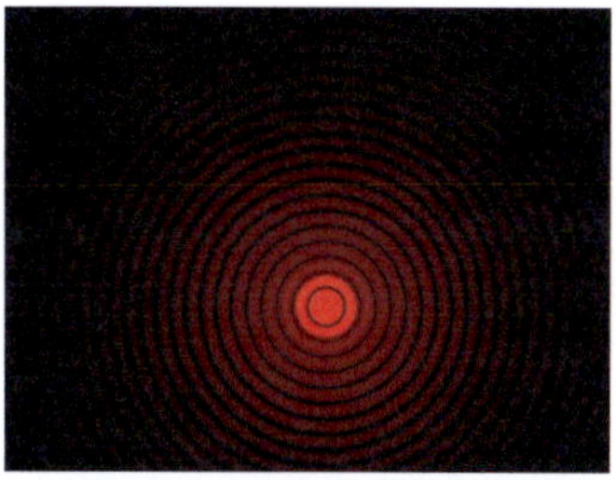

Figure 4.10: Diffraction pattern by passing a laser beam through a 90 μm circular aperture. Image from Wikipedia [Wika].

Although diffraction can happen all over the imaging scene, like at the edges of the objects or at a rough surface, a prominent appearance of diffraction is when light passes through the aperture. Increasing the aperture size reduces the effect, however, any finite aperture leads to some level of diffraction. This degrades the focusability of a point light source, even when lenses are aberration-free, and limits the smallest lateral distance d_r between the images of two incoherent point sources that the optical system is able to resolve. This is known as the *Rayleigh criterion* [Goo17] which is given as

$$d_\mathrm{r} = 1.22\frac{f\lambda}{D}. \tag{4.13}$$

When light hits a rough surface, it diffracts and the illuminated points appear as sources of secondary spherical waves, which interfere with each other. With an incoherent light source, illuminated points are incoherent with respect to each other and the superposition of the waves averages out the phase differences and thus creates a uniform intensity distribution. In case of a spatially coherent light source (e.g. a laser) and a surface rough enough to create all phase differences in $[0,2\pi)$, the interference of the diffracted waves forms a random intensity pattern, known as the *speckle pattern*.

Imaging a speckle pattern by yet another diffracting optical element (e.g. a lens system), forms a so-called *subjective speckle pattern*, whose speckle size essentially depends on the f-number of the imaging system. Figure 4.11 compares the subjective speckle pattern for two f-numbers. Reducing the f-number (increasing aperture area) generally reduces the diffraction effect in both coherent and incoherent imaging; however, this also leads to a shallower depth of field and further aberrations.

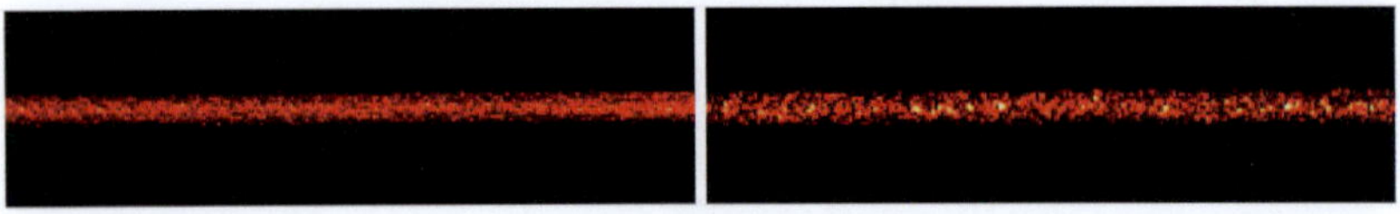

Figure 4.11: Subjective speckle of a laser line illuminated on a rough surface, taken with f-numbers 2 for the left image and 22 for the right image. Notice the increase in the speckle size with the increase of the f-number.

Aberrations

As depicted in figure 4.9, a perfect imaging lens creates a spherical wave at the exit pupil, with its center on the sensor plane. Any deficiencies in the optical system causing a deviation from the reference wavefront is denoted as an aberration. Aberrations are generally either chromatic or monochromatic [Hec02]. Chromatic aberrations are caused by the varying refractive index of a lens with wavelength, thus different wave lengths form slightly different spherical waves at the exit pupil. Monochromatic aberrations are caused by the imperfection of the optical system to focus a monochromatic light. This can either be caused by the lens geometry or optical misconfiguration, or due to the oversimplifying assumptions typically made for optical derivations. A typical example of the latter is the *paraxial approximation,* in which one assumes that rays entering the optical system hold a very small angle to the optical axis. Rays not satisfying those assumptions cause aberrations. Typically, choosing a wider aperture strengthens the aberration effects, mainly because more non-paraxial rays enter the optical system.

Defocus as an Aberration

A familiar aberration is *defocus,* in which the center of the spherical wave at the exit pupil is either in front or behind the image plane, yielding a blurred image. All scene points on a plane of distance d_g to the lens can be sharply imaged by a corresponding image plane of distance b to the lens, indicated by the lens equation. Therefore, only a set of scene points which are in a particular range of distance to the lens can be sharply imaged. Since the camera sensor has a limited resolution, as long as the blurred imaged point lies within a pixel, the image is said to be sharp enough. Therefore, each optical imaging system can tolerate a displacement of Δb from the optimal focus point, which can be translated into an allowed displacement in the scene space Δd_g, keeping the image still sharp [Bey15]. Δd_g is also known as the *depth of field* and decreases by widening the aperture approximately proportional to $\frac{1}{D}$.

Simulating Optical Effects

Section 4.3 discussed the deficiencies of typical geometric optic simulations in mimicking interference effects. Therefore, one requires either phenomenological simulations [Ber16b] or dedicated optical simulations [Equ06] to incorporate such wave optics effects. In this thesis, especially with the focus of simulating images illuminated by a laser, the imaging optic is modeled as a system whose response is determined by a *Point Spread Function (PSF)*. This way, optical effects such as aperture diffraction and aberrations can be simulated as a filtering step on the ideal images predicted by ray tracing methods. The underlying theories for such a systematic modeling of the optic is provided in the field of *Fourier optics*. This modeling is valid as long as the diffracting elements are large compared to the wavelength of light.

Simulating Optical Effects in Fourier Optics

In Fourier optics, an optical system is modeled as a linear system with a PSF [Goo17], which determines the response of the optic to the ideal image. Thus, the resulting image can be simulated by convolution of the PSF with the ideal image, or equivalently, by a multiplication in the frequency domain using Fourier transforms. A variety of optical simulations in the literature have already utilized this systematic perspective towards optical imaging systems [Fli04] [Fie14].

The definition of this linear system, however, depends on the coherence of the light source. If the incoming light to the system is incoherent, the system is linear on the intensities I of the ideal image. Thus the output intensity image in this case can be directly calculated by a convolution of the ideal image with the system incoherent PSF. If the illumination has some level of spatial coherence (e.g. laser light or other light sources within their coherence length), the system is no more linear on the intensities, but rather acts linearly on the wave field of the image E^{f}, which is the complex electrical field of the monochromatic light. The response of the optics can, therefore, be formulated as in equation 4.14 for incoherent imaging or using equation 4.15 for the coherent case. Here, h^{inc} denotes the incoherent PSF and h^{coh} the coherent one, with x and y being the image space coordinates. $I_{\mathrm{o}}^{\mathrm{inc}}$ represents the resulting image of incoherent imaging, and $E_{\mathrm{o}}^{\mathrm{f}}$ refers to the response wave field in coherent imaging.

$$I_{\mathrm{o}}^{\mathrm{inc}}(x,y) = I(x,y) * h^{\mathrm{inc}}(x,y) \tag{4.14}$$

$$E_{\mathrm{o}}^{\mathrm{f}}(x,y) = E^{\mathrm{f}}(x,y) * h^{\mathrm{coh}}(x,y) \tag{4.15}$$

Our eyes, as well as all sensor chips, are only sensitive to light irradiance. The irradiance of a light wave is proportional to the squared of its electrical field magnitude [Goo17] as given by

$$I(x,y) \propto \left| E^{\mathrm{f}}(x,y) \right|^2 . \tag{4.16}$$

The wave field is a complex term $E^{\mathrm{f}} = |E^{\mathrm{f}}| e^{j\angle E^{\mathrm{f}}} \propto \sqrt{I} e^{j\angle E^{\mathrm{f}}}$, whose amplitude is proportional to square root of the light intensity (equation 4.16), and its phase $e^{j\angle E^{\mathrm{f}}}$ is dependent on the optical path the wave has traveled and the superposition of the interfering waves. For correctly simulating interference patterns which appear in coherent imaging systems, the phase of the wave field is the deciding factor. If a common phase is set for the whole wave field, the coherent formulation reduces to the incoherent case.

In terms of intensities, coherent imaging introduces non-linear effects on the final intensity image. To better interpret the process of imaging in the coherent case, equations 4.15 and 4.16 can be integrated as below to yield the intensity image resulting from a coherent imaging system.

$$I_o^{\mathrm{coh}}(x,y) = \left| (\sqrt{I(x,y)} e^{j\angle E^{\mathrm{f}}(x,y)}) * h^{\mathrm{coh}}(x,y) \right|^2 \tag{4.17}$$

Some optical measurement techniques, such as interferometry, directly process the interference patterns. For simulation of such images, the exact optical path of the light must be traced and translated into the corresponding phase. In other coherent imaging scenarios, such as laser triangulation, the calculation of the exact phases is not essential; nevertheless, the statistics of the interference pattern must be correctly simulated. When laser light is scattered by a surface whose roughness profile has variations larger than the wavelength, the phase of the whole wave field is assumed to be independently uniformly distributed in $[0,2\pi)$ [Ber16b]. The subjective speckle pattern can then be simulated by inserting independently generated uniform random phases in equation 4.17 and setting $I(x,y)$ to the ideal geometric optic image computed by ray tracing.

Frequency Analysis of Optical Imaging

Computationally, it is more convenient to consider the systematic perspective presented in equations 4.14 and 4.15 in the frequency domain, by calculating the following Fourier transforms, where f_x and f_y refer to the frequency components and $\mathscr{F}$ represents the Fourier transform operator.

$$\mathcal{I}(f_x,f_y) = \mathscr{F}\{I(x,y)\} \tag{4.18}$$

$$\mathcal{H}^{\mathrm{O}}(f_x,f_y) = \mathscr{F}\{h^{\mathrm{inc}}(x,y)\} \tag{4.19}$$

$$\mathcal{H}^{\mathrm{A}}(f_x,f_y) = \mathscr{F}\left\{h^{\mathrm{coh}}(x,y)\right\} \tag{4.20}$$

The Fourier transform of the incoherent PSF, $\mathcal{H}^{\mathrm{O}}$, is called the *Optical Transfer Function (OTF)* and in the coherent case, $\mathcal{H}^{\mathrm{A}}$, is denoted by the *Amplitude Transfer Function (ATF)*. As both ATF and OTF belong to the same optical system, they are naturally related to each other. Goodmann has shown that the OTF is the normalized autocorrelation function of the ATF [Goo17]. Thus, knowing the ATF is enough to describe an optical system in both coherent and incoherent imaging cases.

Using a frequency analysis approach, the convolution with a linear space-invariant PSF is replaced with a multiplication and the final intensity images will be obtained by an inverse Fourier transform given by

$$I_o^{\mathrm{inc}}(x,y) = \mathscr{F}^{-1}\left\{\mathcal{I}(f_x,f_y)\,\mathcal{H}^{\mathrm{O}}(f_x,f_y)\right\}, \tag{4.21}$$

$$I_o^{\mathrm{coh}}(x,y) = \left|\mathscr{F}^{-1}\left\{\mathscr{F}\left\{\sqrt{I(x,y)}e^{j\angle E^{\mathrm{f}}(x,y)}\right\}\mathcal{H}^{\mathrm{A}}(f_x,f_y)\right\}\right|^2. \tag{4.22}$$

For both formulations, $I(x,y)$ can be set to the ideal image predicted by graphical rendering methods. In principle, by knowing the exact ATF or OTF and with the assumption of linearity and space-invariance of the optical system, additional imaging phenomena can be introduced to the simulated images by an image processing step. We can usually only approximate the system transfer function, and therefore, the optical effects will be also approximative. In the light transport simulation step, it is important to keep track of coherent and incoherent light components on the sensor and induce the corresponding phase factor to the coherent rays which reach the sensor. Coherent and incoherent image components must be differently filtered and then added together.

To incorporate several optical effects such as diffraction and aberrations, it will then suffice to know the ATF and OTF associated to these phenomena. The next two parts will briefly introduce Fourier optics modeling of aperture diffraction and aberration effects.

Simulating Aperture Diffraction

Diffraction effects associated with the aperture are directly related to the shape of the aperture, indicated by the *pupil function* $P(x,y)$. P is a binary function, indicating the light blocking area with zero and the unblocking area with one. Goodman [Goo17] has shown that for a symmetrical pupil function, the ATF can be derived as given in equation 4.23. d_e in this equation refers to the distance of the exit pupil to the sensor, λ is the wavelength, and (f_x,f_y) refer to the spatial frequencies.

$$\mathcal{H}^\mathrm{A}(f_x,f_y) = P(d_\mathrm{e}\,\lambda f_x, d_\mathrm{e}\,\lambda f_y) \tag{4.23}$$

For instance, the ATF of a circular aperture with diameter D and distance d_e to the sensor, is given by the following equation. In this case, the ATF is a disk in the frequency domain, i.e. a low-pass filter.

$$\mathcal{H}^\mathrm{A}(f_x,f_y) = \mathrm{circ}\left(2\lambda\, d_\mathrm{e}\frac{\sqrt{f_x^2+f_y^2}}{D}\right), \tag{4.24}$$

$$\mathrm{circ}(r) := \left\{\begin{array}{ll} 1, & \text{for } r \leq 1 \\ 0, & \text{otherwise} \end{array}\right\}.$$

If the lens aberrations are negligible, the aperture function alone is enough to simulate the whole imaging optics [Moh18a]. In this case the optic is known to be *diffraction-limited*. For the whole imaging system to be diffraction-limited though, the resolution of the sensor must be equal or better than the Rayleigh resolution in order to resolve what the optic is capable to image.

Figure 4.12 compares the effect of aperture diffraction on imaging an ideal intensity pattern, in coherent and incoherent imaging cases. As it can be seen, the speckles in coherent imaging degrade the image much more than the blurring effect in incoherent diffraction. Details on computational methods for these simulations can be found in the book by Voelz [Voe11].

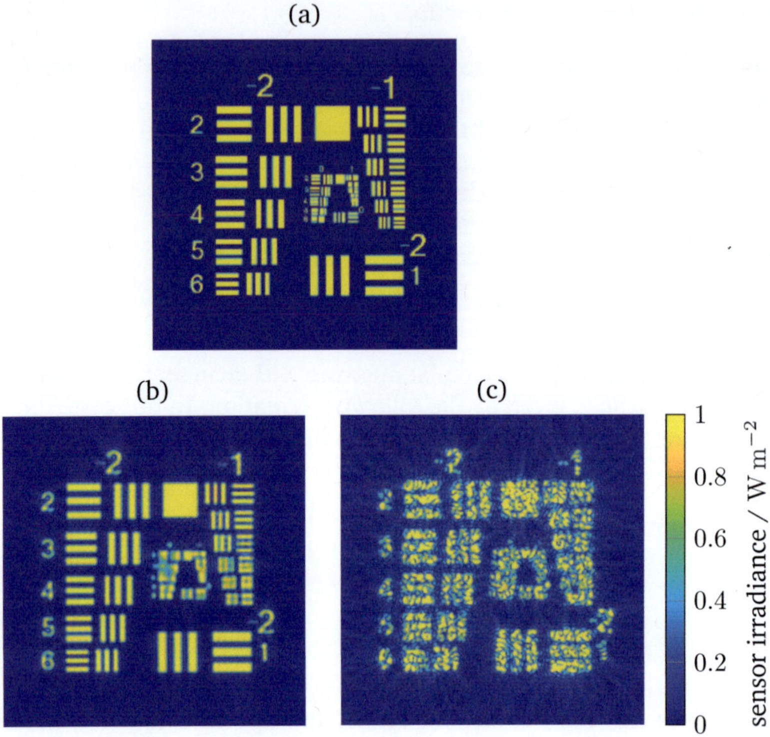

Figure 4.12: Coherent vs. incoherent imaging, with $f^{\#} = 22$. (a): ideal irradiance (i.e. intensity) on a sensor of size $1.45\,\mathrm{mm} \times 1.45\,\mathrm{mm}$, (b): simulated aperture diffraction assuming incoherent imaging, (c): simulated aperture diffraction in coherent imaging with $\lambda = 660\,\mathrm{nm}$ and uniform random phase.

The Rayleigh limit describes the resolution of the optical system only in the incoherent case. Resolution in coherent imaging is more difficult to study because depending on the actual phases, it can perform better or worse than the incoherent case [Goo17]. Nevertheless, incoherent imaging is in general considered to deliver better images [van06].

Simulating Aberrations

As discussed earlier, aberrations occur when the exit pupil wavefront has any deviations from a perfectly spherical wave which should ideally come to focus on the sensor. This means, aberrations cause a path-length error of $W(x,y)$ to the exiting wavefront, as if a phase shifting plate is placed in the aperture [Goo17].

With this in mind, the *generalized pupil function* [Goo17] integrating both the pupil shape and aberrations is given in the equation below:

$$\mathcal{P}(x,y) = P(x,y) \exp\left(\frac{j2\pi}{\lambda} W(x,y)\right). \tag{4.25}$$

Consequently, the ATF in the aberrated case can be calculated in a similar manner as given in equation 4.23, but this time using the generalized pupil function

$$\mathcal{H}^{\mathrm{A}}(f_x,f_y) = \mathcal{P}(d_{\mathrm{e}}\lambda f_x, d_{\mathrm{e}}\lambda f_y). \tag{4.26}$$

It has to be noted that most aberrations depend on the depth or lateral position of the image point, and thus, they cannot be modeled as a shift invariant system. This is obvious in out-of-focus effects that different depths experience different blurring levels. This can make the filtering step more difficult, nevertheless, it can be handled by acquiring additional depth information from the ray tracing step and applying a variable blurring kernel for filtering. Simulation of out-of-focus effects using Fourier optics methods for a pattern of constant depth to the camera will be studied in the next chapter, section 5.3.3.

When defocus is the only aberration of interest to be simulated, it is more convenient to simulate it in the light transport step, by including a lens and an aperture in the ray tracing. If the wavefront deformations can be calculated in advance, the Fourier optics simulations introduced in this section are more convenient to apply.

4.7.3 Sensor

The result of the previous simulation steps is an irradiance profile on the sensor, which is essentially an analog signal. The role of the imaging sensor is to measure the accumulated light energy during the time the sensor is exposed to light, i.e. the exposure time, and transform it to a discrete digital intensity image by an Analog to Digital Converter (ADC). The sensor measurement and sampling is one of the important sources of stochastic noise in the images, and therefore, it is important to incorporate the characteristics of a sensor in the simulations to evaluate its performance in a particular imaging scenario.

A sensor is composed of a 2D grid of light sensitive pixels. A pixel sensor integrates the incoming irradiance $E(x,y)$ both over the pixel area A_{p} and the exposure time t_{exp}, leading to the total energy accumulated on the pixel. Neglecting temporal differences of the incoming light and assuming a monochromatic light with frequency ν, the number of photons μ_{p} hitting a pixel can be approximated by

$$\mu_{\mathrm{p}} = t_{\mathrm{exp}} \frac{\int_{A_{\mathrm{p}}} E(x,y)\mathrm{d}x\mathrm{d}y}{h\nu}, \tag{4.27}$$

where $h\nu$ refers to the energy of one photon with frequency ν.

Arriving photons induce an electrical voltage in the pixel sensor, which is measured, amplified, and finally converted to a digital signal [EMV16]. The transformation steps from photons to intensities introduce stochastic noise to the signal, leading to a mean intensity value as well as an intensity-dependent variance. For a reliable simulation, both the average behavior and the stochastic noise of a sensor must be incorporated.

The *EMVA standard 1288* [EMV16] for the first time introduced a common guideline for the camera producers to conduct standard experiments to accompany their products with the corresponding specifications. This model aims at systematically modeling the statistical transformation of photon energies to intensity values. Fortunately, many manufacturers have already adopted the standard, which provides a good opportunity for integrating the EMVA 1288 model in the image simulation framework for a wide variety of available camera sensors. In what follows, the components of this standard will be introduced.

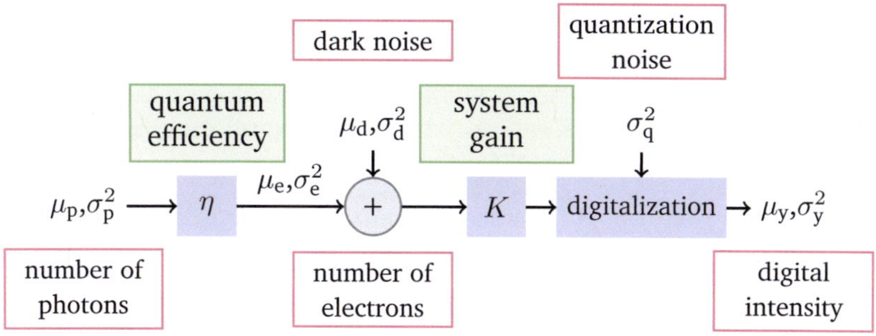

Figure 4.13: EMVA 1288 linear model of a sensor pixel [EMV16].

EMVA Standard 1288

The EMVA 1288 standard introduced by the European Machine Vision Association (EMVA) [3] models the process of image formation on a camera sensor as a linear model, as displayed in figure 4.13. This model covers a wide range of off-the-shelf camera sensors typically used in machine vision setups. In the following, the main components of the model are described.

Incoming Photons

The input to this model is the number of photons hitting a pixel sensor. Because light sources emit photons at random times, the number of photons reaching a spot in a given time interval is a random variable with a Poisson distribution. The fluctuations of the number of photons are referred to as the *shot noise*, which is caused by the random nature of photon emissions from light sources. Equation 4.27 derived earlier actually calculates the average number of photons μ_p. From the Poisson distribution we know that its variance is given by $\sigma_p^2 = \mu_p$.

Photons to Electrical Voltage

From the total number of photons, a fraction determined by the wavelength-dependent *quantum efficiency* η is absorbed, which induces $\mu_e = \eta\mu_p$ electrons in the sensor pixel. The quantum efficiency is a

[3]https://www.emva.org/

positive wavelength-dependent factor less than one. The accumulated charge on the pixel sensor induces a voltage to a capacitor, which is read out by the sensor and further amplified by the system gain factor K. The unit of system gain is DN/e$^-$, in which DN (digital unit) is actually a dimensionless unit but is used for the sake of clarity.

All the noise relating to the sensor read-out and amplification can be modeled as an additive signal independent normally distributed *dark noise* with mean μ_d and variance σ_d^2. μ_d is usually non-zero which means there are typically some thermally induced electrons in the sensor even when there are no input photons. Dark noise and its variance increase linearly with the exposure time and exponentially with the temperature.

Digitalization

After the amplification with the system gain, the resulting value is quantized and saved as a digital intensity. The quantization process introduces a uniformly distributed noise to the values with zero mean and variance σ_q^2 equal to $1/12$ of the quantization interval (variance of uniform distribution is $1/12$ of the quantization interval).

The result of the whole sensing and digitalization process leads to an average intensity μ_y with variance σ_y^2, given by

$$\mu_\mathrm{y} = K(\eta\mu_\mathrm{p} + \mu_\mathrm{d}), \tag{4.28}$$

$$\sigma_\mathrm{y}^2 = K^2(\eta^2\sigma_\mathrm{p}^2 + \sigma_\mathrm{d}^2) + \sigma_\mathrm{q}^2. \tag{4.29}$$

Color Cameras

The mechanism described in section 4.7.3 explains how gray scale intensities emerge from the incoming photons. Acquisition of colors in cameras happens by different quantum efficiencies for different wavelengths. With the red, green, and blue being the most commonly used color components, there are three different pixel types with high quantum efficiencies for the intended wavelengths. The color pixels, however, are not only sensitive to one particular wavelength, but rather exhibit a *spectral response* over a range of wavelengths. Figure 4.14 shows the quantum efficiency curves for a sample color camera.

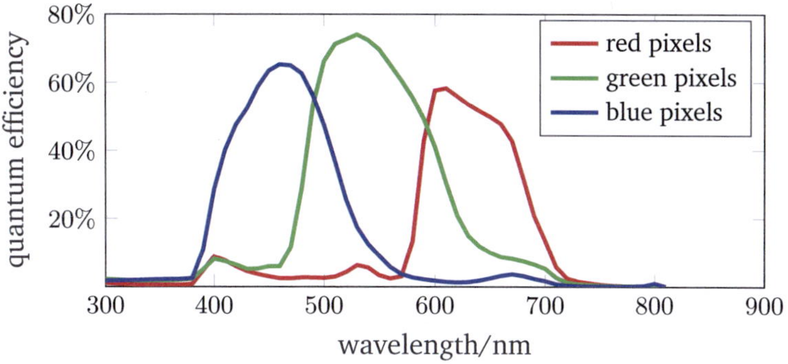

Figure 4.14: Quantum efficiency curves for BFLY-PGE-23S6C-C camera from FLIR Integrated Imaging Solutions Inc. [FLI17].

Figure 4.15: A typical Bayer filter grid. Image from Wikipedia [Wikb].

Most color cameras use a single chip with an arrangement of 50% green, 25% red, and 25% blue pixels, known as a *Bayer filter*. In such a filter, each square of four neighboring pixels will have one red, one blue, and two green pixels, similar to figure 4.15. The distribution of colors mimics the sensitivity of human eye and thus provides a higher resolution for green. The image directly resulting from the color filter is called a *raw image*, which has actually false colors. By *demosaicing*, the missing colors will be interpolated, to estimate all three color channels for each pixel.

In addition to demosaicing, a process called *white balance correction* is also needed to balance the amount of red, green, and blue intensities. This is due to the fact that the quantum efficiencies are typically higher for the green color, and the images would look rather greenish without white balance correction.

Apart from Bayer filters, there are also other technologies where more than one sensor chip is used. Traditionally, 3-sensor cameras have been used in which the RGB color components are split into three separate sensors using a beam-splitter [Bey15]. More recently, the FOVEON X3 sensor [4] stacks three layers of silicon sensors on top of each other. Due to the fact that longer wavelengths (red) penetrate in silicon deeper than shorter wavelengths (blue), three layers of transparent silicon sensors of blue, green, and red, record all three color channels for each pixel.

Camera Simulation in this Thesis

This chapter studies the simulation process for both monochromatic and color cameras. Although for the special application of this thesis, which is on laser triangulation, the monochromatic cameras are the prevailing choice, this thesis also considers simulating color cameras in addition to monochrome ones. Considering the inspection systems in a broader sense, there can be more complex inspection scenarios where the color plays a role, such as when inspecting color-related features on the surface, or even in the application of laser triangulation, in case several laser lines with different colors are used. Therefore, it is left as an expert choice, whether or not a color camera is considered in the planning.

Among the different types of color cameras, for the simulation and planning purposes of this thesis only Bayer-filter-based color cameras are taken into account.

4.8 Simulation Results

Figure 4.16 shows a collage of a real camera image and the corresponding simulated image using the framework proposed in this chapter. This image shows the cylinder head under laser line illumination. The greenish appearance of the image is due to simulating the raw camera image directly after demosaicing, without white balance correction. Direct comparison against raw images help us avoid the extra, often not exactly known, data processing procedures on the cameras. The image exposure is adjusted so that the laser line can be imaged without being overexposed. This is why the unilluminated parts of the cylinder head look dark on

[4] http://www.foveon.com

the image. Figure 4.16 also shows a magnified view of the real and simulated laser line, which visually proves that the laser profile, intensity, and speckle texture, have been realistically reproduced.

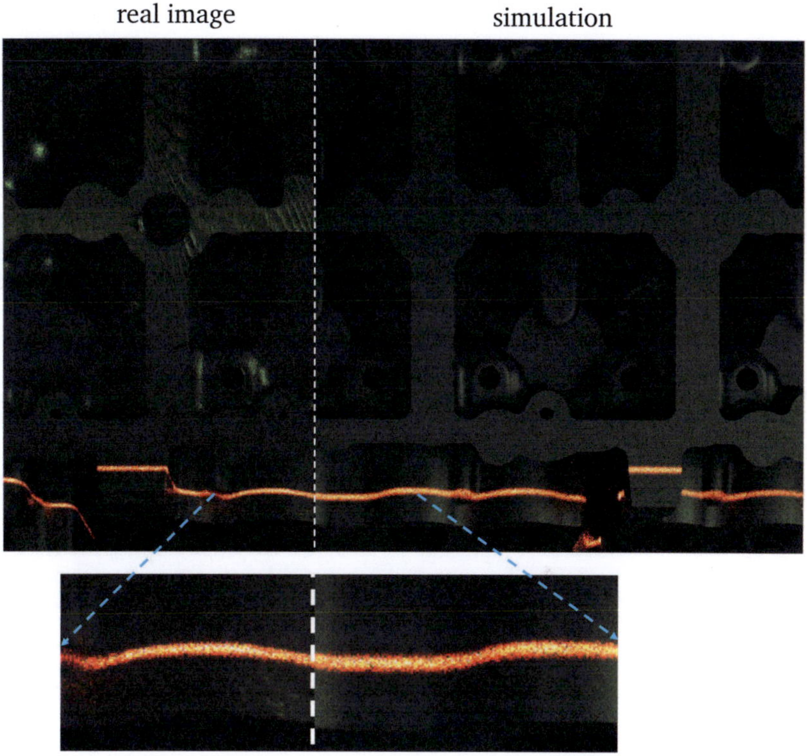

Figure 4.16: This image shows a cylinder head illuminated with a laser line. (left): real image with $f^{\#} = 11$ and $t_{\text{exp}} = 811\,\text{ms}$, (right): simulated image using the proposed sensor-realistic simulation framework.

Figure 4.17 shows the same real and simulated images after applying a white balance correction algorithm to both images. This algorithm simply multiplies the red, green, and blue channels of an image with factors to balance the three color channels. This simulation corresponds to f-number 11 with a focal length of 16 mm. The geometrical and optical parameters of the laser and the camera were calibrated and integrated into the simulations, to generate an image with the same field of view and with comparable intensities. The light sources used in this experiment include both the laser line and the incoherent light sources (usual ceiling lamps and a window with daylight) in the lab.

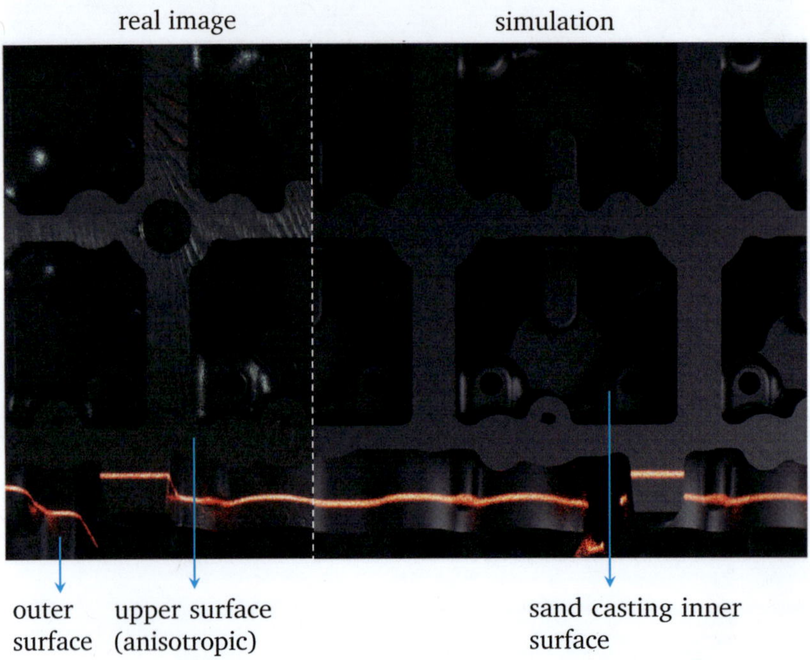

Figure 4.17: Same images of figure 4.16 after applying a white balance correction procedure. Different types of surfaces in the cylinder head object are annotated in this figure.

The light transport simulation for the results of this chapter are carried out using the Mitsuba renderer [Wen10]. Ray tracing was separately carried out for the coherent laser light and the incoherent ambient light, in order to process the laser irradiance on the sensor for inclusion of the speckles (diffraction effect). In order to simulate speckles when they are smaller than a pixel, the image was rendered with a higher resolution, where a pixel is sub-sampled with a grid of 3×3 sub-pixels.

Each sub-pixel is then sampled with 1024 sample rays. After this step, the image is down-sampled to the original size by considering the average irradiance generated within a pixel. The aberrations of the utilized lens were considered negligible. The rendering time for this image was about 10 hours, using 8 cores of a CPU at 3.70 GHz.

Since Mitsuba is a spectral renderer, it can be used to render spectral images. Spectral rendering is required for modeling the sensor spectral response to the incoherent light source. To do so, ray tracing results were exported for bandwidth bins of 10 nm. All bins together cover the spectral range of 360 nm to 830 nm. As the laser bandwidth is small, for simulating the laser light, spectral imaging was dedicated only to the bin which contained the wavelength of the laser. Simulation of the lab lights required all spectral bins.

After the simulation of the light transport and the optical effects, the resulting incoherent and coherent irradiance patterns were added together. For the sensor simulations, the full EMVA 1288 data-sheet for the BFLY-PGE-23S6C-C sensor including quantum efficiency curves of figure 4.14 was taken into account. The actual exposure time of 811 ms, corresponding to the real image, was used for integrating light on the pixels and calculating the number of incoming photons in the simulation.

The object consisted of at least three different surface textures which also showed some variations along the surface. These surface types are annotated in figure 4.17. The outer surface of the cylinder head (the part which is illuminated by the laser light) and the sand casting inner parts of the model were subject to BRDF and microscopic roughness measurements. The measured BRDFs were used to model the surface reflectance in the simulations. The flat upper surface is additionally machined and thus, shows an anisotropic appearance. This surface was not subject to BRDF measurements due to its high variations along the surface and complexities in the BRDF measurements. For this anisotropic surface, the BRDF parameters of the outer surface were used for the simulations. Differences between the real and the simulated image in the upper anisotropic surface area are, therefore, more distinctly visible.

Figure 4.18 gives a collage of another pair of real and simulated images, in which the laser line illuminates a different part of the cylinder head. The real image is captured with the same lens as in the previous result, with f-number 2 and an exposure time of 25 ms. Figure 4.19 displays the same pair of images after white balance correction.Slight differences in the intensity of the cylinder head and the highlights on the surface correspond to the inaccuracies in modeling the ambient light in the lab environment and the surface BRDF. As it can be seen in these figures, the laser intensity and profile are realistically reproduced. The next chapter includes further information regarding the experiments for surface BRDF and roughness measurements, as well as measurements regarding the lens and the laser. Moreover, the intermediate results during several steps of the simulation procedure will be discussed there.

real image simulation

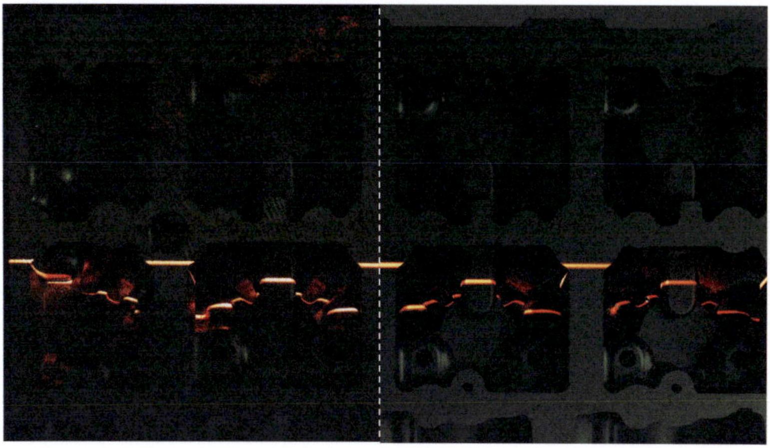

Figure 4.18: (left): real image with $f^{\#} = 2$ and $t_{\text{exp}} = 25\,\text{ms}$, (right): simulated image using the sensor-realistic simulation framework.

real image simulation

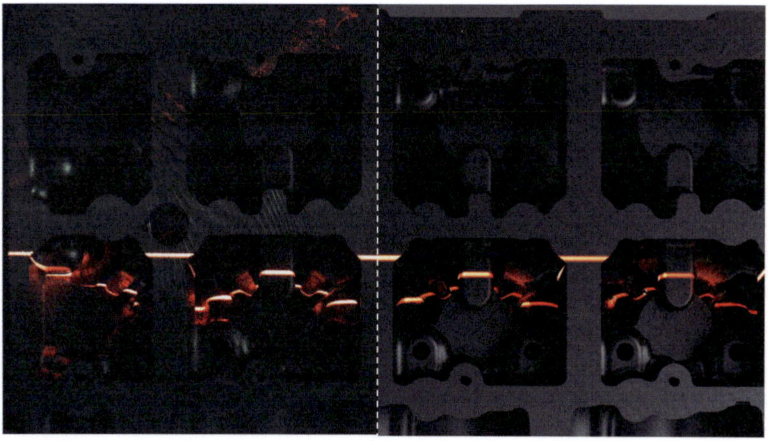

Figure 4.19: Same images of figure 4.18 after applying white balance correction.

4.9 Conclusion and Discussion

This chapter studied the problem of simulating the image formation process with a special focus on a realistic simulation of optical imaging systems. After an introduction to the prevailing computer graphics techniques for image synthesis, a framework for the sensor-realistic simulation of images was proposed. The framework extended geometric optics ray tracing techniques with additional post processing for simulation of wave optics effects, with special focus on coherent light sources and the spectral response of a given sensor.

The simulation results indicate that it is indeed possible to generate very realistic images of optical imaging systems, using state of the art rendering engines, extended with additional components to simulate the relevant optical and digitalization effects. Different optical phenomena can appear differently in various imaging systems, and therefore, it is important to recognize and model the dominating factors and include them in the simulations. Therefore, the speckle effect, which is a special phenomena related to lasers, was specifically modeled in this chapter. Nevertheless, the introduced concepts for Fourier optics simulations can also be beneficial to the simulation of other optical imaging systems as well.

As it can be seen in the simulation results, many details of the imaging scene must be known to yield a realistic simulation. Difficulties in controlling the ambient light, non-cooperative surfaces for BRDF measurements, varying BRDFs along the surface, surface deviations from the CAD models, and inaccuracies in lens, cameras, and light source specifications, can make the realistic simulations more difficult to achieve. In general more information about the imaging scene will always contribute to the simulation realism, however, scene measurements become very costly and time consuming at some point.

Machine vision experts who would like to deploy inspection planning systems in the future will need to decide about which details may have more prominent effects on the measurement results and how much they would like to invest in acquiring better measurements from the surfaces and light sources.

5 Simulation Verification

A challenging concept which has been relatively rarely addressed when utilizing simulated images is an objective *simulation verification*. Verification is meant to evaluate the correctness and quality of the simulations. The majority of the works in this regard rely on evaluating the believability of the synthesized images. Believability is always tied with the perception of a human observer and is biased towards his/her experiences, memories, and the evaluation method [Sun01]. There have also been a few objective verification metrics [Ulb06], such as pixel-wise error metrics, comparison against radiometric measurements, and perception-based metrics. The latter are supposed to be similar to human verification, only that the human perception procedure is formalized and analytically applied.

This chapter focuses on verifying the simulation framework discussed earlier for the simulation of the entire imaging chain in a simplified inspection scenario. A special focus of this chapter is on defining objective verification criteria for evaluating the suitability of simulated images for planning machine vision inspection setups. With the special application of this thesis to laser triangulation, the inspection scenario is dedicated to imaging a laser line incident on metal surfaces under different imaging conditions.

5.1 Scope of Verifications

It is important to precisely determine the scope in which simulations are being compared against real images. In this thesis, it is assumed that the simulated geometry is sufficiently correct, including a consistent CAD model, correct sensor field of view and resolution as well as accurate positions for the objects, sensors, and illumination sources. As these simulation aspects constitute the basics of graphical simulations, they will not be explicitly verified here. The main scope of verifications in this chapter encompasses the optical, photometric, and radiometric features of simulations, attributing to a correct reproduction of the actual signal to noise ratio.

To verify rendered images which are to represent the reality for some quantitative measurement, verifications are needed at two different levels: the **signal level** and the **application level**. At the signal level, the signal values stored in the pixel intensities of the real and simulated images must be compared to verify the realistic reproduction of the images. The application level is concerned with the performance of the image processing algorithms on simulated images and their suitability for the final intended application. This comparison can be performed in terms of the uncertainties in 2D feature detection on the image, which further leads to stochastic noise in the final measurement.

5.2 Experiments with Imaging a Laser Line

The experiments for simulation verification follow the scenario depicted in figure 5.1, where the laser line projector illuminates a piece of an approximately flat metal surface. The imaging scenario has been intentionally chosen simple to facilitate accurate physical measurements in each step and provide sufficient control over the influencing factors. The light transport is particularly simplified, including only two paths, one from the light source to the surface and a further path towards the camera. Therefore, the experiments mainly aim at verifying the correct simulation of the optical effects and the sensor, which have been often missing in previous works.

Experimental Setup

Figure 5.2 shows the experimental setup. In this setup, the camera is installed on an axis with adjustable height and looks perpendicularly on the surface. The laser line projector with a measured power of 23 mW is placed on a rotation arm which allows one to adjust the laser incident angle θ_{inc}. For imaging, a 16 mm Fujinon lens is used with manually adjustable f-number and focus. On the sensor side, a color (Blackfly BFLY-PGE-23S6C) and a monochrome camera sensor (Blackfly BFLY-PGE-13E4M), both from FLIR [1] with global shutter and available EMVA 1288 specifications have been separately utilized for capturing images. The sample surface used for the experiments is a 7 cm×7 cm part cut from the body of the cylinder head object, as illustrated in figure 5.3. As seen in figure 5.2, the laser line is projected over the flat part of the surface.

The parameters which have been been varied during the experiments include: camera distance to surface d_{c}, camera focus distance $d_{\mathrm{c}}^{\mathrm{foc}}$, f-number $f^{\#}$, exposure time t_{exp}, and the camera sensor. For further quick references to the parameters, table 5.1 gives an overview of the degrees of freedom in the experiments with their corresponding range of values. The fixed setup parameters are summarized in table 5.2. Table 5.3 gives the sensor specifications as well as the EMVA 1288 data relevant for the simulation of the two sensors.

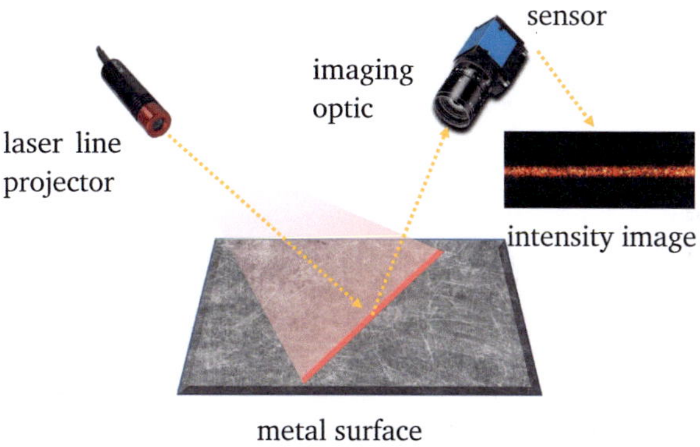

Figure 5.1: Laser line imaging scenario for simulation verification.

[1] https://www.flir.com/

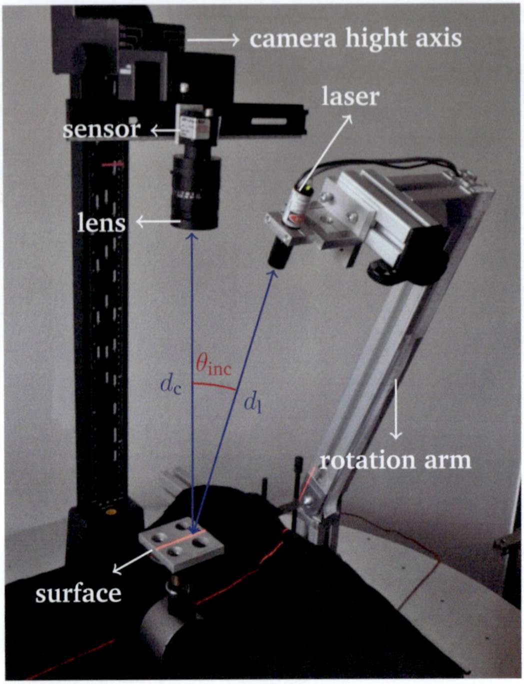

Figure 5.2: Experimental setup for image acquisition. d_{c} and d_{l} correspond to the distances of the camera and laser projection points to the surface and θ_{inc} denotes the laser incident angle.

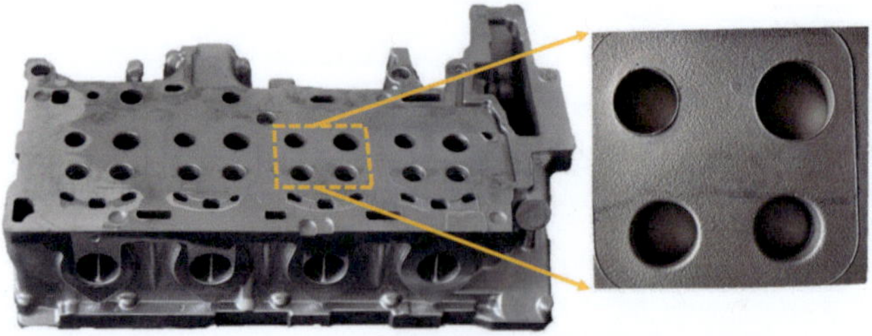

Figure 5.3: Sample surface of size 7 cm×7 cm extracted from the cylinder head body for surface measurements and the simulation verification experiments.

Table 5.1: List of variable parameters in the experiments

Parameter	Value range
camera distance to surface d_c	[0.2 m,0.5 m]
laser distance to surface d_l	[0.1 m,0.5 m]
f-number $f^{\#}$	1.4 - 22
camera focus distance d_c^{foc}	[0.2 m,0.5 m]
exposure time t_{exp}	[0 ms, 1630 ms]

Table 5.2: List of constant parameters in the experiments

Parameter	Value
objective focal length f	16 mm
incident angle θ_{inc}	45°
laser power p_W	23 mW
laser distance to surface d_l	0.36 m
laser wavelength λ	661 nm
laser divergence δ	0.24 mrad
laser fan angle	60°
laser focus distance	0.9 m
monochrome camera field of view	19°×23°
color camera field of view	24°×35°

Table 5.3: Specification of the camera sensors used in the experiments

Sensor	Pixel Size	Image Grid	Image Gain	Saturation capacity	Quantum efficiency (660 nm)	Dark noise μ_d	Valid bits
color	5.86 μm	1200 × 1920	0.53 DN/e$^-$	33 456 e$^-$	R: 48% G: 9% B: 3%	15.06 e$^-$	10
mono-chrome	5.3 μm	1024 × 1280	0.16 DN/e$^-$	9893 e$^-$	53%	27.57 e$^-$	10

Setting Parameters and the Calibration Procedure

Among the variable setup parameters, the f-number was manually adjusted on the lens and the exposure time was programmatically controlled on the sensor. The laser incident angle θ_{inc} was manually adjusted with the rotation arm and a goniometer. A number of parameters were extracted from the devices' data sheets, including the laser divergence δ, laser fan angle, and the objective focal length f. The laser wavelength and power were measured using a power meter. The laser distance d_{l} was estimated based on the length of the projected laser line and the laser fan angle, and kept unchanged after the calibration. The laser focus distance was also experimentally estimated by observing the distance in which the projected laser profile was at the thinest.

The only parameter that required constant recalibration was the camera distance d_{c} and the camera focus distance $d_{\mathrm{c}}^{\mathrm{foc}}$. To estimate $d_{\mathrm{c}}^{\mathrm{foc}}$, the camera was focused at the surface, where a calibration scale was placed. Using the calibration scale, the distance of the camera to the surface was estimated, which was also equal to the camera distance d_{c} in this case. Keeping the focus unchanged, the camera height was changed relative to this calibration point by means of the linear height axis, allowing the adjustment of d_{c} while keeping the focus distance $d_{\mathrm{c}}^{\mathrm{foc}}$.

All the calibrated distances, including d_{c}, $d_{\mathrm{c}}^{\mathrm{foc}}$, d_{l}, and the laser focus distance have been estimated to be accurate within 5 mm uncertainty.

Image Acquisition and Sample Images

The purpose of the experimental image acquisition was to take several images with different setup parameters in order to provide the ground truth data for comparison against the simulations. In these experiments, the only light source of interest was the laser light and therefore, the lab light sources were turned off and the window in the lab was covered with a curtain. In spite of this action, there was inevitably some ambient light in the lab, emitted by a computer monitor which was needed for the experiments, and the light which entered the room through the curtain. As the exposure for acquiring images of a laser light must be relatively low to avoid overexposure of the bright laser light, the dim ambient light in the imaging workspace was considered negligible.

By varying the setup parameters of table 5.1, a number of 1872 images with the color sensor and 2184 images using the monochrome sensor were captured for the verification process. Figure 5.4 displays a number of sample images taken with the experimental setup under different imaging conditions.

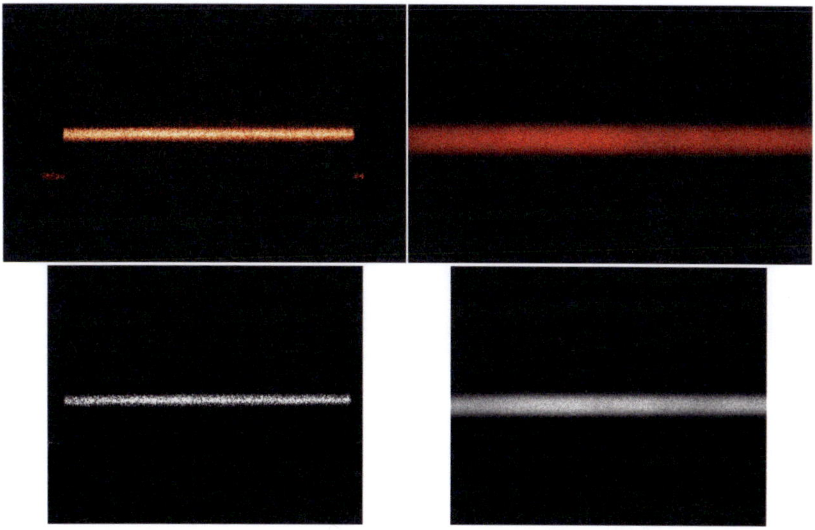

Figure 5.4: Sample images taken with the experimental setup, using the color and the monochrome sensor, in two different distances. The images on the right are defocused. Difference in the size of the color and the gray scale images is caused by the different camera field of views.

5.3 Sensor-Realistic Simulation Process

After an introduction to the experimental setup, sections 5.3.1 to 5.3.4 go through the simulation process to synthesize the images captured in the experimental setup. As the simulation framework of figure 4.7 suggests, every physically-based simulation starts with measuring the components of the imaging scene and is further followed by the simulation of the light transport, optical imaging, and the sensor. Throughout the following sections, intermediate simulation results will be also presented.

5.3.1 Scene Measurements

For physically-based simulations, the surfaces participating in the imaging scene are one of the challenging elements to be measured in terms of their BRDFs and roughness profiles. Accurate surface measurements play a key role in a realistic appearance.

Light sources are the other important elements of an imaging scene which should be measured in terms of their power and the intensity profile. Light source manufacturers often provide users with technical information which can be used in simulations.

Another factor which must be estimated and taken into account is the transmission efficiency T_{tr} of the optical imaging, as discussed previously in section 4.7.1. T_{tr} appears as a scale factor to correct the actual radiation energy reaching the sensor.

BRDF measurements

The sample surface material extracted from the inspection object has been through a BRDF measurement process. This measurement was performed using a robot-assisted BRDF measurement system shown in figure 5.5, and was carried out in Fraunhofer IOSB in Ettlingen. This figure also illustrates the geometry of the system. The light source, a laser of 650 nm wavelength, illuminates the sample by an inclination angle $\theta_{\mathrm{l}} \in [0°, 90°]$ using a motorized circular arm. The robot arm moves the optical detector to a desired outgoing direction indicated by the angles θ_{d} and ϕ_{d}, to calculate the amount of scattered light in this direction. The detector inclination angle θ_{d} can be varied in the interval $\theta_{\mathrm{d}} \in [0°, 90°]$. Due to collision issues, the detector azimuthal angle ϕ_{d} was limited to the interval $\phi_{\mathrm{d}} \in [-134°, 134°]$. During the measurements, all three angles were sampled with a step of 2°. A *spectralon*, assumed as a diffuse reference surface with the constant BRDF $\rho_{\mathrm{r}} = \frac{1}{\pi}$, was used to calibrate the measurements.

Figure 5.6 illustrates the measured surface BRDF values, for a constant laser inclination of θ_{l}=60°. The BRDF has its highest values near the specular reflection direction.

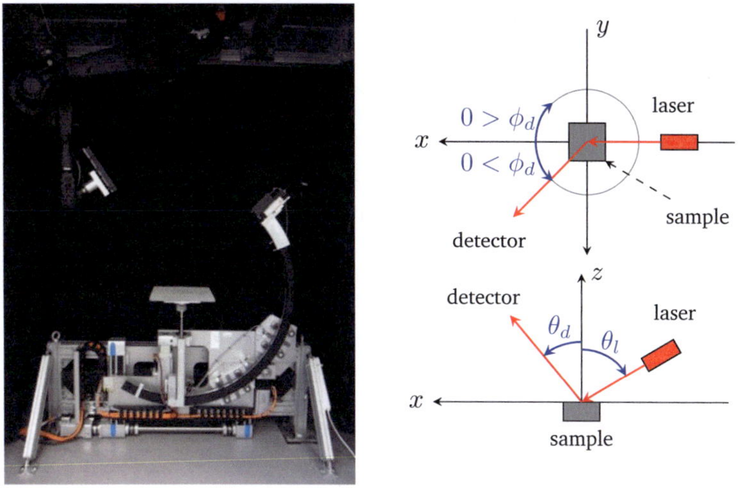

Figure 5.5: (right): BRDF measurement system, with optical detector on the left, laser source on the right, and sample in the middle. (right, above): Top view of the BRDF measurement setup. (right, below): Side view of the BRDF measurement setup.

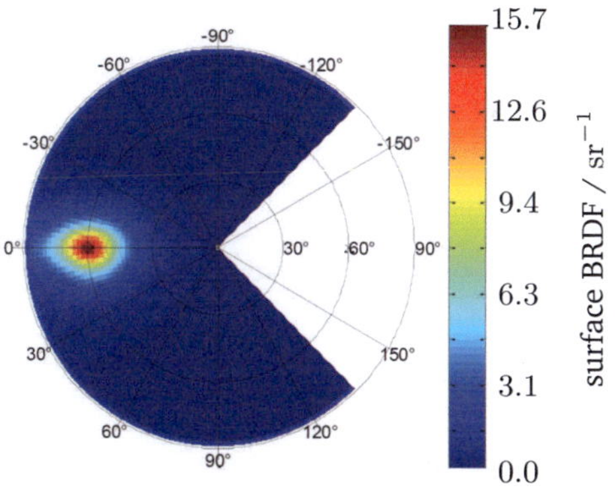

Figure 5.6: Measured BRDF illustrated for a constant laser inclination of $\theta_l = 60°$. Circular contours indicate the detector inclination θ_d and radial lines refer to azimuthal angle ϕ_d. The uncovered area is the unmeasurable region due to collision of the laser and the detector arms.

Roughness Measurements

Without considering the roughness profile, surfaces would look very smooth in the simulations. The microscopic structures of a surface introduce local changes to the orientation of the surface normal and thus create an intensity variation along the surface, conveying a sense of roughness to the observer. In computer graphic terms, this intensity variation is also known as *texture*. One way to integrate surface roughness in simulations is to use the height field to calculate a normal field for the surface. BRDF evaluations on each surface point for shading can then be calculated using the normal field instead of the normal in the global surface geometry. The intensity variations which will be introduced in this way produce an approximation of the actual surface texture.

In computer graphics terms, this method of incorporating microscopic surface structure without explicitly modeling the height field in the object geometry is known as *normal mapping*. This method is an approximation in which the masking and shadowing effects of the microscopic surface will be neglected. It is, however, a popular method for generating a visual complexity for the surface without adding much complexity to its geometry [Sch17]. The scale on which the normal maps are measured is highly related to the BRDF measurement scale. In the next section this topic will be elaborated.

To incorporate surface roughness into simulations, the surface height field was measured using Leica DCM3D microscope with a 20x magnification and a field of view of $636.61\,\mu\text{m} \times 477.25\,\mu\text{m}$. To cover a larger measurement area, several overlapping measurements were made and stitched together. Figure 5.7 shows the resulting height field measurement which covers an area of $3.4\,\text{mm} \times 2.7\,\text{mm}$. The measurements were carried out using confocal microscopy [Web96] with an uncertainty less than 15 nm in height.

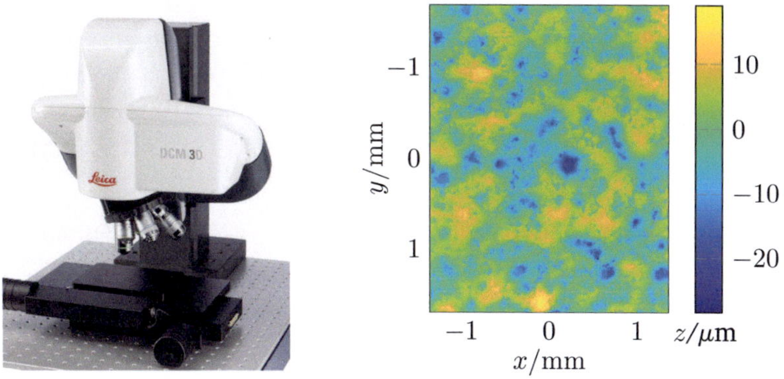

Figure 5.7: (left): Leica DCM3D microscope used for profile measurements with 20x confocal objective, (right): measured height field of the surface, with a standard deviation of 5.4μm. The measured height field of size 3.4 mm×2.7 mm is generated by stitching several overlapping measurements.

Scale Dependency of BRDFs and Normal Maps

A fundamental difficulty in measuring a BRDF is its dependency on the scale of the measurement and the resolution of the imaging system. Any light beam used for measuring the BRDF, illuminates the surface in some nonzero area, and thus, the scattered light is an averaged BRDF over the entire illuminated spot. Surface variations which are non-resolvable by the imaging system must be modeled in terms of the BRDF, whereas resolvable structures must be integrated to the geometry, for example as a normal map or directly as height variations. Choosing the correct scale depends mainly on the local resolution of the imaging system on the surface. This adds a further dimension to BRDFs, imposing a considerable difficulty in correctly measuring them. Pak in his work [Pak17] has mathematically studied the evolution of BRDFs through different scales. Due to the complexity of this topic, the scale dependency has been ignored in this thesis and the normal maps and the BRDF are kept constant for different resolutions. This approximation can of course cause slight deviations between the real and simulated images.

Laser Measurements and Modeling

Light source manufacturers usually provide useful information about the power and intensity profile of their products. It is, however, recommendable to measure the power or, if possible, the profile of the light source prior to simulations, in order to account for possible variations caused by the applied voltage, device aging, or unit-to-unit variations. The light source used in the experiments is a laser line projector, which is generated by spreading the light of a laser beam over a line through special optics. The power and wavelength of the employed laser were measured by removing the line generating lens, and focusing the beam inside a power meter probe. Based on the measurements, the laser provides 23 mW of power at 661 nm wavelength.

In this section, first the profile of a Gaussian laser beam is studied and later the description will be extended to laser lines. The laser line used in the experiments is approximated to follow the properties of a perfect Gaussian beam.

Laser beams: Laser emitters create beams with different properties. A commonly used type of laser beam is known as the *Gaussian beam*. Perpendicular to the propagation direction, these beams create a laser spot with a Gaussian profile. Eichler and Eichler in their book [Eic15], describe the intensity distribution (i.e. irradiance profile) of such a beam propagating in z-direction by

$$I(x,z) = I_{\text{max}} \exp\left(\frac{-2x^2}{w^2(z)}\right). \tag{5.1}$$

As illustrated in figure 5.8, $w(z)$ refers to the *beam width*, which indicates the spread of the beam. By convention, the focus plane of a laser is chosen to be at $z = 0$, and thus the beam width takes its minimum at $w_0 = w(0)$. As it can be seen in figure 5.8, the beam width increases by increasing the distance to the laser focus plane, which is mathematically given as below [Eic15]. In this equation, λ is the wavelength of the laser.

$$w(z) = w_0\sqrt{1 + \frac{z^2\lambda^2}{\pi^2 w_0^4}} \tag{5.2}$$

For distances far enough from the focus distance $z \gg 0$, the beam width can be linearly approximated as $w(z) \approx \frac{\lambda z}{\pi w_0}$, with the slope $\delta = \frac{\lambda}{\pi w_0}$ being known as the *divergence angle*. The divergence angle is usually given by the manufacturer in radians and can be used to derive w_0 as well as $w(z)$. The only unknown parameter to fully derive the laser profile from equation 5.1 is I_{max}. This parameter can be calculated by knowing the total laser power p_{w}. This will be explicitly derived for laser lines in the following section.

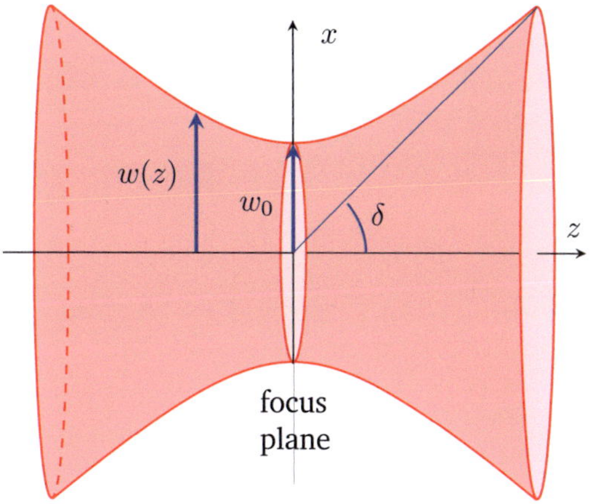

Figure 5.8: Visualization of a laser beam propagation, focus, and divergence angle.

Laser lines: To create *structured illumination* for machine vision inspection purposes, special lenses transform the laser beam into a particular structure, such as a line or a grid. A *cylindrical lens* is a cost-efficient solution for generating a laser line, but unfortunately transfers the beam Gaussian profile along the line, as shown in figure 5.9, which makes the laser line exponentially dimmer at both ends of the laser line. To generate an approximately uniform intensity over the line, a *Powell lens* redistributes the light along the laser line and yields a much better uniformity [Opt18]. Figure 5.10 visualizes the simulation of the intensity profile of such a laser line, assuming a perfectly uniform intensity distribution by the Powell lens. In the cross section of the laser profile (i.e. y-axis in figure 5.10), the Powell lens still generates a Gaussian profile.

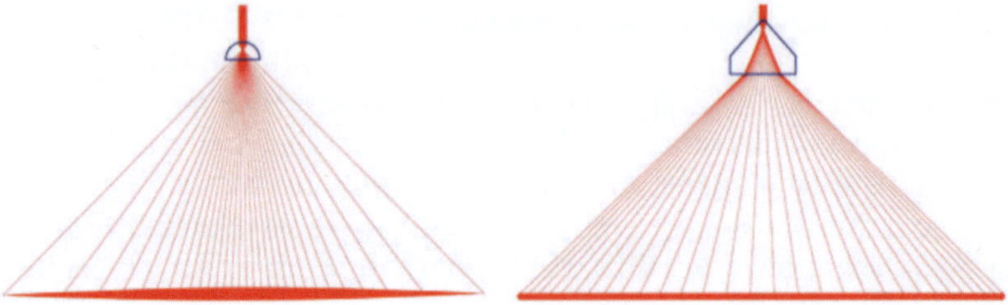

Figure 5.9: Comparison of laser line profiles generated by a cylindrical lens (left) and a Powell lens (right) [Opt18].

By Integrating the total intensity of a laser line of length L_l and setting it equal to the total power p_w as below

$$p_\mathrm{w} = I_\mathrm{max} \int_{-\infty}^{\infty} \int_{-L_\mathrm{l}/2}^{L_\mathrm{l}/2} \exp\left(\frac{-2x^2}{w^2(z)}\right) \mathrm{d}x \, \mathrm{d}y = L_\mathrm{l} \frac{\sqrt{2\pi}}{2} w(z) \, I_\mathrm{max}, \quad (5.3)$$

the maximum intensity can be derived for the laser line as below for every desired distance z from the focus plane by

$$I_\mathrm{max} = \frac{2\, p_\mathrm{w}}{\sqrt{2\pi} w(z) L_\mathrm{l}}. \quad (5.4)$$

This way, all the parameters to describe the emitted laser irradiance for any given point in the space can be extracted. Experiments of this thesis are also done using a Powell lens.

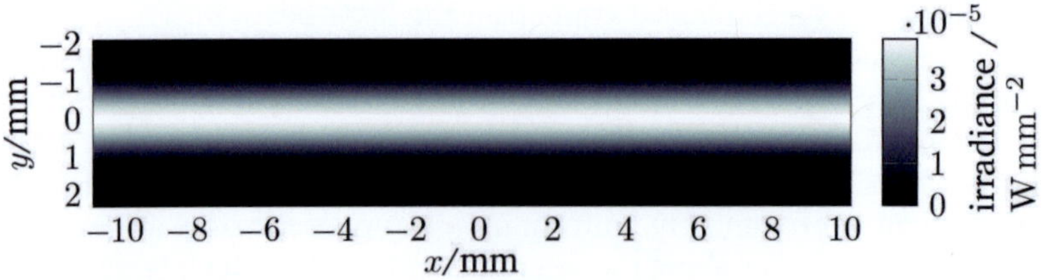

Figure 5.10: Simulated laser irradiance. Simulation parameters include: laser power 23 mW, laser focus distance 0.9 m, divergence angle 0.27 mrad, and a surface of distance 0.35 m to laser source.

Measuring Lens Transmission Efficiency

To estimate the transmission efficiency of the 16 mm Fujinon lens, the same experiment for laser power measurement was repeated, but this time the laser beam was focused inside the power meter probe through the lens. The ratio of the laser power measured with and without the lens gives an estimate of the transmission efficiency T_{tr}. Based on the experiments, T_{tr} was estimated to be 87%.

5.3.2 Light Transport Simulation

Compared to typical ray tracing applications, the scenario of figure 5.1 is rather simple in terms of light transport. Ignoring multiple reflections on the roughness scale, the simple flat geometry of the surface in the experiments requires simulating two steps in the light transport: laser illumination on the surface which was derived in section 5.3.1 and scattering of that light which is governed by the BRDF and the surface normal field. In the experiments of this chapter, no MC-based path sampling was implemented due to the simplified geometry. The main focus of these experiments concerns the optical and sensor simulations.

After calculating the laser irradiance profile on the surface, each surface point acts as a scattering element. Using the measured normal field, each such surface element has a local normal direction, using which the laser incident angle on that element is calculated (i.e. as in normal mapping). The scattered radiance in the direction of the camera will be then evaluated by means of the measured BRDF.

In these simulations, the light path sampling is not extended to cover the whole aperture, rather only the main ray passing through the center of the objective is traced, assuming a pin-hole camera model. Thus the result of light transport simulation is a radiance pattern on the sensor and not the irradiance. In computer graphics, aperture integration is usually part of the ray tracing by using lenses and tracing rays through them. In the experiments of this chapter, the role of the aperture is modeled in the optical simulations, which will be discussed in the next section.

Figure 5.11 shows the sensor radiance simulated with a resolution of $0.3\,\mu\mathrm{m}$ on the sensor, using the measured BRDF and the normal field. For a better visualization of the induced texture, the surface is assumed to be uniformly illuminated. Some artifacts due to stitching of the measured normal field and potential errors in height field measurements can be seen in the figure.

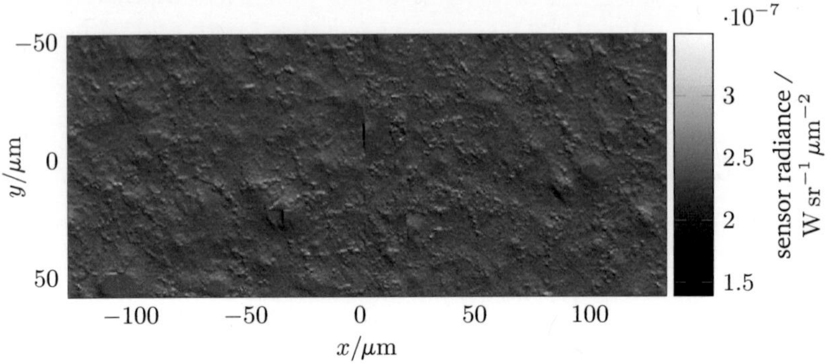

Figure 5.11: A small region of the simulated sensor radiance with a resolution of $0.3\,\mu$m, corresponding to an imaged surface area of $2.5\,$mm$\times 6.2\,$mm illuminated with an irradiance of $1\,\mu$W/μm^2.

5.3.3 Optical Imaging Simulation

Section 4.7.1 in the previous chapter covered the necessary background on simulating the optical imaging in a machine vision system. In summary, the important phenomena to take into account are: accumulation of light over the aperture (if not already done during light transport), aperture diffraction, and lens aberrations. In what follows, simulation of these phenomena for the imaging scenario of interest will be discussed.

Aperture Integration

Assuming the solid angle subtended by the aperture is small, equation 4.11 gives a good approximation of the integrated amount of light entering the aperture. This equation has been used to calculate the irradiance pattern on the sensor, by setting the radiance values $L_s(\boldsymbol{x_p}, \boldsymbol{r}_c)$ to the radiance calculated in the light transport simulation step.

Diffraction and Speckles

The simulation scenario in this chapter contains a laser light source, thus the coherent variant of the Fourier optics modeling should be used. To this end, the system ATF (Fourier transform of the aperture function) determines the response of the optical system to diffraction, according to equation 4.22. The correct choice of the wavefront phase factor $\angle E^{\mathrm{f}}$ in this equation plays the central role in simulating the interference patterns. As the surface used for the experiments is rough at the wavelength scale, it is valid to assume that the incoming wavefront to the lens, formed by the superposition of scattered waves from the surface, contains independently distributed random phases in $[0,2\pi)$. $I(x,y)$ in equation 4.22, is set to the ideal irradiance pattern obtained from the previous step.

To calculate the system ATF, $\mathcal{H}^{\mathrm{A}}(f_x,f_y)$, it suffices to know the aperture shape and the focal length of the objective. In the simulations, the aperture is assumed to be circular whose diameter is calculated by knowing the f-number and the focal length. Calculation of a circular ATF is straightforward using equation 4.24. The result of this simulation step is another irradiance pattern, however, with diffraction effects (i.e. speckles in this case) being introduced. Figure 5.12 visualizes the simulated irradiance pattern on the sensor after aperture integration and diffraction modeling, for imaging the laser profile previously seen in figure 5.10. The speckle pattern can be recognized on this image.

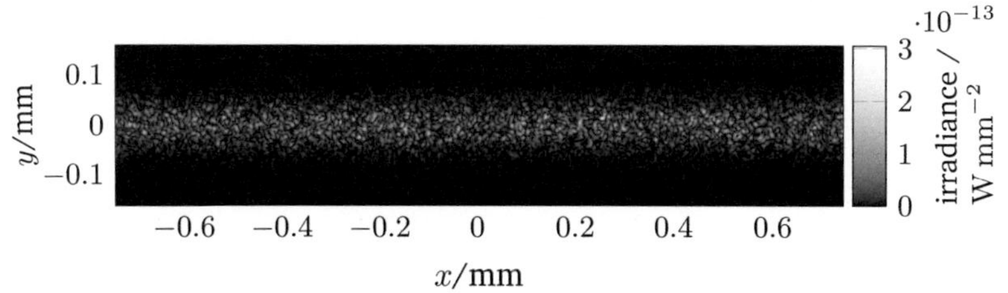

Figure 5.12: Sensor irradiance pattern by imaging the laser profile of figure 5.10, with $f^{\#} = 16$, from a distance of $d_{\mathrm{c}} = 0.35\,\mathrm{m}$.

Defocus as an Aberration

The blurring effects due to defocus can affect machine vision inspection systems in different ways. Therefore, it is important to take them into account. The verification experiments of this thesis include both focused and defocused images. In ray tracing, depth of field can be simulated by collecting rays of light over the aperture and tracing rays through the lenses. Alternatively, defocus can be also modeled as a sort of aberration in Fourier optics, as discussed in section 4.7.2. Since single depth images are captured in the experiments, it is straightforwards to model the depth of field as a part of the optical simulations using the generalized pupil function in equation 4.25, as discussed in the previous chapter. This method significantly reduces the rendering time for the numerous images of the verification process and avoids the need to trace trays through the lens system. To do so, it suffices to calculate the path-length error of the wavefront $W(x,y)$ exiting the objective at the exit pupil.

As Goodman shows [Goo17], in order for a spherical wave leaving the exit pupil (on an on-axis point) to ideally come to focus on an image plane of distance d_e, its phase on the image plane $\phi_\mathrm{foc}(x,y)$ must be given by

$$\phi_\mathrm{foc}(x,y) = -\frac{\pi}{\lambda\, d_\mathrm{e}}\left(x^2+y^2\right). \tag{5.5}$$

With a focusing error, the convergence distance of the exiting wavefront is some other distance $d_\mathrm{e}^\mathrm{def}$, inducing a different phase $\phi_\mathrm{def}(x,y)$. The path-length error $W(x,y)$ required for building the generalized pupil function of equation 4.25 can be calculated as

$$W(x,y) = \frac{\phi_\mathrm{def}(x,y) - \phi_\mathrm{foc}(x,y)}{2\pi/\lambda} = -0.5\left(\frac{1}{d_\mathrm{e}^\mathrm{def}} - \frac{1}{d_\mathrm{e}}\right)\left(x^2+y^2\right). \tag{5.6}$$

Based on the distance d_g of the scene point to the objective, the ideal distance of the lens to the exit pupil, d_e, can be calculated using the *lens equation*

$$d_\mathrm{e} = \frac{1}{\left(\frac{1}{f} - \frac{1}{d_\mathrm{g}}\right)}.$$

In the imaging scenario, $d_{\mathrm{e}}^{\mathrm{def}}$ is known based on the setup calibration. Thus, the path-error can be fully calculated to yield the generalized pupil function for on-axis points. In the experiments, the path-length error of off-axis points were also approximated with the same function, and thus, the same generalized aperture function was used to introduce diffraction and defocus effects to the ideal irradiance pattern. Other chromatic or monochromatic aberrations were considered negligible and thus, not included in the simulations.

Figure 5.13 shows two sampled simulations including focused and strongly defocused laser lines. Note that this simulation approach correctly keeps the speckles in focus, although the overall profile is blurred. This is consistent with the physics of speckle pattern formation.

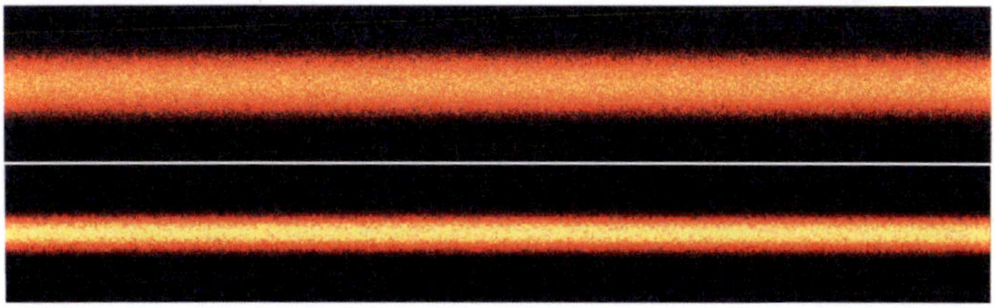

Figure 5.13: Simulations with $f\# = 2$ and $d_{\mathrm{c}}^{\mathrm{foc}} = 0.25\,\mathrm{m}$. (bottom): focused case where $d_{\mathrm{c}}^{\mathrm{foc}} = d_{\mathrm{c}}$, (top): defocused case with the camera moved $0.1\,\mathrm{m}$ closer to the surface ($d_{\mathrm{c}} = 0.15\,\mathrm{m}$). Note that the speckles are fully in focus, only the overall profile is blurred.

5.3.4 Sensor Simulation

Monochromatic cameras are most often used for applications of laser triangulation as they provide a better resolution on the image. Color cameras sacrifice the sensor resolution for color filtering but they are interesting in inspections where color contains some information, for instance, when using several lasers with different wavelengths. Color cameras provide three intensity channels with possibly different signal and noise statistics, thus they are interesting for simulation verifications for different intensity profiles, as well as the simulation of a Bayer filter. For this reason, the experiments of this thesis are separately carried out for a monochrome and a color sensor. The specifications of the sensors were introduced in table 5.3. The simulation process follows the linear model of a sensor pixel, as introduced by the EMVA 1288 standard. This model was introduced in section 4.7.3.

In order to control the extra signal processing steps automatically applied by most camera sensors, software development kits provided by the producers can be used to control additional data processing steps, such as white balance correction and image gain, as well as to access the raw image data as directly acquired from the color filter. For the experiments, all extra functionalities of the sensor were programmatically turned off, in order to access the raw data directly measured by the pixel sensors.

5.4 Verification

In this section, the image formation framework introduced earlier will be verified against real images captured in the experimental setup. Before starting with the quantitative verifications though, a visual comparison of simulations and real images can be very insightful. Figure 5.14 provides a side-by-side comparison of some sample images with different optical and geometrical configurations. The high visual resemblance of the images conveys a potentially good approximation of the first and second order statistics of the image signal. This means, if an expert intends to configure an inspection setup merely based on a visual evaluation, realistic simulations can turn out to be so photorealistic that they will not affect the performance of a human.

The effect of using synthetic images on image processing algorithms and the final measurement application is, however, harder to interpret from a visual comparison. To gain a comprehensive verification, simulations are compared against real images at two different levels, starting from the average intensity signal in section 5.4.1, up to the effect of using simulated images on the ultimate application in section 5.4.2.

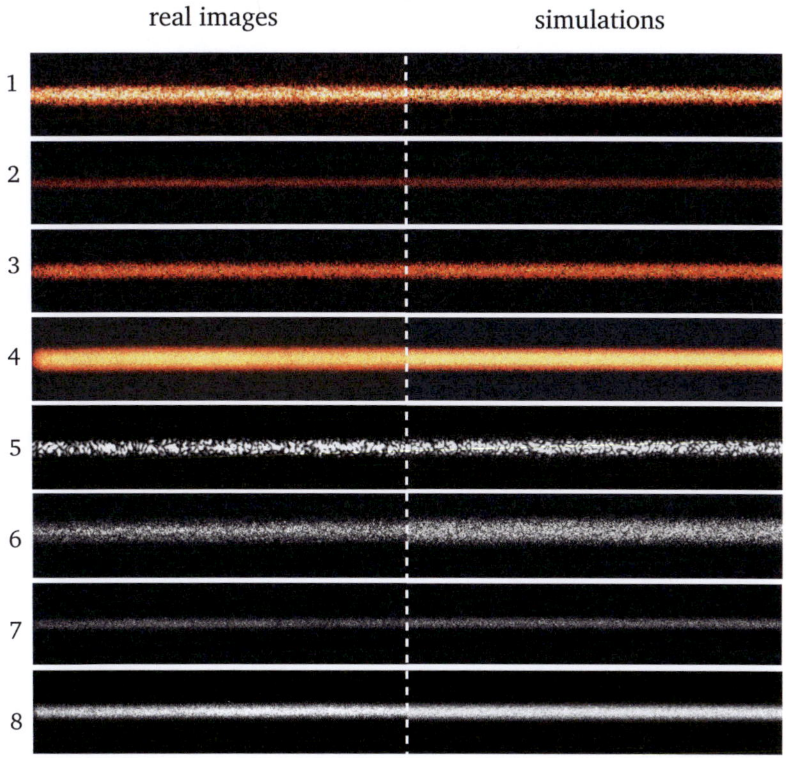

Figure 5.14: Simulated vs. real images acquired in the experimental setup. Side-by-side pairs correspond to cropped regions of the same size on both images. Magnification of the images may be different based on the setup configurations. Image specific parameters include:

1. $d_c = 0.40\,\mathrm{m}$, $f^{\#} = 16$, $d_c^{\mathrm{foc}} = 0.45\,\mathrm{m}$, $t_{\mathrm{exp}} = 812\,\mathrm{ms}$, color
2. $d_c = 0.20\,\mathrm{m}$, $f^{\#} = 8$, $d_c^{\mathrm{foc}} = 0.35\,\mathrm{m}$, $t_{\mathrm{exp}} = 13\,\mathrm{ms}$, color
3. $d_c = 0.40\,\mathrm{m}$, $f^{\#} = 5.6$, $d_c^{\mathrm{foc}} = 0.25\,\mathrm{m}$, $t_{\mathrm{exp}} = 26\,\mathrm{ms}$, color
4. $d_c = 0.30\,\mathrm{m}$, $f^{\#} = 2$, $d_c^{\mathrm{foc}} = 0.45\,\mathrm{m}$, $t_{\mathrm{exp}} = 13\,\mathrm{ms}$, color
5. $d_c = 0.50\,\mathrm{m}$, $f^{\#} = 22$, $d_c^{\mathrm{foc}} = 0.40\,\mathrm{m}$, $t_{\mathrm{exp}} = 100\,\mathrm{ms}$, monochrome
6. $d_c = 0.10\,\mathrm{m}$, $f^{\#} = 22$, $d_c^{\mathrm{foc}} = 0.25\,\mathrm{m}$, $t_{\mathrm{exp}} = 50\,\mathrm{ms}$, monochrome
7. $d_c = 0.35\,\mathrm{m}$, $f^{\#} = 4$, $d_c^{\mathrm{foc}} = 0.50\,\mathrm{m}$, $t_{\mathrm{exp}} = 0.8\,\mathrm{ms}$, monochrome
8. $d_c = 0.25\,\mathrm{m}$, $f^{\#} = 4$, $d_c^{\mathrm{foc}} = 0.40\,\mathrm{m}$, $t_{\mathrm{exp}} = 3\,\mathrm{ms}$, monochrome

5.4.1 Verification at Signal Level

Figure 5.15 looks closely at the average signal profiles of two sample pairs of simulated and real images in different intensity channels. The average profile is calculated by averaging the 2D Gaussian profile perpendicular to the laser line along the whole image (i.e. average profile along the columns of the image). As it can be seen in figure 5.15, the overall form of the profiles are closely predicted, which indicates a consistent modeling of the laser profile, surface reflectance, and sensor spectral response. Around the peak intensities of figure 5.15, the simulations seem to slightly underestimate the actual intensities in these examples.

In order to study the intensity discrepancies in a comprehensive way, the *relative simulated intensity error* is defined to quantify the relative error in the maximum intensities of the averaged laser profiles, as given by

$$e_{\mathrm{i}} = \frac{I_{\mathrm{p}}^{\mathrm{real}} - I_{\mathrm{p}}^{\mathrm{sim}}}{I_{\mathrm{p}}^{\mathrm{real}}} \times 100. \tag{5.7}$$

In this equation, $I_{\mathrm{p}}^{\mathrm{real}}$ and $I_{\mathrm{p}}^{\mathrm{sim}}$ represent the peak intensities of the average laser intensity profile in the real and the simulated image, respectively.

Figure 5.16 displays the statistics of e_{i} for the RGB channels of the color sensor, as well as the gray scale intensities of the monochrome sensor. These statistics are extracted by taking all experimental images into account. The horizontal axis in these figures represents the normalized exposure time $t_{\mathrm{exp}}^{\mathrm{n}}$, which scales the exposure time with a factor to compensate the effect of f-number on the exposure. $t_{\mathrm{exp}}^{\mathrm{n}}$ allows one to sort the images based on their intensity levels. In other words, linear increase of the values on the horizontal axis corresponds to a linear increase of the amount of the incoming light to the sensor. This quantity, in this case, is defined as

$$t_{\mathrm{exp}}^{\mathrm{n}} = t_{\mathrm{exp}} \left(\frac{22}{f\#} \right)^2, \tag{5.8}$$

which normalizes the exposure time for different f-numbers against the exposure time for f-number 22.

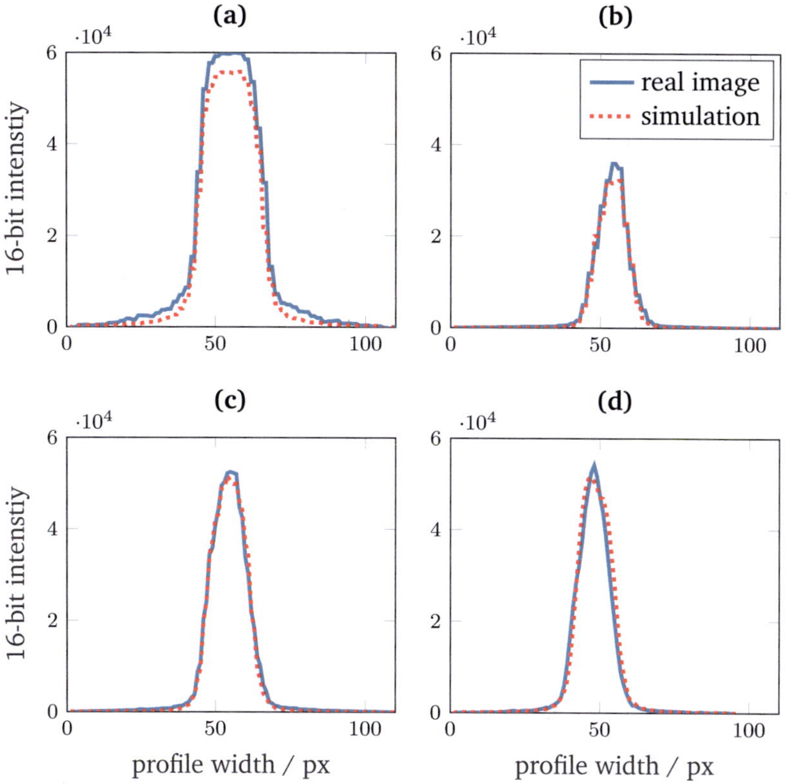

Figure 5.15: Comparison of average laser intensity profiles over the columns of images (1) and (5) of figure 5.14. **(a)**: red channel of image 1, **(b)**: blue channel of image 1, **(c)**: green channel of image 1, **(d)**: gray scale intensity of image 5.

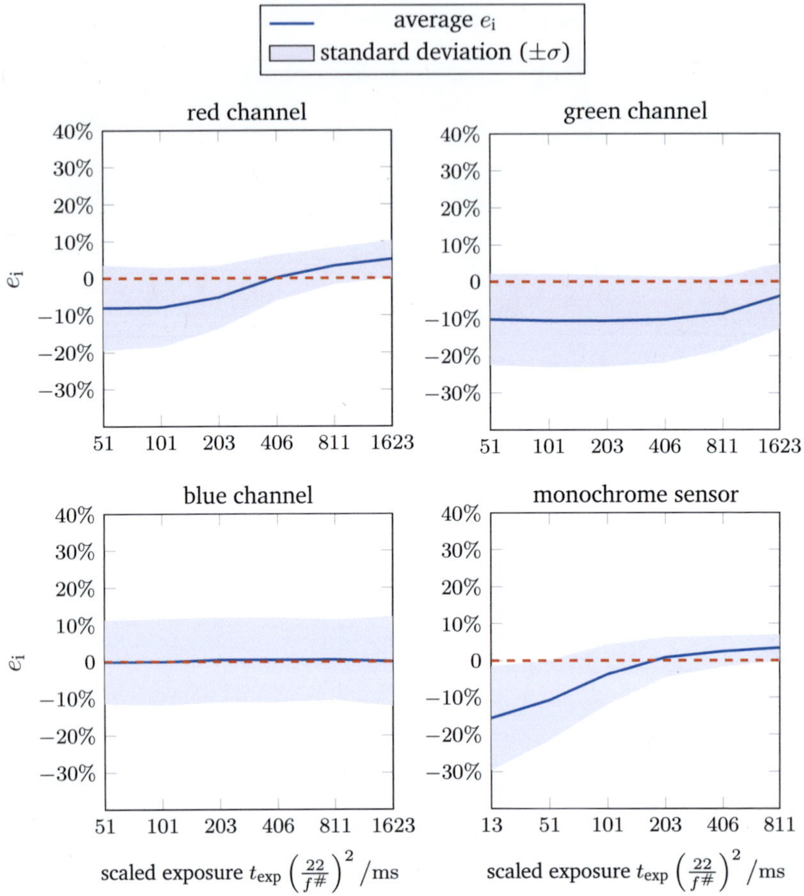

Figure 5.16: Statistics of the "relative simulated intensity error" e_i vs. image exposure. The horizontal axis represents exposure time normalized against the f-number, which is an indicator of the amount of light reaching the sensor. Shaded area corresponds to one standard deviation ($\pm\sigma$). Due to the lower saturation capacity of the monochrome sensor, the exposure range for this sensor contains shorter exposure times.

Analysis and Discussion

As it can be seen in figure 5.16, the blue channel of the color camera has exhibited a good fit to the real intensities, with about 10% standard deviation. The discrepancies in the rest of the intensity channels follow some nonlinear systematic trend. In low intensity images, the simulations tend to overestimate the intensities between 10% to 15% on average, whereas the discrepancies decrease as the sensors are more exposed to light. Since the simulation method and the experimental condition has been the same for both sensors, the overestimation of light in the red, green, and the monochrome channel should mostly correspond to potential deviations from the actual quantum efficiency values. As the sensor is exposed to more light, the intensity values approach the saturation threshold and therefore, the discrepancies of the intensities as well as their standard deviations decrease.

At high exposure values, the red channel of the color sensor and the monochrome sensor tend to slightly underestimate the intensities. This must correspond to underestimated saturation capacities of the sensors. For moderate exposure values, the simulated intensities seem to fit well to the real values.

In summary, the visual image comparison and the statistical analysis indicate that, it is possible to closely predict the intensity values of a real image, without any additional post-processing or manual correction, provided sufficient information from the imaging scene. Although many factors can contribute to intensity deviations, including nonlinearities in the sensor model and the ambient light, it is indeed possible to predict the intensity levels with acceptable approximations, which are hard to distinguish by human eyes.

In addition to intensities, another interesting aspect to verify at this level is the correct reproduction of the image noise. In these images, noise appears mostly as speckles, but also as sensor noise. At the signal level, the comparison of the generated noise and the speckle pattern will be left as a visual comparison of the side-by-side images of figure 5.14. On the application level, however, this chapter provides a comprehensive quantitative verification of the effect of image noise on the measurement uncertainties.

5.4.2 Verification at Application Level

While the topic of the previous section was to evaluate the simulations in terms of the visual impression and the intensity level, the main focus of this section is to evaluate how similarly the image processing algorithms perform on real and simulated images. In addition, it is of importance to quantify how much discrepancy the simulation-based inspection evaluation will introduce in the final measurement value.

Verification of image processing uncertainty: An indicator of the performance of the image processing algorithm in a laser triangulation application is the uncertainty in detecting the laser profile on the image. In this thesis, the laser detection uncertainty u_{px}, which is expressed in pixel unit, is used to verify the simulations at the image level. To calculate this quantity, the laser peak detection algorithm is separately applied to the laser profile in each column of the image to calculate the center of the profile. This algorithm is introduced in appendix section A. u_{px} is then estimated as the standard deviation of the detected profile center over the columns of the image.

Figure 5.17 compares the actual uncertainty of the laser detection algorithm to the resulting uncertainty when applying the same algorithm on the simulated images. This comparison includes images of both sensors at three different camera distances with varying f-numbers.

Verification of height measurement uncertainty: Using the methods of chapter 3 for propagation of uncertainties, u_{px} can be used to calculate the corresponding uncertainty in height measurement u_{h}. For the simple geometry of the experimental setup, u_{h} can be also calculated using equation 1.2 in chapter 1, which yields

$$u_{\mathrm{h}} = \frac{u_{\mathrm{px}} \times \text{pixel size}}{\tan(\theta_{\mathrm{inc}}) \times m}.$$

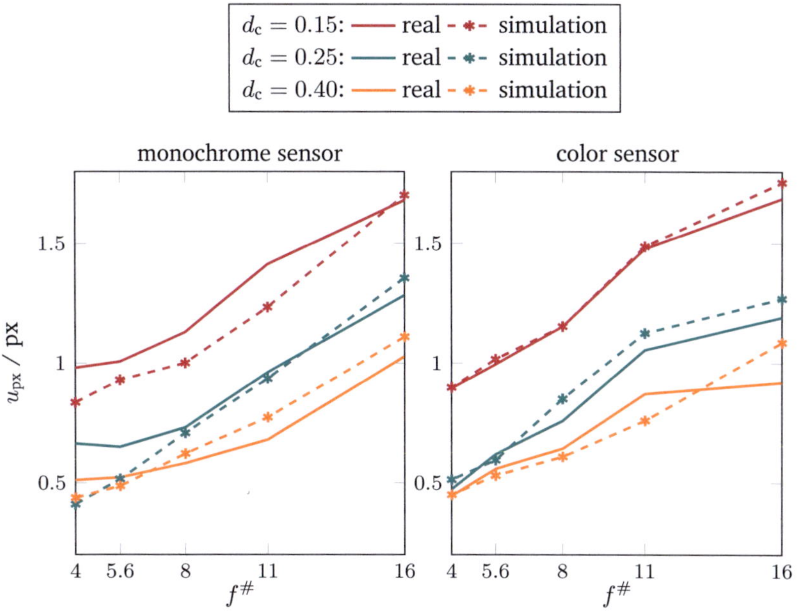

Figure 5.17: Comparison of laser detection uncertainty in real and simulated images, for three series of images with different sensors, camera distances, and varying f-number. Other constant parameters include $t_{exp} = 25\,\text{ms}$ and $d_c^{foc} = 0.3\,\text{m}$.

Multiplication with the pixel size transforms u_{px} from pixel unit to the metric unit on the sensor. The magnification m of the imaging setup can be estimated as $m = \frac{f}{d_c}$ and $\theta_{inc} = 45°$. Thus u_h can be calculated as:

$$u_h = \frac{u_{px} \times d_c \times \text{pixel size}}{f}. \tag{5.9}$$

Figure 5.18 displays the previous series in terms of height measurement uncertainty. Note that the series with closer camera distances d_c generally has higher uncertainties on the image u_{px}, because of a higher magnification. When propagating the uncertainties to the height measurement, the effect of distance changes the order of the series and those with shorter distances will exhibit smaller u_h.

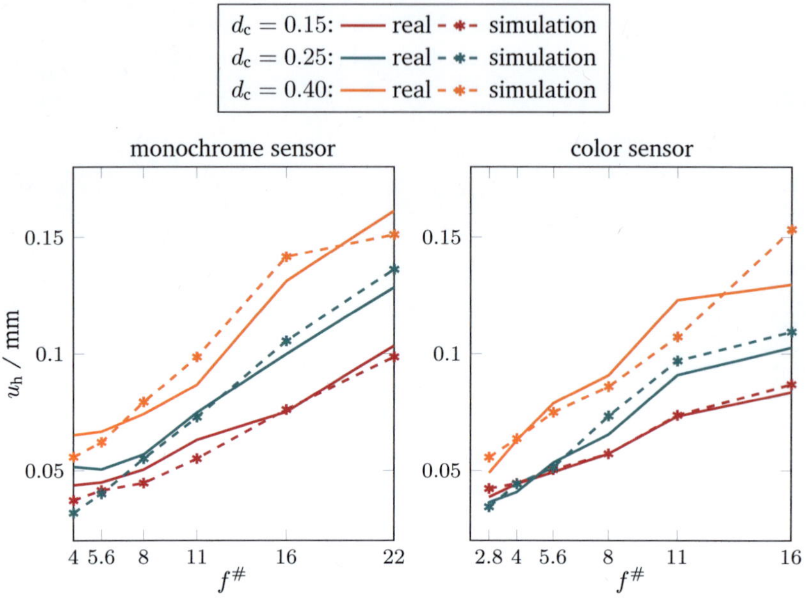

Figure 5.18: Comparison of the height measurement uncertainties corresponding to the same series in figure 5.17.

Although slight differences from the actual values are inevitable, figures 5.17 and 5.18 demonstrate that simulations could be used to correctly predict the behavior of both sensors under different imaging conditions. Figure 5.19 demonstrates similar comparisons for other series of images at a constant camera distance $d_c = 0.25\,\mathrm{m}$ with varying focus distance and f-number. Although the height measurement uncertainties are partly over- or underestimated, the general trends are correctly predicted, which can be already very useful for the inspection planning phase.

The plots presented in this section were dedicated to some selected series of images for demonstration purposes. For making a comprehensive statement though, such trends must be analyzed on many more images, covering all adjustable parameters, which is exactly the topic of the next part.

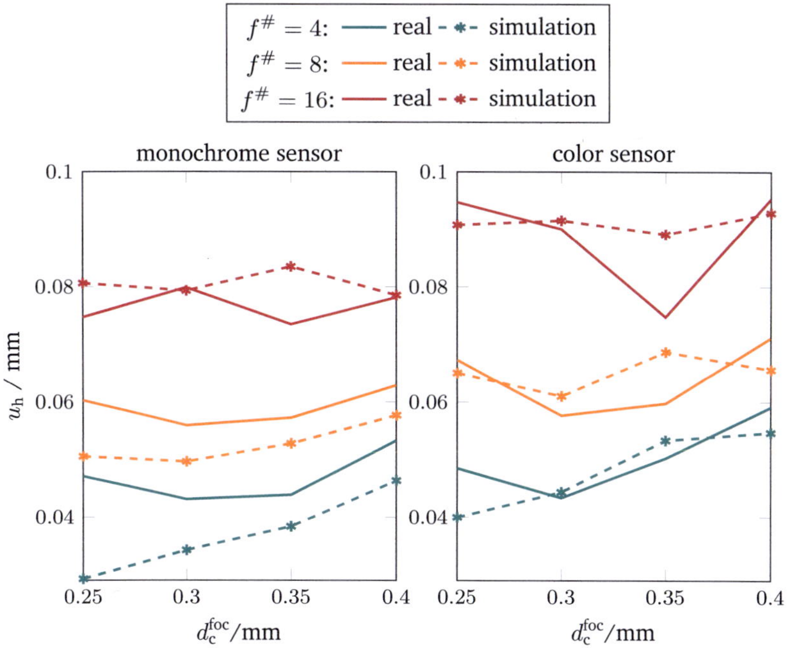

Figure 5.19: Comparison of height measurement uncertainty in real and simulated images vs. focus distance. Camera distance is at 0.25 m and all images have the same normalized exposure.

Relative Simulated Uncertainty Error

An indicator of the simulation error at the application level is the discrepancy between the actual height uncertainty $u_{\mathrm{h}}^{\mathrm{real}}$ with the same metric extracted from simulations $u_{\mathrm{h}}^{\mathrm{sim}}$. The *relative simulated uncertainty error*

$$e_{\mathrm{u}} = \frac{u_{\mathrm{h}}^{\mathrm{real}} - u_{\mathrm{h}}^{\mathrm{sim}}}{u_{\mathrm{h}}^{\mathrm{real}}} \times 100, \tag{5.10}$$

expresses this error as a percentage, normalized against the actual height uncertainty extracted from the real image. Note that, according to equation 5.9, this ratio remains the same if instead of height uncertainties, image level uncertainties (u_{px}) are used to derive e_{u}. Therefore, this metric is independent of the uncertainty propagation approach.

To statistically evaluate the simulation error in terms of measurement uncertainty, e_u has been calculated for all pairs of simulated and real images, including 1872 images of the color sensor and 2184 images of the monochrome one under variable imaging conditions as given in table 5.1. The following part provides a statistical analysis of the results along with a discussion.

Analysis and Discussion

The captured experimental images cover a range of geometrical and optical parameters which were varied during the experiments. Therefore, the relative simulated uncertainty error e_u can be expressed in terms of several parameters, including camera distance d_c, camera focus distance d_c^{foc}, exposure time t_{exp}, f-number $f^{\#}$, and the utilized sensor. Figures 5.20 to 5.23 illustrate the results of analyzing the statistics of e_u in terms of different imaging parameters for both the color and the monochrome sensor.

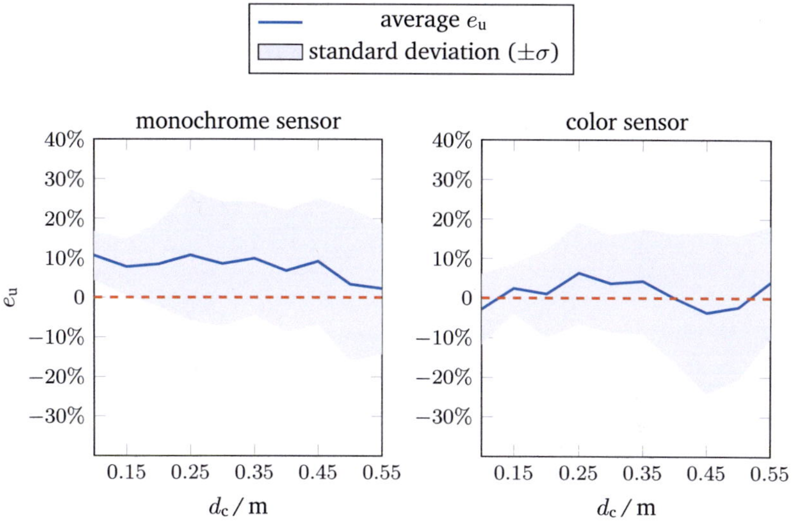

Figure 5.20: Relative simulated uncertainty error e_u vs. camera distance.

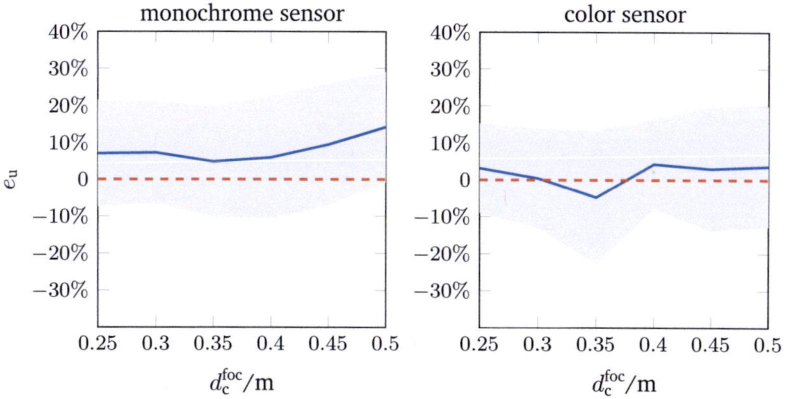

Figure 5.21: Relative simulated uncertainty error e_u vs. camera focus distance.

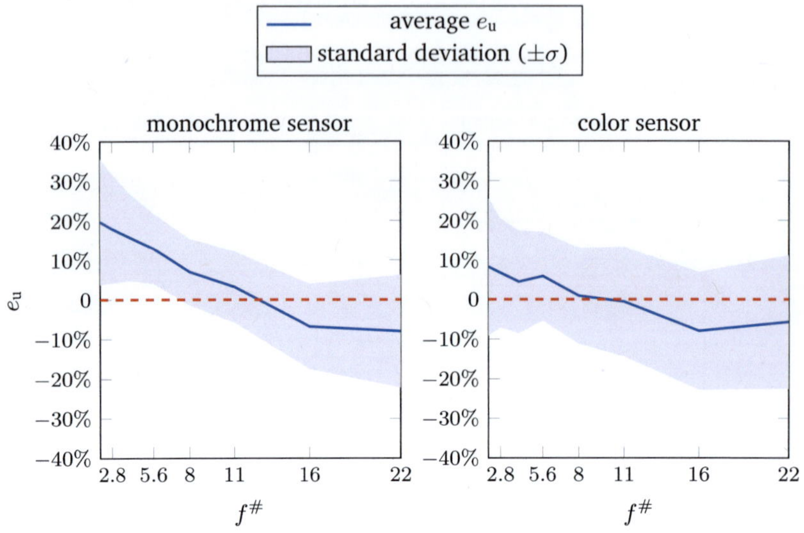

Figure 5.22: Relative simulated uncertainty error e_u vs. f-number.

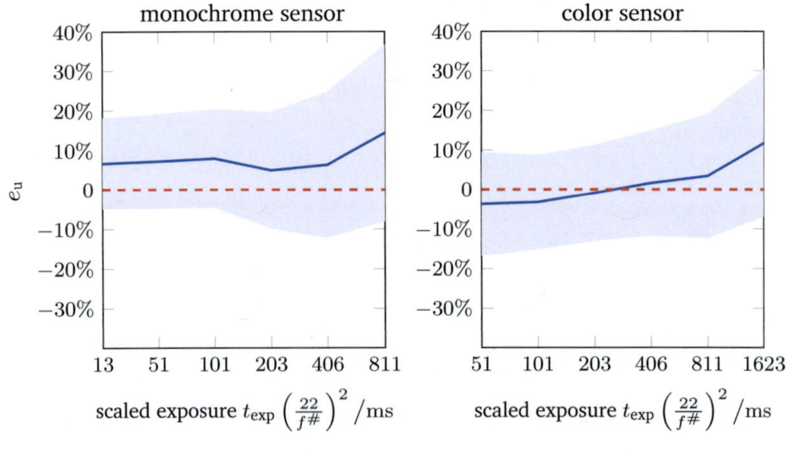

Figure 5.23: Relative simulated uncertainty error e_u vs. normalized exposure time.

The statistical analysis of e_u with respect to different parameters generally shows that the simulation process has been successful in reproducing similar behavior as of a real imaging measurement system, with no more than 20% error on average. This can be a good approximation for inspection planning. In the planning phase, it is not necessarily vital to predict absolute values, rather it suffices if the simulations can reproduce the reality in a way so as to distinguish potentially good setup constellations from bad ones. We have to take into account that it is extremely difficult, if not impossible, to perfectly replicate the reality, as a slight improvement on the simulations corresponds to a significantly higher complexity in methods and requires much more detail from the scene. In the rest of this section, the statistical results will be discussed in more detail.

Looking at the statistics of the simulation error, a systematic bias as well as some stochastic deviation can be observed. There can be plenty of factors contributing to the systematic bias, including, among the others, inaccuracies in the BRDF and roughness measurements, unknown environmental light, inaccuracies in setup calibration, lens distortion, variations of the EMVA 1288 data among the units of the same series and between the individual pixels, and numerical inaccuracies in the frequency analysis of Fourier optics methods. In addition, simulations are typically associated with plenty of oversimplifying assumptions, which in this case included the paraxial approximations, modeling the laser as a perfect Gaussian beam, using a linear model for the sensor spectral response, and assuming uniform radiance over the aperture when integrating light through the optic. As all those factors influence the simulations in a tied way, it can turn out to be very difficult to identify the actual cause of discrepancy.

For each sensor, the simulation errors are defined in a 5-dimensional space (see variable experimental parameters in table 5.1). Figures 5.20 to 5.23 illustrate this error in four plots, each containing a projection of the values over one of the parameters. Generally, the color sensor seems to have been simulated with a better approximation. Since the simulation method and the experiments have been the same for both sensors, discrepancies between the two sensors must be associated with inaccuracies in the EMVA 1288 data or the linear sensor model.

Figure 5.20 illustrates the simulation error with respect to the camera distance d_c. It can be observed that the e_u standard deviation has increased with the camera distance. This behavior is to a great extend associated with the inaccuracies in camera distance calibration, since the calibration precision decreases as the images are taken from further distances. Generally, the average error with respect to the distance is no more than 6% and 10%, for the color and the monochrome sensor respectively.

Figure 5.21 studies the statistics of e_u with respect to the focus distance. Note that for a constant focus distance d_c^{foc} images from all different camera distances have been taken, therefore the standard deviation remained almost constant along the whole plot (in contrast to figure 5.20). The color sensor exhibits a specially good fit to the simulation results, with an average error of less than 5% in this case.

The trend of simulation error with respect to the f-number is depicted in figure 5.22. This plot is particularly interesting in verifying the correct simulation of the speckles. Although speckles are caused by complicated wave optics phenomena, this figure indicates that their effects on the real images can be well reproduced, with an error of no more than 20% on the measurement uncertainty. In addition, it can be seen that the statistics of e_u show a systematic dependency on the f-number.

For smaller f-numbers the simulations underestimate the actual measurement uncertainty by an average of 8% for the color sensor and 20% for the monochromatic one. Small f-numbers indicate a wide aperture, which makes the lens aberrations more dominant and paraxial approximations less correct. Thus, it is expectable for the simulations to underestimate the actual influencing factors. F-numbers 8 to 16 exhibit a good match, whereas simulations tend to overestimate the height uncertainty by increasing the f-number.

To verify if modeling the aperture as a perfect circle could have led to the systematic simulation error for higher f-numbers, the entire simulation verification was repeated for a more exact aperture shape. In these experiments, the circular aperture was replaced by a decagon (polygon with 10 sides), to represent the 10 rotating blades in the Fujinon objective aperture. The trend of the simulation error, however, exhibited negligible changes. Therefore, the author associates the trend of error in this case to inaccuracies in manually setting the f-number on the objective. Since speckle formation is very sensitive to the aperture size, slight inaccuracies in modeling the aperture area can influence the speckle size and consequently, the estimated measurement uncertainties.

The last analysis in figure 5.23 belongs to studying the trend of simulation error with respect to the exposure. Since different f-numbers require significantly different exposure times to deliver the same intensity, exposure time in this plot is normalized against the f-number (similar to the previous analysis in figure 5.16). Deviations from the actual EMVA 1288 data and, similarly, the error in manually setting the f-number values on the objective have contributed to the dependency of the simulation error on the exposure.

5.5 Conclusion

The experiments of this thesis for simulation verification indicate that it is essentially achievable to simulate optical imaging systems with acceptable accuracy, using available computer graphics and optical simulation techniques. The methods used for simulations do not pose any extraordinary complexity to the conventional rendering techniques and they were verified to approximate the uncertainty of the measurement system with no more than 20% error. These results can be considered as a starting point for the machine vision industries, to trust simulation-based inspection planning systems more than before and to invest time and money in acquiring more information from the surfaces and light sources for sensor-realistic simulations and eventually, the automatic inspection planning.

6 Application to a Cylinder Head Inspection Planning

This chapter brings together all the topics discussed earlier and applies the automatic planning workflow to the laser triangulation application introduced in chapter 1. The main focus of this chapter is to demonstrate and discuss the results of the different inspection planning methods. For planning the surface coverage, the performance of several optimization algorithms as well as the results of manual human planning will be compared. Further on, the planning results for optimum inspection sensitivity to uncertainty factors will be demonstrated. At the end, the planning is dedicated to optimizing the optical parameters, such as the f-number and the exposure time, for minimizing the uncertainties at the image processing level.

The coverage and the uncertainty planning tasks in this chapter concern the geometrical degrees of freedom of the imaging setup. For both planning problems, the same setup geometry and constraints have been used. Chapter 2 already introduced the planning approach, setup geometry, constraints, and the assumptions of the planning application. A summary can be found in section 2.4. For further details, the reader is requested to refer to that section.

On the simulation side, geometrical planning tasks utilize real-time graphical simulations (based on rasterization) to efficiently determine the effect of setup geometry on surface coverage and the expected coordinates of the measurement points. Optimization of the optical parameters in section 6.4 is based on sensor-realistic simulations.

Before starting with the quantitative analysis of the planning results, it is important to analyze the selected target points on the surface to indicate if all of them can be potentially measured within the admissible degrees of freedom of the optical setup. The next section is dedicated to this concept.

6.1 Measurability of Target Points

The idea behind using target points for the quantification of surface measurements was introduced in chapter 3 (see figure 3.1). It is important to note that most CAD models contain the full geometry of the object, consisting of both the surface and the internal structure. When an automatic method is used to generate uniform points on the surface, the samples can lie anywhere on the model. Completely internal parts of opaque surfaces, which cannot be lit by rays of light, are unmeasurable by optical measurement systems which use visible light. In addition, there can be samples on the surface which are visible but not measurable within the constraints of the optical system. For measuring deep cavities of the cylinder head, for example, often very small triangulation angles are required. Consequently, it is important to distinguish potentially measurable points from the unmeasurable ones for a fair evaluation of the planning method.

For the cylinder head, 23 334 points were initially sampled using the Poisson disk sampling algorithm [Cor12], which uniformly covered the whole model with a resolution of about 5 mm. The samples were further analyzed for proper light reachability using ray tracing methods. As illustrated in figure 6.1, a point is considered potentially measurable if there exist at least a pair of rays holding an angle $\tau \geq \tau_0$, which reach the point without being occluded by the rest of the scene. Based on the parameter constraints of table 2.1, τ_0 was set to 10°. Using ray tracing on GPUs, it is possible to cast millions of such rays within seconds and trace if they actually reach the point. For each sampled point, 2^{16} random pairs of rays with $\tau \geq 10^\circ$ were generated. If at least one such pair reached the point, it was cleared as measurable and set as a target point for planning.

In computer graphics, a technique called *ambient occlusion analysis* [Mil94] is applied to quantify how much ambient light reaches certain parts of the scene and the values are used for shading to create a better 3D perception. In this thesis, the ambient occlusion analysis was performed with the extra constraint on the triangulation angle to determine the target points which do not receive light from the environment, i.e. invisible target points. After this step, the number of target points for planning was reduced to 19 080.

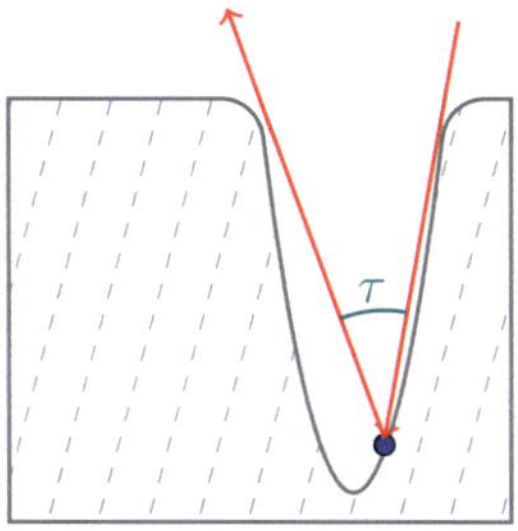

Figure 6.1: Analysis of target points for measurability.

6.2 Coverage Planning

This section is dedicated to the analysis of the coverage planning results produced by different optimization algorithms. The surface coverage is evaluated as the percentage of target points covered by the inspection plan. As discussed in section 3.2, target point coverage is indicated based on a given lateral resolution δ_r. This means that a target point is considered as covered, if evaluating the simulated images leads to a measurement point within a distance δ_r from it. In the rest of this section, a lateral resolution of 3 mm is considered for all planning results.

The planning follows the general approach of the iterative greedy method, as given in algorithm 3. For finding the *next best scan* in each planning iteration, all continuous optimization algorithms introduced in chapter 2 are separately utilized. The configuration details of each algorithm are provided in table 6.1. These parameters are mostly empirically chosen based on the algorithms performances. For PSO, however, several standardizations have been proposed which give recommendations on configuring the algorithm. The PSO version implemented in this thesis is mostly based on the standardization given in 2007 by Bratton and Kennedy [Bra07].

Table 6.1: Configuration of the optimization algorithms

Optimization	Parameter	Value
Simulated Annealing (SA)	T_{start}	4×10^{26} K
	max iterations	3000
	temperature at iteration k	$T_{\text{start}} \left(1 - \frac{k}{3000}\right)^3$
	number of restarts	50
Genetic Algorithm (GA)	population size	200
	generation count	50
	α_{c}	0.7
	α_{m}	0.3
Particle Swarm (PSO)	swarm size	50
	c_l,c_g	1.19
	number of restarts	5
Measurability Matrix (MM)	number of view point samples	1 500 000

6.2.1 Empirical Human Planning

Comparing the automatic planning results with the empirical performance of a human expert provides insight into how much, and if at all, the human performance can be improved using automatic planning. Even for an empirical planning, a simulation environment can be extremely beneficial because of its convenience in visualizing every desired configuration just by entering the parameters. This way, the expert can potentially explore more of the solution space compared to the conventional experimental trial and error approach.

The empirical coverage planning of this thesis was carried out by the author with the help of an interactive real-time simulation environment. The author has made the best effort to perform a fair planning and to avoid any bias due to the knowledge of the automatic planning results.

The experience with the empirical planning indicated that human empirical planning is much easier at the beginning when most of the surface is still uncovered, and gets considerably more difficult as it continues to cover the remaining unmeasured regions. For this reason, the empirical planning had to be stopped at measurement 15. Another noticeable difference with the automatic planning is that an optimization algorithm might spend several hours for finding a good solution but a human typically gets tired within an hour of fine-tuning each measurement and thus resorts to solutions found within this time.

Without a simulation environment to assist the expert, the empirical planning is expected to be significantly more challenging with potentially inferior results.

6.2.2 Results & Discussion

Figure 6.2 demonstrates the results of coverage planning for different optimization algorithms, up to 40 optimized measurements. Table 6.2 gives a summary of these results, indicating the number of measurements required for each algorithm to achieve 90% and 95% surface coverage.

All the curves indicate that the iterative greedy approach towards planning tends to make big improvements at the beginning while the contributions of the remaining measurements considerably decrease. This is the natural cost of using the greedy approximation in return of its significant complexity reduction.

Among the chosen algorithms, PSO demonstrates the best performance with 10 and 16 measurements for achieving 90% and 95% surface coverage, respectively.

The MM (measurability matrix) optimization results correspond to the re-implementation of the discrete planning proposed by Scott [Sco09], which was introduced in chapter 2 section 2.2.1. This method shows

Table 6.2: Summary of coverage planning results

Optimization Algorithm	Measurements for 90% coverage	Measurements for 95% coverage
SA	17	29
GA	12	22
PSO	10	16
MM	13	23

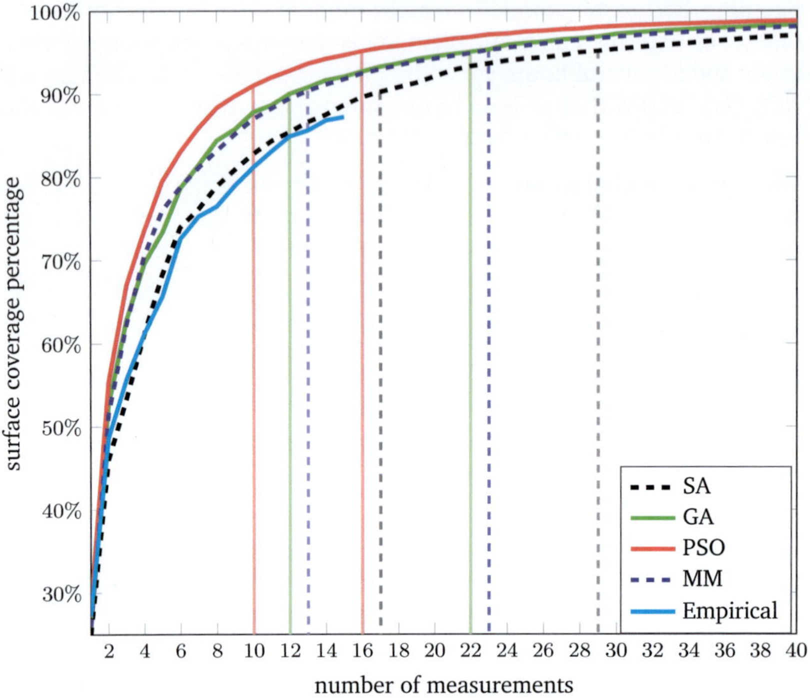

Figure 6.2: Coverage planning results vs. number of measurements. The curve points reaching 90% and 95% coverage are marked for each algorithm.

a very similar performance to the GA algorithm. In order to fill the required measurability matrix, 1.5 million samples of the design space were randomly chosen. With 19080 target points, the measurability matrix is of size 1 500 000×19080, which must be split into small patches and written on the hard disk. In addition, the sufficient number of function samples for this method directly depends on the gain function complexity and its dimensionality, which is often hard to tell at the beginning. As increasing this number to 20 million led to negligible changes in the result, the selected number of function evaluations for these results are considered to be sufficient.

The GA algorithm has led to a slightly better plan compared to MM, with clearly less function evaluations (i.e. 10^4) and no overhead for reading and writing from the hard disk. Planning with GA resulted in 12 and 22 measurements for achieving 90% and 95% surface coverage, respectively. The largest number of proposed measurements corresponds to the SA algorithm. This could be predicted as the SA searches the design space with only one search particle, whereas PSO and GA can benefit from the overall intelligence resulting from the communication/reproduction of the particles/population.

The empirical planning has slightly outperformed the SA algorithm at the beginning, but it falls behind as the planning proceeds and the task becomes more difficult for a human. In general, all automatic planning methods have shown a better performance compared to the empirical human planing. This confirms the important role of automation and artificial intelligence for inspection planning, especially when it comes to measuring complex surfaces.

Among the implemented automatic methods, the PSO algorithm has delivered the most efficient inspection plan. Generally, all automatic planning algorithms could reach over 97% surface coverage with 40 measurements, however, the improvements are very slow for surface coverage over 95%.

It is worth to mention that the performance of such probabilistic algorithms are dependent on the configuration of their heuristic parameters. Therefore, some changes in the results are expected by varying those parameters. As the PSO setting can be adjusted based on available standards, and considering its good performance in the coverage planning, this algorithm is potentially a very good choice for inspection planning or for other optimization applications.

Table 6.3 lists the 9-dimensional sets of parameters corresponding to measurements 1, 2, 3, and 10, proposed by the PSO coverage planning. As the cylinder head model contains deep cavities, most proposed triangulation angles contain very small values or they are exactly equal to the lower limit which was set to 10°.

Table 6.4 visualizes the PSO coverage planning results during these four steps of the proposed inspection plan. In this table, the red fan illustrates the laser line projector and the blue box close to it represents the camera.

The world coordinate axes are also shown, with respect to which all geometric transformations are calculated. As discussed in chapter 2, the scan direction is considered to be the x-axis, which is colored in red here. The second column visualizes the covered surface up to the specified measurement. For a better visual impression, the surface color has been interpolated based on the distance to the closest measurement point with a Gaussian kernel of width 5 mm. In this color map, purple indicates covered surface points (within 3 mm resolution) whereas yellow represents the surface area whose distance to the closest measurement is larger than 15 mm. The visualization images of table 6.4 correspond to the parameters of table 6.3.

Figure 6.3 visualizes the resulting point cloud by applying the first 10 measurements proposed by PSO coverage planning, corresponding to 91% surface coverage. The transparent view in this image provides a visualization of the measurement points acquired from the complex hard-to-reach areas of the object, including the deep intake and outtake manifolds.

Table 6.3: Optimized geometric parameters in PSO planning

Scan	Parameters								
	$d_{\mathbf{c}}$	τ	$\phi_{\mathbf{c}}$	$\theta_{\mathbf{c}}$	$\alpha_{\mathbf{o}}$	$\beta_{\mathbf{o}}$	$\gamma_{\mathbf{o}}$	Δy	Δz
1	0.44 m	10°	131°	51°	185°	150°	145°	−0.2 m	−0.17 m
2	0.23 m	10°	189°	60°	306°	232°	188°	0 m	−0.06 m
3	0.3 m	12°	215°	62°	153°	139°	208°	0.11 m	−0.09 m
10	0.28 m	12°	5°	62°	150°	63°	194°	−0.1 m	−0.1 m

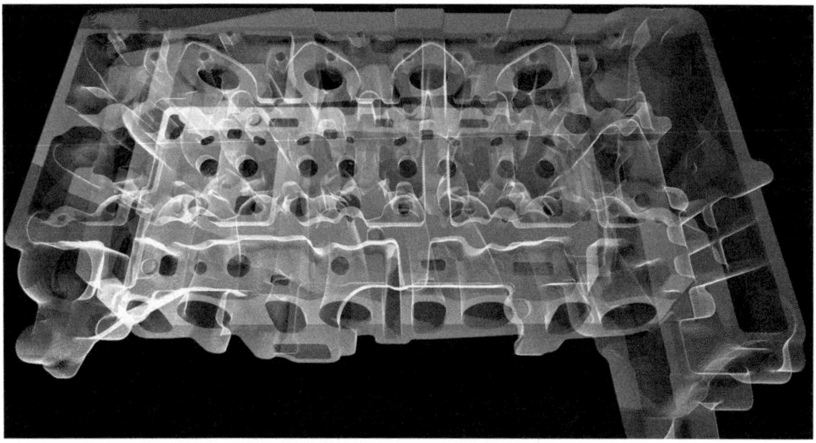

Figure 6.3: A transparent view of the point cloud resulting from applying 10 measurements proposed by the PSO coverage planning. It can be seen that most of the intake and outtake manifolds of the cylinder head have been covered.

Table 6.4: Visualization of PSO coverage planning results

	Geometry	Coverage Visualization	
1	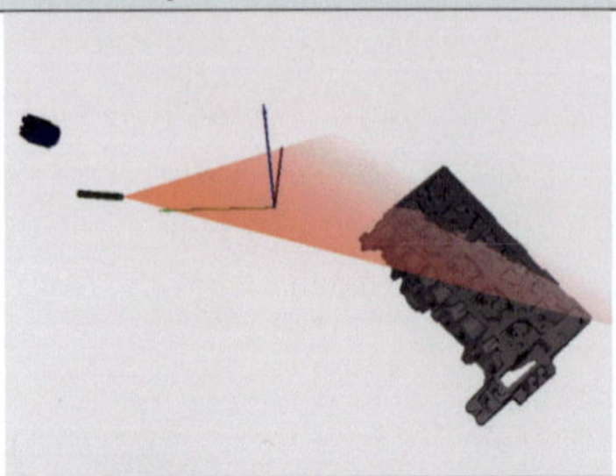	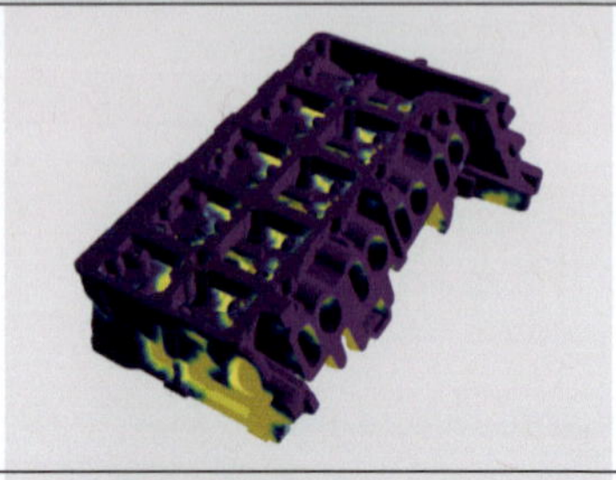	28%
2	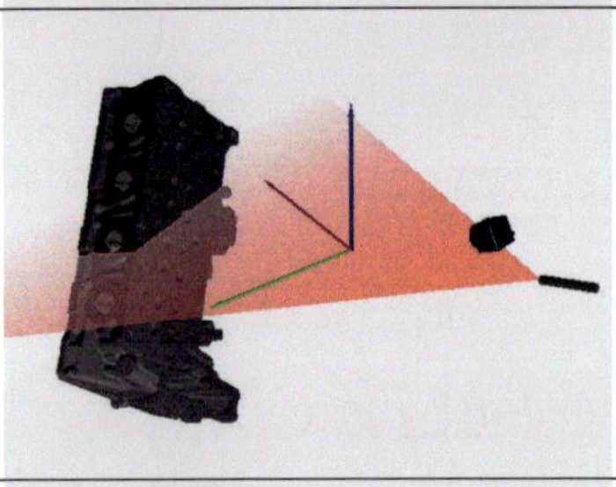	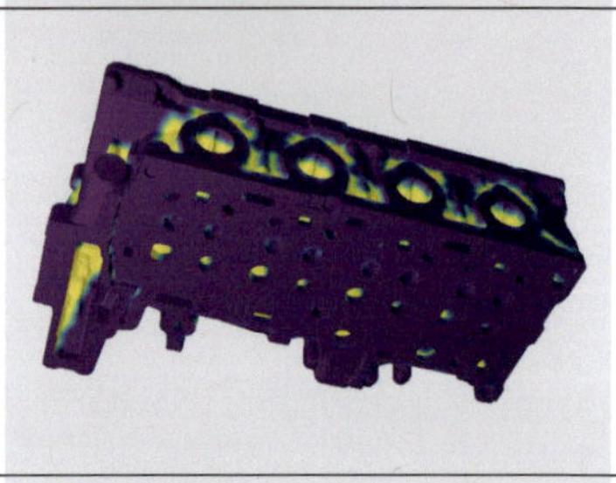	55%
3	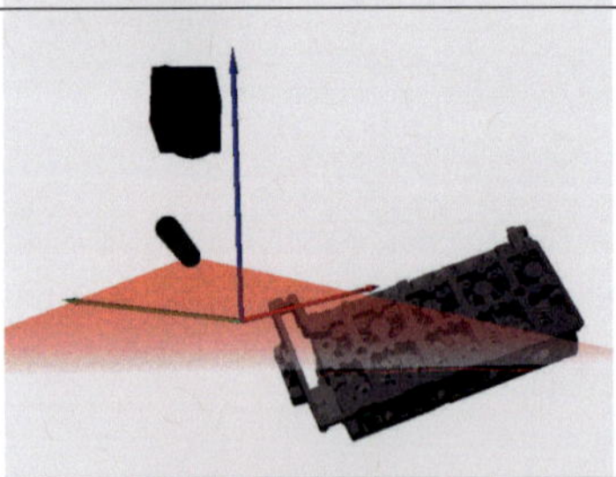	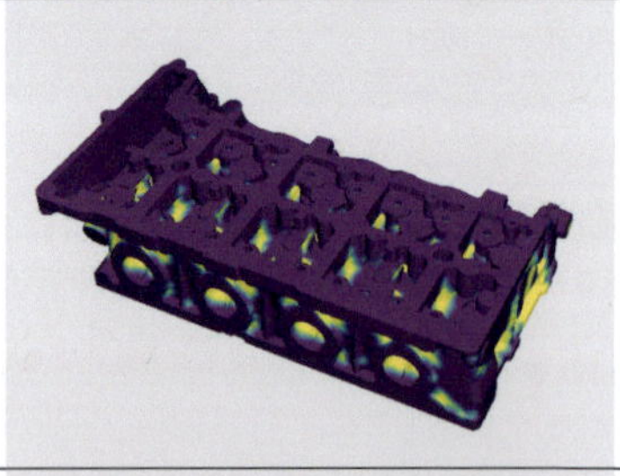	63%
10	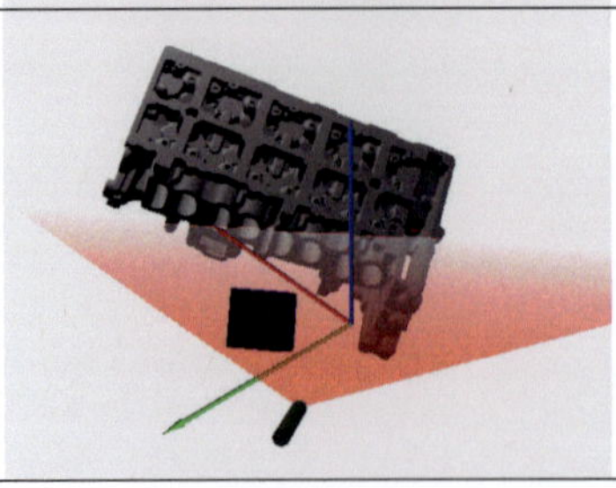		91%

6.2.3 Run-Time & Implementation

The bottle-neck in the execution time of the inspection planning methods is the simulation part. Even real-time simulations are time-consuming when it comes to the evaluation of thousands of setup constellations. The simulation run-time is also dependent on the constellation of the measurement. If a measurement is captured from a close view, the object can remain in the field of view of the camera for hundreds of frames during the linear scan, whereas other measurements may only include a few frames.

The run-time reports of this thesis correspond to a Dell Precision workstation, with an Intel(R) Xeon(R) CPU at 3.70 GHz, 16 GB of main memory, and an ADATA SSD hard disc for quick write and read access. The average run-times of the PSO, GA, and the SA algorithms per single measurement were estimated to be 1.9 h, 2.6 h, and 1.6 h, respectively. Therefore, optimizations for 40 measurements were maximally carried out within 5 days for the GA algorithm, while all the others converged much faster.

The main run-time overhead of the MM algorithm is associated with storing the measurability matrix. In these experiments, building the matrix took about 20 h. As all the measurements are planned using the same matrix, this approach is run-time efficient if numerous measurements are to be planned. The main implementation consideration is the memory overhead which exponentially grows with the dimensionality of the problem.

6.3 Uncertainty Planning

Coverage planning results presented in the previous section only concern the coverage of the target points, using the planning gain function of equation 3.1. As discussed in chapter 3, a measurement can show different sensitivities to the stochastic noise, depending on its parameters. For instance, smaller triangulation angles lead to higher uncertainties in the height measurement for constant inaccuracy in laser detection on the image. This section extends the results of coverage planning by inclusion of the measurement uncertainty. In chapter 3, quantification and propagation of uncertainties were exclusively studied. In this section, a brief overview of the uncertainty evaluation procedure for the experiments of this chapter will be given.

6.3.1 Uncertainty Propagation and Inference

For the uncertainty planning experiments, a value of 0.2 px uncertainty was assumed as the standard deviation for the laser detection algorithm (see chapter 3). Using the uncertainty propagation approach, the sensitivity of measuring each 3D point to this noisy data was calculated using the derivations discussed in section 3.3.1. The setup calibration inaccuracies were neglected here as they can be often modeled as systematic error and corrected.

Having estimated the covariances of every measured point for several measurements, the surface inference method introduced in section 3.4 was used to fuse the information of several measurements and estimate an a posteriori standard deviation $u(\boldsymbol{p}_j)$ for each target point $\boldsymbol{p}_j$. The a priori standard deviation for the surface before applying any measurement was set to 10 mm, which is a pretty high value compared to typical uncertainties in laser triangulation measurements. With this approach, uncertainty planning takes both the covered and the uncovered target points into account, by considering the uncertainty of the unmeasured ones equal to the a priori uncertainty.

For the process of surface inference, the strategies introduced in section 3.4.1 for adaptation of the GP regression have been applied. To satisfy the smoothness requirement, the local inference for each target point was slightly adapted to include not only a local neighborhood of measurement points, but also the neighborhood was constrained to be smooth. To this end, only those neighboring measurement points were included in the inference whose local surface normal exhibited less than 30° difference to that of the target point.

6.3.2 Gain Functions

Chapter 3.2 introduced a potential gain function for uncertainty planning. This chapter looks more closely at the practical usage of this function in the optimizations. To assist the discussion of this section, $f^u(\boldsymbol{\theta})$ is stated again in the equation below:

$$f^u(\boldsymbol{\theta}) = \sum_{j=1}^{k} U_s\left(\frac{s_t(\boldsymbol{p}_j)}{4} - u(\boldsymbol{p}_j,\boldsymbol{\theta})\right).$$

This function calculates the number of target points which were measured with an admissible uncertainty, i.e. $u(\boldsymbol{p}_j,\boldsymbol{\theta}) \leq \frac{s_\mathrm{t}(\boldsymbol{p}_j)}{4}$ with an inspection plan $\boldsymbol{\theta}$. Therefore, it is indifferent for the gain function if a target point is not measured at all or it is measured with an uncertainty higher than the threshold value. If some hard-to-reach areas cannot be measured with the admissible uncertainty at all, this gain function potentially allows them to be totally unmeasured. In addition, it does not reward any reduction in the uncertainty unless it enters the admissible region. Smooth changes in the gain function and gradual rewards when moving towards better solutions can potentially improve the optimization results. In what follows, two modifications to the original gain function will be introduced here which will be evaluated in terms of their performance on the uncertainty planning later.

Total Uncertainty

The first option is to avoid hard decisions of the U_s function, e.g. by penalizing each target point based on the squared difference of its uncertainty to the admissible value. Based on this idea, an alternative gain function can be formulated as below. In this thesis, this function is referred to as the *Total Uncertainty (TU)* gain function.

$$f^{\mathrm{TU}}(\boldsymbol{\theta}) = -\sum_{j=1}^{k} P_\mathrm{s}^2\left(u(\boldsymbol{p}_j,\boldsymbol{\theta}) - \frac{s_\mathrm{t}(\boldsymbol{p}_j)}{4}\right), \tag{6.1}$$

The penalty function $P_\mathrm{s}(x)$ is defined in equation 6.2. This function returns positive values unchanged and maps negative values to zero. This way, the target points with already admissible uncertainty will be assigned to zero costs and others will be penalized based on their gap to the admissible uncertainty value. The negative sign in equation 6.1 changes all penalty terms to gain terms to keep this function consistent with the rest of gain functions defined in this thesis.

$$P_\mathrm{s}(x) = \left\{ \begin{array}{cc} x, & \text{for } x \geq 0 \\ 0, & \text{otherwise} \end{array} \right\} \tag{6.2}$$

Relaxed Admissibility

Another alternative is adding further terms to the original gain function. As the admissibility threshold $\frac{s_t(\boldsymbol{p}_i)}{4}$ can turn out to often be very small, a second weighted term with a relaxed admissibility threshold u_{rel} can be added to regulate the gain function, as given by

$$f^{\mathrm{RA}}(\boldsymbol{\theta}) = \alpha \sum_{j=1}^{k} U_{\mathrm{s}} \left(\frac{s_{\mathrm{t}}(\boldsymbol{p}_j)}{4} - u(\boldsymbol{p}_j,\boldsymbol{\theta}) \right) + (1-\alpha) \sum_{j=1}^{k} U_{\mathrm{s}} \left(u_{\mathrm{rel}} - u(\boldsymbol{p}_j,\boldsymbol{\theta}) \right), \tag{6.3}$$

in which the term $U_{\mathrm{s}}\left(u_{\mathrm{rel}} - u(\boldsymbol{p}_j,\boldsymbol{\theta})\right)$ calculates the number of target points which are measured up to some relaxed admissibility threshold $u(\boldsymbol{p}_j,\boldsymbol{\theta}) < u_{\mathrm{rel}}$.

The admissible target points are counted in both terms, whereas the covered target points with some higher uncertainty are only taken into account in the second term. Therefore, the gain function is still guiding towards covering the most admissible points, however, with a regularization term that can potentially improve the results. Especially those target points which cannot be measured within the small admissibility limit, but may be measured within the relaxed threshold, will be subject to improvements with this regularization term. In the upcoming analysis of the results, this function will be referred to as the *Relaxed Admissibility (RA)* gain function.

The factor α weights the influence of the two terms, so that setting $\alpha = 1$ reduces the gain function to its original form and using $\alpha = 0$ dismisses the original threshold and tries to bring all target points within the relaxed limit.

The rest of this section presents and discusses the uncertainty planning results for the different gain function alternatives. In these experiments, the admissibility threshold $\frac{s_{\mathrm{t}}}{4}$ is calculated for a specification tolerance of $s_{\mathrm{t}} = 0.2\,\mathrm{mm}$ (i.e. admissibility threshold of $0.05\,\mathrm{mm}$). The relaxed threshold for regularizations is set to $1\,\mathrm{mm}$.

Table 6.5: Summary of uncertainty planning parameters

Parameter	Value
assumed uncertainty in laser detection	0.2 px
surface a priori uncertainty σ_{pr}	10 mm
lateral resolution δ_r for inference	3 mm
inspection tolerance s_t	0.2 mm
admissibility threshold $\frac{s_t}{4}$	0.05 mm
relaxed admissibility threshold u_{rel}	1 mm

6.3.3 Results & Discussion

Table 6.5 provides a summary of all the parameters used for uncertainty planning. Similar to the coverage planning experiments, the measurements for uncertainty planning are also selected in an iterative greedy manner. In this section, however, only the PSO algorithm, which led to the best performance in the previous results, is used for the optimizations. The discussions of this section are targeted towards comparing the performance of different gain functions.

Both the TU and RA gain functions were applied to uncertainty planning. Figure 6.4 illustrates the planning results for 4 different RA variants with different α values as well as the results of using the TU function. The top plot in figure 6.4 shows the improvements in surface coverage within 0.05 mm uncertainty (i.e. the admissibility threshold) by increasing the number of measurements. The plot below shows the same metric extracted from the same plans but considering the relaxed threshold.

As expected, the TU gain function has led to the best overall surface uncertainty, but the achieved values lie mostly outside the admissibility limit. As the initial 10 mm uncertainty for the unmeasured target points causes relatively high penalties to the TU function, it has shown a tendency in covering the most surface area, even if the corresponding uncertainty is higher than the admissible threshold.

The RA function with $\alpha = 1$ has completely the opposite strategy, in which only admissible surface points are rewarded. The corresponding planning results also agree with this interpretation. As it can be seen in figure 6.4, most of the measurements selected by this planning gain

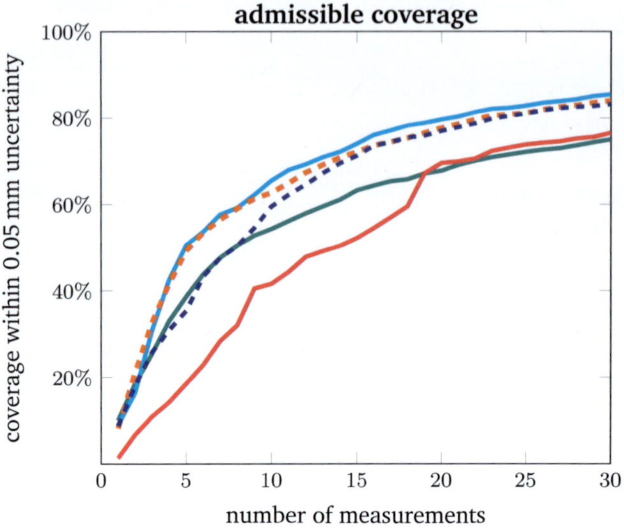

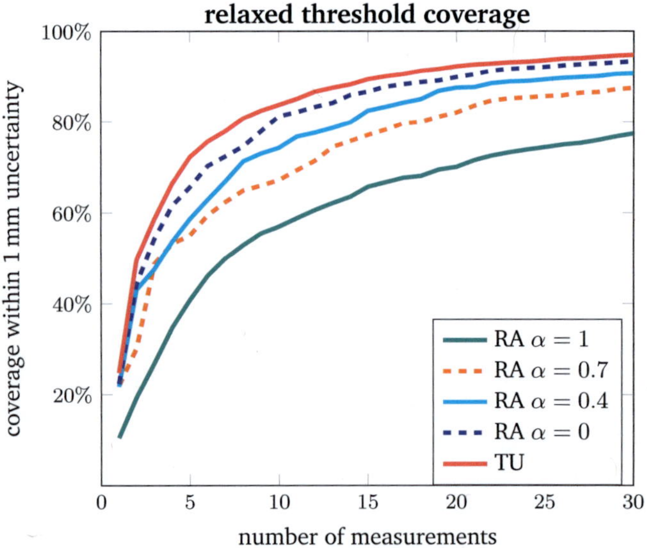

Figure 6.4: Uncertainty planning results vs. number of measurements. **(top)**: target points coverage with $u \leq 0.05\,\mathrm{mm}$ (admissible), **(bottom)**: target points coverage with $u \leq 1\,\mathrm{mm}$ (relaxed admissibility). For each gain function both results correspond to the same plan.

function only deliver admissible measurements and the rest of the surface is left unmeasured.

For a better visualization, figure 6.5 compares the proportion of the surface coverage within the admissible threshold vs. the coverage percentage between the relaxed and the admissible thresholds. This figure is provided for a few selected measurements from figure 6.4.

Choosing intermediate values for α has shown to result in the best balance between achieving the most admissible measurements and overall coverage with the relaxed uncertainty threshold. For a low number of measurements, the best performance corresponds to $\alpha = 0.4$. As the number of measurements increases, the fusion of more and more measurements lead to further reduction of uncertainties and, therefore, the RA function with α values 0.7, 0.4, and 0 lead to comparable results.

It is interesting to see that decreasing α has not only yielded a better overall uncertainty on the surface, but it has also increased the percentage of admissible points. This is because the relaxed admissibility threshold term can reward the gain function as soon as it enters a promising region in the design space, which might be still inadmissible but lead to admissible results in further iterations.

Although the improvement rate generally decreases by adding more measurements, the overall results always improve by considering longer plans. It is indeed a matter of an expert decision when to stop planning further measurements. Generally, it is recommendable to continue to longer plans at first to get an overview on how the planning results develop. The experts can then reduce the plan length based on the achieved performance. In this thesis, 80% coverage with admissible uncertainty was considered as the criteria for plan length sufficiency. Table 6.6 contains the number of required measurements for each implemented gain function to achieve 80% coverage within the admissible uncertainty. For higher coverage thresholds, the planning ends up with much longer plans and consequently requires significantly longer runtime. In order to be able to compare several uncertainty planning approaches within an affordable time budget, the coverage threshold was set to 80%.

Figure 6.6 shows a visualization of the uncertainty planning results on the surface for coverage with both the admissible and the relaxed admissibility thresholds, illustrated as different color maps.

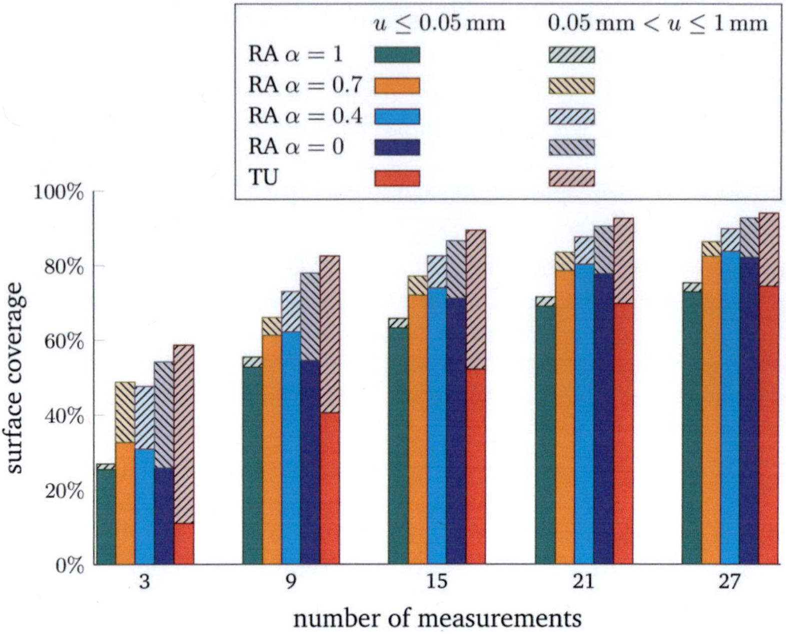

Figure 6.5: Comparison of the covered surface within the admissible uncertainty threshold ($u < 0.05\,\mathrm{mm}$), and the coverage with uncertainties between the admissible and relaxed threshold ($0.05\,\mathrm{mm} < u \leq 1\,\mathrm{mm}$). These results correspond to selected measurements from figure 6.4.

Table 6.6: Summary of uncertainty planning results.

Uncertainty gain function	**Measurements for 80% admissible coverage**
RA $\alpha = 1$	>30
RA $\alpha = 0.7$	23
RA $\alpha = 0.4$	21
RA $\alpha = 0$	24
TU	>30

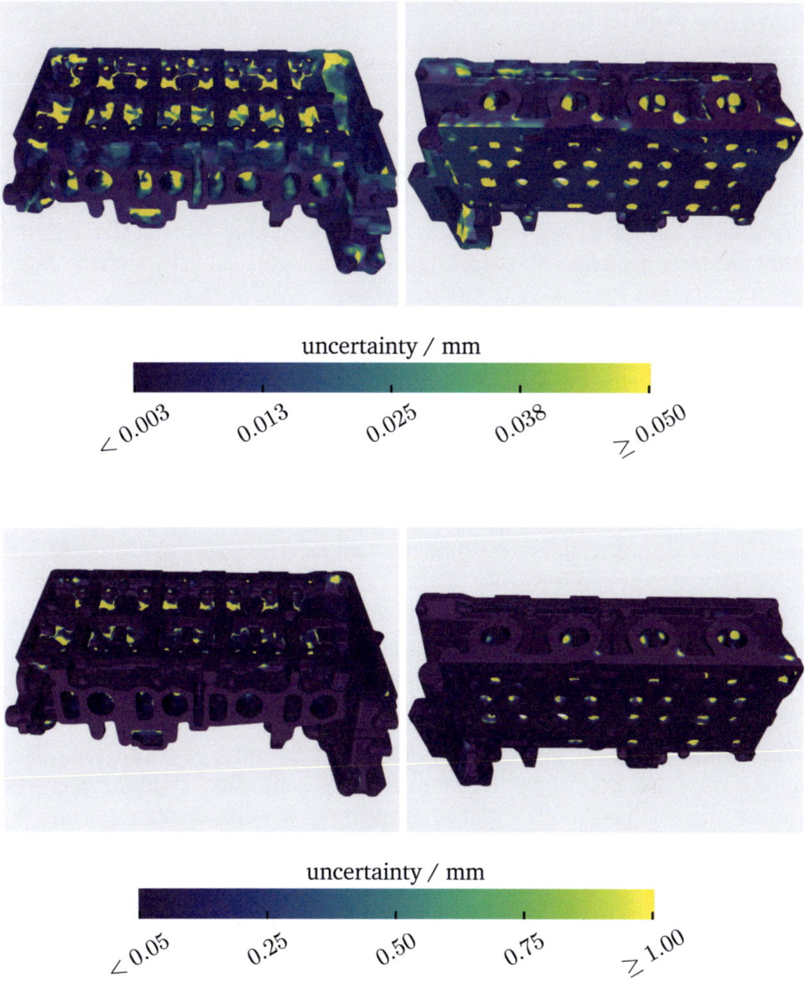

Figure 6.6: Visualization of the estimated measurement uncertainties for planning with the gain function RA $\alpha = 0.4$ and considering 21 optimized measurements (80% admissible coverage). (top): visualization of coverage with admissible uncertainty, (bottom): visualization of coverage within the relaxed uncertainty threshold.

Run-Time Performance

Uncertainty planning took on average 4.3 h for each single measurement, using the PSO optimization in a single run without random restarts. The significant increase in the run-time compared to the coverage planning is associated with the execution overhead of the probabilistic surface inference method. This way, optimizations for 40 measurements would take about a week to complete with the employed hardware. This runtime may not be a big concern for designing an inspection setup which might be in operation for a long time after that.

6.4 Planning for Optical Parameters

The last two sections discussed the problem of planning the geometrical degrees of freedom of the setup for the best coverage or the least sensitivity to stochastic noise. When the image acquisition constellation is determined that way, the optical parameters can still play a significant role in the signal to noise ratio of the image. The exposure time t_{exp} for instance controls the intensity of the image by setting the duration of the time in which the sensor is exposed to light. The f-number $f^{\#} = \frac{f}{D}$, on the other hand, determines the aperture diameter D, which influences the diffraction effect, depth of field, and also the amount of light reaching the sensor.

The configuration of the optical parameters for images containing laser light is especially more challenging. Smaller f-numbers (wider apertures) reduce the diffraction effects, i.e. resulting in smaller speckles, while the depth of field will be also significantly decreased, which in turn leads to blurring effects.

This section exclusively focuses on optimizing the f-number and exposure time to achieve the optimal laser detectability in the images. To this end, the sensor-realistic simulation framework introduced in chapter 4 will be utilized. In this part, all components of the proposed simulation framework have been included to produce realistic images.

6.4.1 Sensor-realistic Simulations

This chapter considers a general imaging scene, with the full cylinder head model, a laser light source, an incoherent area light source with uniform intensity in the visible spectrum, and constant ambient light. For simulation of the light transport (ray tracing), the Mitsuba physically based renderer [Wen10] is utilized. The imaging scene for ray tracing already includes a thin lens model, for modeling out-of-focus blurring. To achieve a better visibility of the imaging object on the images, an ambient light factor with low intensity was also included in ray tracing.

In order to simulate laser speckles, spectral ray tracing was carried out separately for the laser light and the incoherent light sources (area and ambient light). Only the image component corresponding to the laser light has been subject to modeling the diffraction effects using the coherent optical PSF (see section 4.7.1). Both the coherent and the incoherent image components were then added together after the speckle modeling in order to calculate the sensor spectral response. The sensor model used for these simulations corresponds to the same color sensor used in the experiments of chapter 5 (see table 5.3).

Similar to the simulation results of chapter 4, the images were first rendered with super-sampling (each pixel sampled with 9 sub-pixels), in order to realistically simulate the speckles which are smaller than a pixel. After modeling the laser speckles, the image is down-sampled to the original size by averaging the irradiance within a pixel. For ray tracing, each sub-pixel was sampled by 512 rays (i.e. a pixel was sampled by 9×512 rays). To reduce the simulation time, the rendering was only dedicated to the region on the image containing the laser light. This reduced the image size from 1920×1200 to 1540×480. Each single rendering of such images took about 2.5 hours. For more information regarding the simulation process, the reader can refer to the details of simulation results in chapter 4, section 4.8.

In this chapter, planning optical parameters will be demonstrated on the image level for a selected image frame. Figure 6.7 shows this image under several imaging conditions. Similar to the results of chapter 4, the greenish look of these images is due to simulation of raw camera images, which contain higher intensities in the green channel. Figure 6.8 displays a magnified view of a portion of the same images for a better visualization of the intensities and their variations.

For smaller f-numbers, the Gaussian profile of the laser line is much better preserved. For images (a) and (b) the speckles are much smaller than the resolution of the image, thus, they have not degraded the laser profile. Due to the limited depth of field, however, blurring effects can be seen on both images, especially on image (a). By increasing the f-number, the blurring effect gradually vanishes but the speckles tend to increase in size. Variations of the exposure time additionally influence the intensity of the images.

6.4.2 Optimization

Due to the complex impact of f-number and exposure time on the signal to noise ratio of the images, an automatic optimization of the optical parameters can be very useful for achieving the best image processing performance. For every machine vision inspection system, the best optical configuration is the one that leads to the best performance of the image processing algorithms for detecting the desired features. By evaluating the image processing performance, cost functions can be defined to quantify the performance of those algorithms and optimize the optical parameters accordingly.

For the application of laser triangulation, the optimality criterion for image processing is to detect the center of the laser profile with the smallest uncertainty. To quantify this, one requires a reference to compare the image processing results against. The reference laser profile for the optimizations was chosen based on the image processing performance on an image with a high laser contrast and without simulating any disturbing factors.

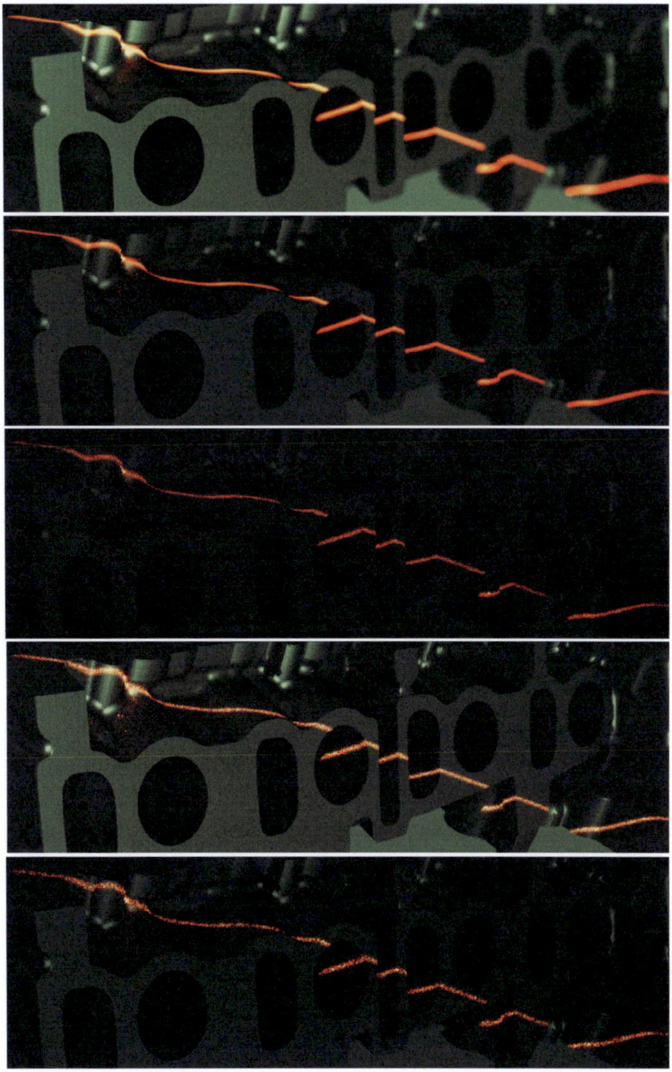

Figure 6.7: Sample simulated images for optical planning. The optical parameters used for simulations are
a) $f^{\#} = 1.4, t_{\text{exp}} = 3\,\text{ms}$, b) $f^{\#} = 2.8, t_{\text{exp}} = 8\,\text{ms}$
c) $f^{\#} = 5.6, t_{\text{exp}} = 13\,\text{ms}$, d) $f^{\#} = 11$, $t_{\text{exp}} = 200\,\text{ms}$, e) $f^{\#} = 22$, $t_{\text{exp}} = 400\,\text{ms}$

a)
b)
c)
d)
e)
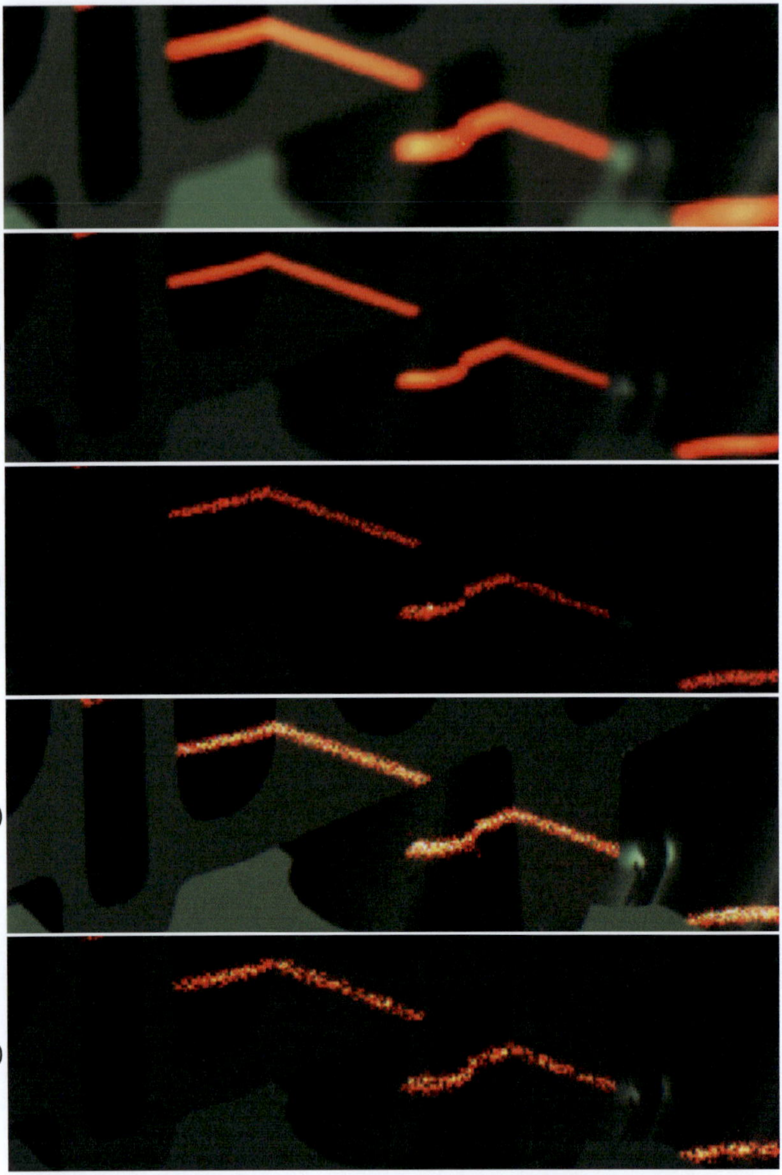

Figure 6.8: Magnified view of the right lower parts of images in figure 6.7.

Figure 6.9 displays the reference image rendered using the rasterization technique. This image is simulated considering only direct light modeling, without accounting for surface roughness, diffraction, aberrations, out of focus effects, sensor noise, and the sensor spectral response. The contrast of the laser profile against the background is also set to be high enough for a robust laser detection. On the plot below this figure, a segment of the extracted laser profile on this image is compared against the detected profile centers in a sensor-realistic image with the optical parameters $f^{\#} = 22$ and $t_{\text{exp}} = 400\,\text{ms}$. The corresponding sensor-realistic image can be seen in sub-figure (e) of figure 6.7.

To optimize the f-number and the exposure time, the light transport simulation (ray tracing) was carried out separately for all the variations of the f-number for the selected lens, in order to simulate the incoming irradiance through the aperture and produce the depth of field effects. The f-number values considered for planning are given by

$$f^{\#} \in \{1.4, 2, 2.8, 4, 5.6, 8, 11, 16, 22\},$$

which correspond to an aperture radius of 11.4 mm to 0.7 mm, considering a 16 mm focal length for the objective.

By applying the optical filtering for diffraction corresponding to each aperture size, the speckle patterns have been introduced. The effect of the exposure time is included in the simulations by applying the sensor intensity integration over time and simulating the sensor spectral response for different exposure times. Finally, the exposure time is independently optimized for each f-number option.

To begin the optimizations, the exposure time interval for f-number 1.4 was empirically chosen to be $t_{\text{exp}} \in [0.2, 12]\,\text{ms}$, in order to cover very low intensities up to over-exposed images. To cover the same exposure range for all f-numbers, the corresponding exposure time interval for f-number $f^{\#}$ was calculated by

$$t_{\text{exp}}(f^{\#}) \in \left[0.2\left(\frac{f^{\#}}{1.4}\right)^2, 12\left(\frac{f^{\#}}{1.4}\right)^2\right]\text{ms}. \tag{6.4}$$

Using the opposite of the approach used for calculating the normalized exposure time in equation 5.8, the scaling factor $(f\#/1.4)^2$ here scales the exposure time interval with respect to the change in the aperture area, so that the range of exposure (amount of light reaching the sensor) for each f-number remains equal. Each exposure time interval is equidistantly sampled with 300 samples. The f-number and its associated optimized exposure time which led to the best image processing performance have then been selected as the optimal parameters.

Before applying the optimizations, it is important to apply a laser profile detection algorithm and properly quantify its performance. The rest of this section briefly covers these two concepts.

Laser Peak Detection

The utilized algorithm for the detection of the laser profile is based on the *ridge detection* method proposed by Steger [Ste98]. This algorithm filters the image with Gaussian partial derivative kernels and uses the results to score the image locations for the presence of a ridge (i.e. a curve or a line with some thickness). In this thesis, the Steger's ridge detection method is used to identify image locations with potentially high chances of containing a ridge. Each image column with a potential ridge is then subject to the classical profile extraction approach using the *center of gravity peak detection* method [Fis96]. This approach can lead to sub-pixel accuracy in the laser profile detection. The signal to noise ratio of the image can highly influence the performance of the algorithm. For more information, the laser peak detection algorithm is presented in more detail in Appendix, section A. Both displayed profiles of figure 6.9 were extracted using this approach.

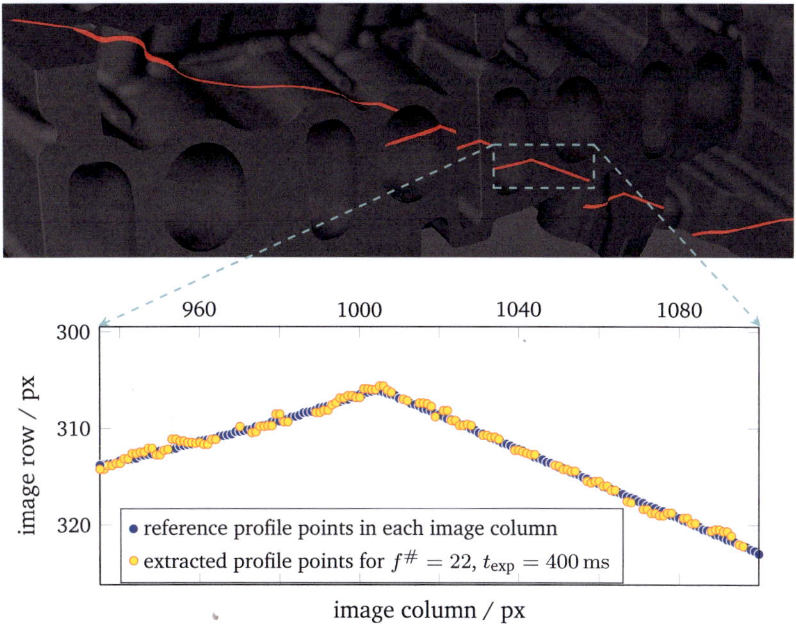

Figure 6.9: (above): Reference image for evaluation of laser detection performance, (below): a portion of the detected laser profile on the reference image vs. the same profile extracted using the sensor realistic image (e) of figure 6.8.

Cost Function

Looking at the extracted profile of figure 6.9, it can be observed that the profile has not been extracted in some image columns, due to dark speckles or a low amount of incoming light. On the columns where a laser profile is detected, the detected image position may slightly deviate from the reference profile.

The performance of the laser detection algorithm can, therefore, be quantified in two terms. On the one hand, the profile coverage rate $\alpha_{\text{cov}} \in [0,1]$, determines the ratio of the length of the extracted laser profile to the complete profile. On the other hand, the fluctuations of the extracted profile around the reference values is formalized in terms of the standard deviation of the differences to the reference profile $u_{\text{px}} \in \mathrm{R}_{\geq 0}$. As both α_{cov} and u_{px} are specific to each rendered image, they can be considered as functions of $f^{\#}$ and t_{exp}. An optical cost function f^{opt} encapsulates both metrics into a single cost function by

$$f^{\text{opt}}\left(f^{\#},t_{\text{exp}}\right) = \alpha_{\text{cov}}\left(f^{\#},t_{\text{exp}}\right) u_{\text{px}}\left(f^{\#},t_{\text{exp}}\right) + \left[1 - \alpha_{\text{cov}}\left(f^{\#},t_{\text{exp}}\right)\right] u_{\text{pr}}, \tag{6.5}$$

where u_{pr} is some prior uncertainty factor much higher than typical standard deviations for laser detection, in order to penalize the uncovered laser profile. For the experiments of this thesis, u_{pr} was set to 3 pixels.

6.4.3 Results & Discussion

Figure 6.10 displays the optimized cost function values for each f-number, which correspond to the optimized exposure times shown in figure 6.12. The results indicate that the best performance corresponds to f-number 2.8 with 9 ms exposure time. The image corresponding to this optical configuration is showed in figure 6.11.

With small f-number values, the out-of-focus blurring effects can slightly degrade the laser detection performance. As the diffraction effects are negligible at wide apertures, increasing the f-number enlarges the depth of field and yields improvements up to f-number 2.8. A further increase of the f-number strengthens the diffraction effects and increases the uncertainty in the laser profile detection.

Figure 6.12 additionally provides a comparison of the optimized exposure times against the curve

$$t_{\text{exp}}\left(f^{\#}\right) = t_{\text{exp}}(1.4)\left(\frac{f^{\#}}{1.4}\right)^{2}. \tag{6.6}$$

By analogy to the previous discussion about equation 6.4, this curve indicates the exposure time that corresponds to the same exposure (overall intensity) for each f-number, as compared to the image with f-number 1.4. The motivation behind this comparison is to study the relative exposure of the optimized images. The curves in figure 6.12 convey that the optimizations tend to increase the intensity of the images as the f-number increases. This can be caused by the intensity variations produced by the speckles. By increasing the intensities, the bright speckles get over-exposed and the dark ones get brighter. This decreases the overall intensity fluctuations and improves the laser detection performance.

Figures 6.13 and 6.14 show the same optimization results in terms the achieved values for u_{px} and their corresponding α_{cov}. According to the simulation-based optimizations, an f-number value of 2.8 with a profile detection uncertainty of 0.29 px and a profile coverage of 98% achieves the best performance. By increasing the f-number, which enlarges the speckles, both the profile coverage and the detection uncertainty deteriorate. The f-number 2.8 seems to have achieved a good balance between depth of field and diffraction effects for the selected image frame.

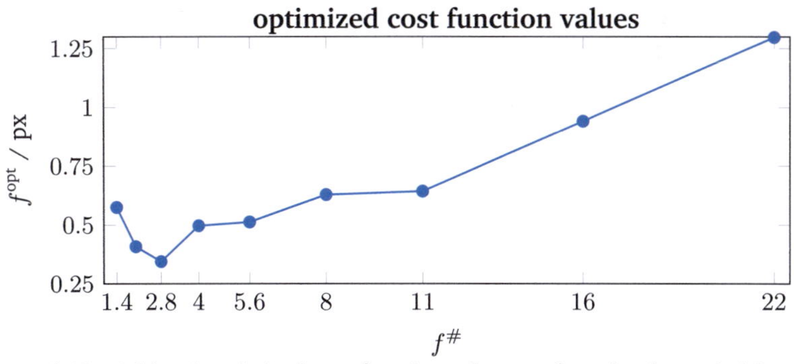

Figure 6.10: Achieved optimized cost function values vs. f-number by optimizing the exposure time for each f-number value.

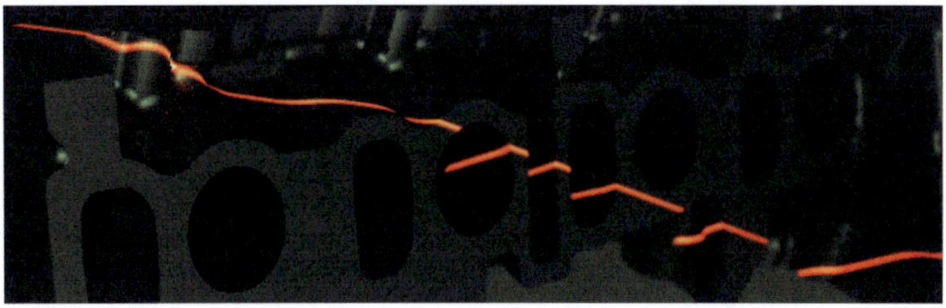

Figure 6.11: Optimized image by applying the optical planning

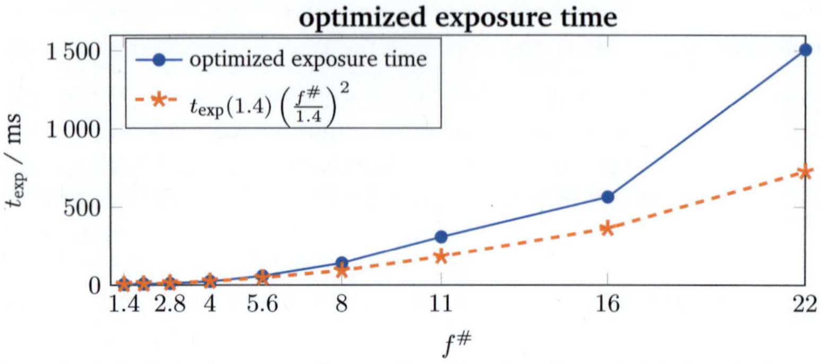

Figure 6.12: Optimized exposure times vs. f-number. For a better insight into the intensity levels, the orange curve indicates the exposure time values needed to yield a constant exposure (intensity) for all f-numbers.

Statistical Analysis of the Results

The statistical analysis of the simulation verification results in the previous chapter (section 5.4.2) revealed that the predicted uncertainties based on simulations can exhibit some systematic as well as stochastic error. Figure 5.22 in chapter 5 illustrated the relative simulated uncertainty error e_{u} with respect to the f-number. Using the results of this analysis, it is possible to draw conclusions about the reliability of the predicted optimization results of this section.

Although e_{u} was previously derived for uncertainties in height measurement, the ratio results in equal values when considering the pixel-level uncertainties as well. Thus, e_{u} can be rewritten as

$$e_{\mathrm{u}} = \frac{u_{\mathrm{px}}^{\mathrm{real}} - u_{\mathrm{px}}^{\mathrm{sim}}}{u_{\mathrm{px}}^{\mathrm{real}}} \times 100. \tag{6.7}$$

Using this equation, the real-world image level uncertainties can be predicted by means of a correction factor, given by

$$u_{\mathrm{px}}^{\mathrm{real}} = \frac{1}{1 - 0.01 e_{\mathrm{u}}} \times u_{\mathrm{px}}^{\mathrm{sim}}. \tag{6.8}$$

In equation 6.8, e_u can be set from the the previous studies in chapter 5, and u_px^sim is the simulation-based uncertainty delivered by the optimizations of the optical parameters.

Figure 6.13 compares the optimization results against the expected real-world uncertainties as well as the estimated spread of the values corresponding to a 95% confidence interval. The expected real-world uncertainties correspond to the optimization results which have been corrected for the expected systematic bias using equation 6.8. The f-number-dependent e_u values used for this correction are based on the verification analysis results of chapter 5. As discussed previously, for smaller f-numbers the simulations slightly underestimate the real-world uncertainties, whereas for larger f-numbers the actual uncertainties are overestimated. However, it can be seen that the bias correction has led to very slight changes to the graph and the overall trend as well as the optimal f-number have not changed. After bias correction, the optimal optical configuration is expected to detect the laser profile with an uncertainty of 0.31 px.

Figure 6.13 further displays a 95% confidence interval for the predicted uncertainties by taking two times the standard deviation of the simulation error into account. This analysis holds the assumption that e_u can be approximated as a Gaussian random variable. For the optimal solution with f-number 2.8, the uncertainties are expected to lie within 0.24 and 0.44 px.

Note that, as the derived correction factor is non-linear with respect to e_u, the shaded area is not symmetric and corresponds to a non-Gaussian distribution. In addition, the statistical analysis for simulation verifications in chapter 5 did not include f-number 1.4 due to technical reasons, and therefore, the statistical plots of figure 6.13 are dedicated to f-number values greater than 1.4.

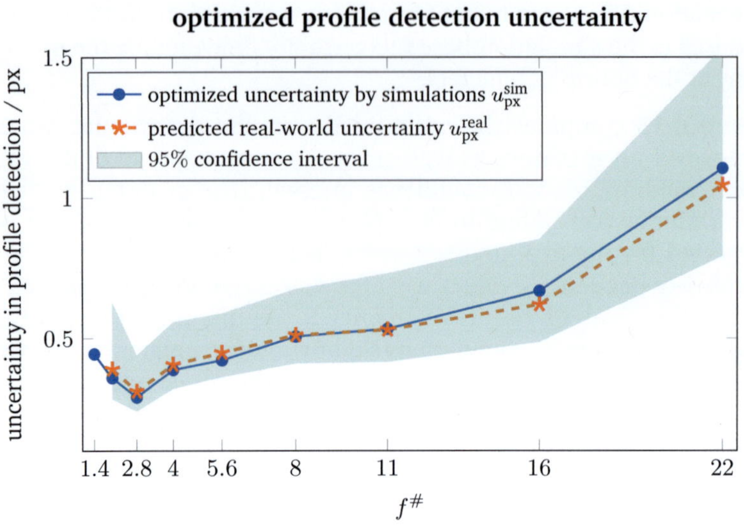

Figure 6.13: Optimized profile detection uncertainties vs. f-number. The uncertainty curves compare the optical optimization results, the corresponding expected uncertainties in real-world, and the predicted spread of the values in a 95% confidence interval.

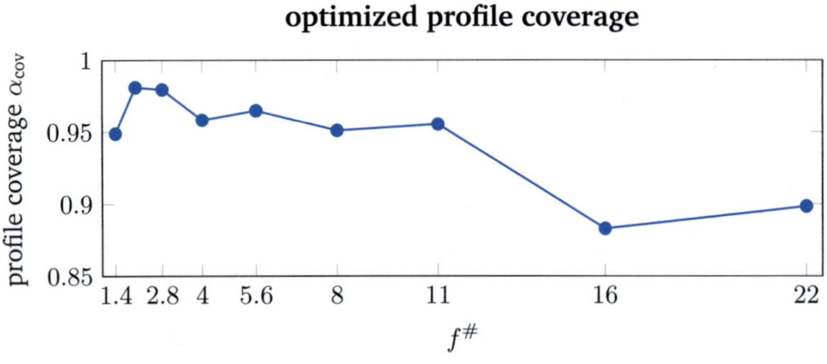

Figure 6.14: Optimized laser profile coverage vs. f-number.

6.5 Concluding Remarks

Uniting all the concepts and methods presented about inspection planning within this thesis, this chapter discussed applying those methods on an actual inspection problem. Section 6.2 started with the optimization of the geometrical degrees of freedom considering only the surface coverage as the planning goal, and within this problem definition, the performance of different optimization algorithms as well as that of a human expert were compared. The results indicate improvements to both the state-of-the-art planning method as well as a human performance.

The uncertainty planning of section 6.3 generalized the coverage planning to include the sensitivities of the inspection to constant stochastic noise in feature detection. Although the input noise is considered constant and probably does not correspond to real-world values, this planning approach can already lead to potentially good setup constellations by minimizing the sensitives to the input noise and thus proposing robust inspection systems.

The third planning problem presented in section 6.4 was concerned with the optimization of optical parameters in order to directly minimize the stochastic noise in detecting the desired features on the images, i.e. the laser profile. The optical planning was demonstrated on a sample image frame and, therefore, the presented results are limited to the imaging use-case selected for the optimizations.

A useful application of the optical planning is to apply frame-based optimizations to the images proposed in the coverage or uncertainty planning. If adjusting the optical parameters during the inspection is not allowed in a frame-based manner, a collection of image frames corresponding to one or more scans can be used together to optimize the average performance of the image processing algorithm throughout the selected measurements. Moreover, the optical planning results can be used to better estimate the real-world uncertainties at the image level, and if necessary, the geometrical uncertainty planning can be repeated with more realistic parameter uncertainties.

7 Conclusion and Outlook

7.1 Conclusion

The optical and geometrical configuration of a machine vision inspection setup and decision making about the number of required measurements have been mainly based on experimental trial and error so far. The main goal in developing this thesis has been to contribute to the inspection planning procedure by proposing automatic and intelligent methods, which not only improve the human performance for complex inspection tasks, but also replace the tedious experimental work.

This thesis studied the automatic inspection planning problem in a comprehensive way, starting from a formal definition up to employing practical tools for implementing a solution. Within this context, a simulation-based planning approach has been proposed, which relies on evaluating the setup constellations by realistic simulations. The content of this thesis is organized in terms of the three main components of the inspection planning problem, namely, simulation, evaluation, and optimization.

The role of simulations in improving the inspection planning procedure is undeniable. Even if a setup is being empirically planned, simulation environments can greatly improve the task by visualizing every desired setup constellation from arbitrary viewpoints and verifying the applicability of different optical devices without imposing the costs of purchasing physical parts and configuring them. With the considerable success of graphical rendering techniques in synthesizing realistic images, simulations can, moreover, be used to generate realistic images which can replicate the actual signal-to-noise-ratio with acceptable accuracy. To adapt the rendering methods to the simulation of optical measurement systems, this thesis proposed to complement conventional ray tracing techniques with additional optical and sensor simulations as a post-processing step.

The simulation results were experimentally verified against more than 4000 real images of a laser line over a measured piece of metal surface in different optical and geometrical constellations. The simulation results not only exhibited a high visual agreement, but they were also able to predict the real measurement uncertainty with no more than 20% error on average. The simulation verification results of this thesis can be seen as a starting point for industries to trust simulation-based inspection planning methods more than before and invest more in acquiring accurate data from the surfaces, light sources, and optical elements, in order to achieve a better simulation quality.

To fully automate the planning procedure, simulations can be integrated with intelligent search algorithms in order to appropriately search the design space of a machine vision setup. This thesis compared the performance of several heuristic continuous optimization algorithms against the results of an empirical human planning as well as the state-of-the-art discrete planning proposed in the literature. The results indicated that the particle swarm optimization (PSO) algorithm outperforms the state of the art and, at the same time, significantly improves the performance of an expert who empirically proposes a plan using an interactive simulation environment. The PSO planning resulted in a plan which covered over 90% of a complicated cylinder head surface with 10 laser triangulation measurements.

This thesis further contributed to the problem of quantifying the information gain of a surface measurement. Within this context, an uncertainty propagation through the measurement and probabilistic surface inference using Gaussian processes were studied, which allow one to score different setup constellations in terms of the amount of information they deliver about the surface.

The proposed methods and concepts were brought together at the end and applied to the inspection planning of a complex cylinder head surface using laser triangulation.

7.2 Outlook to Future Work

For a widespread deployment of automatic inspection planning methods in industries, an essential step to be taken in the future is standardizing specifications and parameters of the participating optical elements. This includes creating a database of conventionally used surface materials with their corresponding roughness profiles and BRDFs, in addition to standard specification parameters for characterizing light sources, lenses, and other optical elements. Before this database can be created, standardized measurements and comprehensive models of the optical elements must be proposed and adopted by the manufacturers. The EMAV standard 1288 has already taken this step for standardizing a model with a set of parameters for describing digital sensors. With all this information available, inspection planning methods can automatically select the most appropriate alternatives of the optical elements in the market and propose a plan including which devices to use and in which configuration.

Another potential for a considerable improvement in inspection planning is to provide dedicated distributed or cloud-based systems for high quality rendering and the optimizations. Rendering an image can be easily parallelized by splitting the image into small patches, and thus such distributed systems can significantly accelerate the simulation. This way, it will be computationally feasible to perform the optical and geometrical planning simultaneously, instead of separating them in two steps for avoiding the high cost of rendering sensor-realistic images for geometrical optimizations. On the optimization side, the allowed intervals for the setup degrees of freedom can be simply divided into several smaller ranges of values and distributed among a number of workstations for a thorough parallel search in the design space. By providing such planning competence centers and especially using a standard database of the optical devices, many industries with different inspection requirements may share a single service provider to receive inspection planning services.

With the advent of automatic inspection planning methods, the human expert will play a supervisory role rather than making direct decisions regarding the setup configuration. An important step in the automatic planning workflow, which was introduced but not further studied in this thesis, is to consider methods for incorporating the expert feedback into the automatic planning. The feedback of the expert can be potentially defined in terms of additional constraints to be taken into account in further optimizations.

Last but not least, we can imagine inspection scenarios in which there is not enough information about the surface under inspection and the surface measurements are not possible (for instance, if one does not want to hurt a surface by cutting a piece out of it and putting it under a microscope) or they are financially not justified. In these cases, an online inspection planning using reinforcement learning approaches can potentially be useful to incrementally build more accurate models from the surfaces and gradually improve the simulation accuracy and consequently the inspection plan.

Bibliography

[Ack08] S. ACKERMANN, F. MENNA, A. SCAMARDELLA, and S. TROISI: 'Digital photogrammetry for high precision 3D measurements in shipbuilding field'. *Proceedings of CIRP International Conference on ICME-Intelligent Computation in Manufacturing Engineering*. 2008 (cit. on p. 7).

[Ake08] T. AKENINE-MOLLER, E. HAINES, and N. HOFFMAN: *Real-time rendering*. AK Peters/CRC Press, 2008 (cit. on pp. 72, 74).

[Ale16] S. M. ALESSIO: *Digital Signal Processing and Spectral Analysis for Scientists*. Springer, 2016 (cit. on p. 60).

[Arv86] J. ARVO: 'Backward ray tracing'. *Developments in Ray Tracing, Computer Graphics, Proceedings of of ACM SIGGRAPH Course Notes*. 1986: pp. 259–263 (cit. on p. 77).

[Bär10] C. BÄR: *Elementare Differentialgeometrie*. 2., überarb. und erw. Aufl. De-Gruyter-Studium. Berlin: DE GRUYTER, 2010 (cit. on p. 69).

[Ber16b] S. BERGMANN, M. MOHAMMADIKAJI, S. IRGENFRIED, H. WÖRN, J. BEYERER, and C. DACHSBACHER: 'A Phenomenological Approach to Integrating Gaussian Beam Properties and Speckle into a Physically-Based Renderer'. *Proceedings of International Workshop on Vision, Modeling, and Visualization*. 2016 (cit. on pp. 89, 91).

[Ber94] J. M. BERNARDO and A. F. M. SMITH: *Bayesian Theory*. Hoboken, NJ, USA: John Wiley & Sons, Inc, 1994 (cit. on p. 50).

[Bey15] J. BEYERER, F. P. LEÓN, and C. FRESE: *Machine Vision: Automated Visual Inspection: Theory, Practice and Applications*. Springer, 2015 (cit. on pp. 1, 2, 7, 66, 69, 86, 89, 100).

[Bra07] D. BRATTON and J. KENNEDY: 'Defining a Standard for Particle Swarm Optimization'. *Proceedings of IEEE Swarm Intelligence Symposium*. 2007: pp. 120–127 (cit. on pp. 30, 145).

[Che00] F. CHEN, G. M. BROWN, and M. SONG: 'Overview of three-dimensional shape measurement using optical methods'. *Optical Engineering* (2000), vol. 39(1): p. 10 (cit. on p. 7).

[Col08] B. M. COLOSIMO, E. G. MOYA, G. MORONI, and S. PETRO: 'Statistical sampling strategies for geometric tolerance inspection by CMM'. *Economic Quality Control* (2008), vol. 23(1): pp. 109–121 (cit. on p. 3).

[Coo84] R. L. COOK, T. PORTER, and L. CARPENTER: 'Distributed ray tracing'. *Proceedings of ACM SIGGRAPH*. Vol. 18. 3. ACM. 1984: pp. 137–145 (cit. on p. 77).

[Cor07] T. H. CORMEN: *Introduction to algorithms*. 2. edition. Cambridge, Mass.: MIT Press, 2007 (cit. on pp. 19, 21).

[Cor12] M. CORSINI, P. CIGNONI, and R. SCOPIGNO: 'Efficient and flexible sampling with blue noise properties of triangular meshes'. *IEEE transactions on visualization and computer graphics* (2012), vol. 18(6): pp. 914–924 (cit. on pp. 39, 40, 144).

[Cow88] C. K. COWAN: 'Model-based synthesis of sensor location'. *Proceedings of IEEE International Conference on Robotics and Automation*. 1988: pp. 900–905 (cit. on pp. 3, 24, 37, 38).

[Di 11] G. DI LEO and A. PAOLILLO: 'Uncertainty evaluation of camera model parameters'. *Proceedings of Instrumentation and Measurement Technology Conference (I2MTC)*. IEEE. 2011: pp. 1–6 (cit. on p. 47).

[Dut06] P. DUTRÉ: *Advanced global illumination*. 2nd ed. AK Petes Boca Raton FL, 2006 (cit. on pp. 66, 70, 75, 76).

[Eic15] H. J. EICHLER and J. EICHLER: *Laser: Bauformen, Strahlführung, Anwendungen*. Springer Berlin Heidelberg, 2015 (cit. on p. 118).

[Ell05] M. M. ELLENRIEDER and H. KOMOTO: 'Model-based automatic calculation and evaluation of camera positions for industrial machine vision'. *Proceedings of Computational Imaging III*. Ed. by C. A. BOUMAN and E. L. MILLER. SPIE, 2005: pp. 467–479 (cit. on p. 38).

[EMV16] EMVA 1288 WORKING GROUP: *EMVA Standard 1288 - Standard for Characterization of Image Sensors and Cameras*. 2016 (cit. on pp. 96, 97).

[Equ06] S. EQUIS and P. JACQUOT: 'Simulation of speckle complex amplitude: advocating the linear model'. *Proceedings of Speckles, From Grains to Flowers*. SPIE, 2006 (cit. on p. 89).

[Fei98] U. FEIGE: 'A threshold of ln n for approximating set cover'. *Journal of the ACM* (1998), vol. 45(4): pp. 634–652 (cit. on p. 21).

[Fie14] R. D. FIETE and B. D. PAUL: 'Modeling the optical transfer function in the imaging chain'. *Optical Engineering* (2014), vol. 53(8) (cit. on p. 90).

[Fis17] M. FISCHER, M. PETZ, and R. TUTSCH: 'Statistical characterization of evaluation strategies for fringe projection systems by means of a model-based noise prediction'. *Journal of Sensors and Sensor Systems* (2017), vol. 6(1): pp. 145–153 (cit. on p. 7).

[Fis96] R. B. FISHER and D. K. NAIDU: 'A Comparison of Algorithms for Subpixel Peak Detection'. *Image Technology*. Ed. by J. L. C. SANZ. Springer Berlin Heidelberg, 1996: pp. 385–404 (cit. on pp. 168, 201).

[Fli04] K. FLIEGEL: 'Modeling and measurement of image sensor characteristics'. *Radio engineering* (2004), vol. 13(4): pp. 27–34 (cit. on p. 90).

[FLI17] FLIR INTEGRATED IMAGING SOLUTIONS INC.: *Imaging performance specification - FLIR blackfly GigE vision*. Version 13.3. Jan. 2017 (cit. on p. 99).

[Flo92] L. M. FLORACK, B. M. ter HAAR ROMENY, J. J. KOENDERINK, and M. A. VIERGEVER: 'Scale and the differential structure of images'. *Image and vision computing* (1992), vol. 10(6): pp. 376–388 (cit. on p. 200).

[Gol97] P. W. GOLDBERG, C. K. I. WILLIAMS, and C. M. BISHOP: 'Regression with input-dependent noise: A Gaussian process treatment'. *Advances in neural information processing systems* (1997), vol. 10: pp. 493–499 (cit. on p. 53).

[Goo17] J. W. GOODMAN: *Introduction to Fourier optics*. Fourth edition. W.H. Freeman Macmillan learning, 2017 (cit. on pp. 67, 88, 90, 92–95, 124).

[Gre97] D. P. GREENBERG, K. E. TORRANCE, P. SHIRLEY, J. ARVO, E. LAFORTUNE, J. A. FERWERDA, B. WALTER, B. TRUMBORE, S. PATTANAIK, and S.-C. FOO: 'A framework for realistic image synthesis'. *Proceedings of Computer graphics and interactive techniques*. 1997: pp. 477–494 (cit. on pp. 78, 82).

[Gro16] M. GRONLE and W. OSTEN: 'View and sensor planning for multi-sensor surface inspection'. *Surface Topography: Metrology and Properties* (2016), vol. 4(2) (cit. on pp. 3, 19, 22, 23, 38).

[Han14] J. HANIKA and C. DACHSBACHER: 'Efficient Monte Carlo rendering with realistic lenses'. *Proceedings of Computer Graphics Forum*. Vol. 33. 2014: pp. 323–332 (cit. on p. 79).

[Har96] R. M. HARALICK: 'Propagating covariance in computer vision'. *International Journal of Pattern Recognition and Artificial Intelligence* (1996), vol. 10(05): pp. 561–572 (cit. on pp. 43, 48).

[Hec02] E. HECHT: *Optics*. Fourth edition. Addison-Wesley, 2002 (cit. on pp. 87, 89).

[Hol15] N. HOLZSCHUCH and R. PACANOWSKI: *A physically accurate reflectance model combining reflection and diffraction*. Research Report RR-8807. INRIA, Nov. 2015: p. 24 (cit. on p. 74).

[Irg17c] S. IRGENFRIED, H. WÖRN, S. BERGMANN, M. MOHAMMADIKAJI, J. BEYERER, and C. DACHSBACHER: 'A Versatile Hardware and Software Toolset for Computer Aided Inspection Planning of Machine Vision Applications'. *Proceedings of Information Systems Architecture and Technology*. Springer, 2017: pp. 326–335 (cit. on p. 3).

[Irg17d] S. IRGENFRIED, H. WÖRN, S. BERGMANN, M. MOHAMMADIKAJI, J. BEYERER, and C. DACHSBACHER: 'CAD-basierter Workflow für den semi-automatischen Entwurf optischer Inspektionssysteme'. *at - Automatisierungstechnik* (2017), vol. 65(6) (cit. on p. 3).

[Ish11] A. ISHEIL, J.-P. GONNET, D. JOANNIC, and J.-F. FONTAINE: 'Systematic error correction of a 3D laser scanning measurement device'. *Optics and Lasers in Engineering* (2011), vol. 49(1): pp. 16–24 (cit. on p. 7).

[ISO17] ISO: *Geometrical product specifications (GPS) – Inspection by measurement of workpieces and measuring equipment – Part 1: Decision rules for verifying conformity or nonconformity with specifications*. ISO 14253-1. Switzerland, 2017 (cit. on p. 41).

[Joi08] JOINT COMMITTEE FOR GUIDES IN METROLOGY (JCGM)": *Evaluation of Measurement data–Guide to the Expression of Uncertainty in Measurement*. JCGM 100:2008. 2008 (cit. on pp. 38, 40, 42).

[Kaj86] J. T. KAJIYA: 'The rendering equation'. *Proceedings of ACM SIGGRAPH*. Vol. 20. 4. ACM. 1986: pp. 143–150 (cit. on pp. 75, 77).

[Kel62] J. B. KELLER: 'Geometrical theory of diffraction'. *JOSA* (1962), vol. 52(2): pp. 116–130 (cit. on p. 79).

[Kol95] C. KOLB, D. MITCHELL, and P. HANRAHAN: 'A realistic camera model for computer graphics'. *Proceedings of ACM SIGGRAPH*. Ed. by S. G. MAIR and R. COOK. New York, USA: ACM Press, 1995: pp. 317–324 (cit. on p. 79).

[Kri15] S. KRIEGEL, C. RINK, T. BODENMÜLLER, and M. SUPPA: 'Efficient next-best-scan planning for autonomous 3D surface reconstruction of unknown objects'. *Journal of Real-Time Image Processing* (2015), vol. 10(4): pp. 611–631 (cit. on p. 4).

[Kun05] H. KUNZMANN, T. PFEIFER, R. SCHMITT, H. SCHWENKE, and A. WECKENMANN: 'Productive Metrology - Adding Value to Manufacture'. *Manufacturing Technology* (2005), vol. 54(2): pp. 155–168 (cit. on p. 1).

[Laf93] E. P. LAFORTUNE and Y. D. WILLEMS: 'Bi-directional path tracing'. *Proceedings of Compugraphics*. 1993: pp. 145–153 (cit. on p. 77).

[Lee97] G. LEE, J. MOU, and Y. SHEN: 'Sampling strategy design for dimensional measurement of geometric features using coordinate measuring machine'. *International Journal of Machine Tools and Manufacture* (1997), vol. 37(7): pp. 917–934 (cit. on p. 39).

[Lob17] F. S. LOBATO and V. STEFFEN JR.: *Multi-Objective Optimization Problems: Concepts and Self-Adaptive Parameters with Mathematical and Engineering Applications*. SpringerBriefs in Mathematics. Springer, 2017 (cit. on p. 25).

[Lon04] P. LONGHURST and A. CHALMERS: 'User validation of image quality assessment algorithms'. *Proceedings of Theory and Practice of Computer Graphics*. IEEE, 2004: pp. 196–202 (cit. on pp. 78, 83).

[Ma12] Y. MA, S. SOATTO, J. KOSECKA, and S. S. SASTRY: *An invitation to 3-d vision: from images to geometric models*. Vol. 26. Springer Science & Business Media, 2012 (cit. on pp. 9, 46).

[Mah11] M. MAHMUD, D. JOANNIC, M. ROY, A. ISHEIL, and J.-F. FONTAINE: '3D part inspection path planning of a laser scanner with control on the uncertainty'. *Computer-Aided Design* (2011), vol. 43(4): pp. 345–355 (cit. on pp. 4, 38).

[Mal03] E. N. MALAMAS, E. G. PETRAKIS, M. ZERVAKIS, L. PETIT, and J.-D. LEGAT: 'A survey on industrial vision systems, applications and tools'. *Image and Vision Computing* (2003), vol. 21(2): pp. 171–188 (cit. on p. 1).

[Mar14] T. C. MARTINS, M. S. G. TSUZUKI, R. Y. TAKIMOTO, A. BARARI, G. B. GALLO, M. A. A. GARCIA, and H. TIBA: 'Algorithmic iterative sampling in coordinate metrology plan for coordinate metrology using dynamic uncertainty analysis'. *Proceedings of International Conference on Industrial Informatics (INDIN)*. IEEE, 2014: pp. 316–319 (cit. on p. 3).

[Mav15] A. MAVRINAC, X. CHEN, and J. L. ALARCON-HERRERA: 'Semiautomatic Model-Based View Planning for Active Triangulation 3-D Inspection Systems'. *IEEE/ASME Transactions on Mechatronics* (2015), vol. 20(2): pp. 799–811 (cit. on pp. 19, 24, 38).

[Mch14] A. MCHUTCHON: 'Nonlinear Modelling and Control using Gaussian Processes'. Dissertation. Department of Engineering, University of Cambridge, 2014 (cit. on pp. 54, 56, 57).

[Mil94] G. MILLER: 'Efficient algorithms for local and global accessibility shading'. *Proceedings of ACM SIGGRAPH*. 1994: pp. 319–326 (cit. on p. 144).

[Moh18a] M. MOHAMMADIKAJI, S. BERGMANN, J. BEYERER, and C. DACHSBACHER: 'Sensor-realistic simulation of images in diffraction-limited imaging systems / Sensorrealistische Simulation von Bildern in beugungsbegrenzten Abbildungssystemen'. *tm-Technisches Messen* (2018), vol. 85(s1): pp. 95–102 (cit. on p. 93).

[Moh18b] M. MOHAMMADIKAJI, S. BERGMANN, S. IRGENFRIED, J. BEYERER, C. DACHSBACHER, and H. WORN: 'Inspection planning for optimized coverage of geometrically complex surfaces'. *Proceedings of Workshop on Metrology for Industry 4.0 and IoT*. IEEE, 2018: pp. 52–67 (cit. on p. 22).

[Moh16] M. MOHAMMADIKAJI, S. BERGMANN, S. IRGENFRIED, J. BEYERER, C. DACHSBACHER, and H. WÖRN: 'A framework for uncertainty propagation in 3D shape measurement using laser triangulation'. *Proceedings of Instrumentation and Measurement Technology Conference*. IEEE, 2016: pp. 1–6 (cit. on pp. 10, 44–46).

[Mor18] G. MORONI and S. PETRÒ: 'Geometric Inspection Planning as a Key Element in Industry 4.0'. *Proceedings of Industry 4.0 model for Advanced Manufacturing*. Springer, 2018: pp. 293–310 (cit. on pp. 2, 3).

[Mor10] G. MORONI and S. PETRÒ: 'Virtual CMM-Based Sampling Strategy Optimization'. *Product Lifecycle Management: Geometric Variations* (2010), vol.: pp. 385–403 (cit. on p. 3).

[Nam99] V. N. NAMBOOTHIRI: 'On determination of sample size in form error evaluation using coordinate metrology'. *International journal of production research* (1999), vol. 37(4): pp. 793–804 (cit. on p. 39).

[Nel65] J. A. NELDER and R. MEAD: 'A Simplex Method for Function Minimization'. *The Computer Journal* (1965), vol. 7(4): pp. 308–313 (cit. on p. 24).

[Opt18] OPTICS CANADA: *Powell Lens Buyer's Guide*. `http://www.laserlineoptics.com/powell_primer.html`. [Online, accessed 28-August-2018]. 2018 (cit. on pp. 119, 120).

[Pak17] A. PAK: 'Scale-related evolution of BRDFs'. *Proceedings of Joint Workshop of Fraunhofer IOSB and Institute for Anthropomatics, Vision and Fusion Laboratory*. Vol. 33. KIT Scientific Publishing. 2017 (cit. on p. 117).

[Pap02] A. PAPOULIS and S. U. PILLAI: *Probability, random variables, and stochastic processes*. Tata McGraw-Hill Education, 2002 (cit. on p. 59).

[Pit99] R. PITO: 'A solution to the next best view problem for automated surface acquisition'. *IEEE Transactions on Pattern Analysis and Machine Intelligence* (1999), vol. 21(10): pp. 1016–1030 (cit. on p. 37).

[Pri03] F. PRIETO, R. LEPAGE, P. BOULANGER, and T. REDARCE: 'A CAD-based 3D data acquisition strategy for inspection'. *Machine Vision and Applications* (2003), vol. 15(2): pp. 76–91 (cit. on pp. 24, 38).

[Ras06] C. E. RASMUSSEN and C. K. I. WILLIAMS: *Gaussian processes for machine learning*. Adaptive computation and machine learning. MIT Press, 2006 (cit. on pp. 50–52, 58).

[Ret17] M.-G. RETZLAFF, J. HANIKA, J. BEYERER, and C. DACHSBACHER: 'Physically based computer graphics for realistic image formation to simulate optical measurement systems'. *Journal of Sensors and Sensor Systems* (2017), vol. 6(1): pp. 171–184 (cit. on pp. 65, 78, 79).

[Reu03] S. E. REUTEBUCH, R. J. MCGAUGHEY, H.-E. ANDERSEN, and W. W. CARSON: 'Accuracy of a high-resolution lidar terrain model under a conifer forest canopy'. *Canadian journal of remote sensing* (2003), vol. 29(5): pp. 527–535 (cit. on p. 7).

[Ros13] M. ROSCHANI and J. BEYERER: 'Planungsbasierte Oberflächeninspektion in der Deflektometrie mittels Greedy-Optimierung'. *tm - Technisches Messen* (2013), vol. 80(6): pp. 189–195 (cit. on p. 24).

[Sch17] V. SCHÜSSLER, E. HEITZ, J. HANIKA, and C. DACHSBACHER: 'Microfacet-based normal mapping for robust Monte Carlo path tracing'. *ACM Transactions on Graphics (TOG)* (2017), vol. 36(6): p. 205 (cit. on p. 116).

[Sco09] W. R. SCOTT: 'Model-based view planning'. *Machine Vision and Applications* (2009), vol. 20(1): pp. 47–69 (cit. on pp. 3, 19, 22, 23, 38, 147).

[Sco03] W. R. SCOTT, G. ROTH, and J.-F. RIVEST: 'View planning for automated three-dimensional object reconstruction and inspection'. *ACM Computing Surveys* (2003), vol. 35(1): pp. 64–96 (cit. on p. 4).

[Shi66] G. E. SHILOV, B. L. GUREVICH, and R. A. SILVERMAN: *Integral, measure and derivative: A unified approach*. Prentice Hall, 1966 (cit. on p. 61).

[Sin12] P. K. SINHA: *Image acquisition and preprocessing for machine vision systems*. SPIE Press, 2012 (cit. on pp. 85, 86).

[Sla97] P. SLAVIK: 'A tight analysis of the greedy algorithm for set cover'. *Journal of Algorithms* (1997), vol. 25(2): pp. 237–254 (cit. on p. 21).

[Sny18] J. A. SNYMAN and D. N. WILKE: *Practical Mathematical Optimization*. Vol. 133. Springer International Publishing, 2018 (cit. on p. 24).

[Som54] A. SOMMERFELD: *Optics: Lectures on theoretical physics*. Academic Press, 1954 (cit. on p. 87).

[Ste98] C. STEGER: 'An unbiased detector of curvilinear structures'. *IEEE Transactions on Pattern Analysis and Machine Intelligence* (1998), vol. 20(2): pp. 113–125 (cit. on pp. 8, 168, 199, 200).

[Ste11] B. STEINERT, H. DAMMERTZ, J. HANIKA, and H. P. A. LENSCH: 'General spectral camera lens simulation'. Vol. 30. 6. 2011: pp. 1643–1654 (cit. on p. 79).

[Sun01] Y. SUN, F. D. FRACCHIA, M. S. DREW, and T. W. CALVERT: 'A spectrally based framework for realistic image synthesis'. *The Visual Computer* (2001), vol. 17(7): pp. 429–444 (cit. on p. 107).

[Sun07] K. V. SUNDSTEDT: 'Rendering and Validation of High-Fidelity Graphics using Region-of-Interest'. Dissertation. Bristol, England: University of Bristol, 2007 (cit. on pp. 78, 83).

[Tar95a] K. A. TARABANIS, R. Y. TSAI, and P. K. ALLEN: 'The MVP sensor planning system for robotic vision tasks'. *IEEE Transactions on Robotics and Automation* (1995), vol. 11(1): pp. 72–85 (cit. on pp. 19, 24, 38).

[Tar95b] G. H. TARBOX and S. N. GOTTSCHLICH: 'Planning for Complete Sensor Coverage in Inspection'. *Computer Vision and Image Understanding* (1995), vol. 61(1): pp. 84–111 (cit. on p. 37).

[Ulb06] C. ULBRICHT, A. WILKIE, and W. PURGATHOFER: 'Verification of Physically Based Rendering Algorithms'. *Computer Graphics Forum* (2006), vol. 25(2): pp. 237–255 (cit. on p. 107).

[van06] S. VAN AERT, D. VAN DYCK, and A. J. DEN DEKKER: 'Resolution of coherent and incoherent imaging systems reconsidered - Classical criteria and a statistical alternative'. *Optics Express* (2006), vol. 14(9): p. 3830 (cit. on p. 94).

[Vea97] E. VEACH: *Robust Monte Carlo methods for light transport simulation*. Vol. 1610. Stanford University PhD thesis, 1997 (cit. on p. 76).

[Voe11] D. G. Voelz: *Computational fourier optics: a MATLAB tutorial*. SPIE press Bellingham, 2011 (cit. on p. 93).

[Wan14] L. Wang and C. Li: 'Spectrum-based kernel length estimation for Gaussian process classification'. *IEEE transactions on cybernetics* (2014), vol. 44(6): pp. 805–816 (cit. on p. 61).

[Web96] R. H. Webb: 'Confocal optical microscopy'. *Report on Progress in Physics* (1996), vol. 59(3): pp. 427–471 (cit. on p. 116).

[Wec06] A. Weckenmann, G. Peggs, and J. Hoffmann: 'Probing systems for dimensional micro-and nano-metrology'. *Measurement Science and Technology* (2006), vol. 17(3): p. 504 (cit. on p. 2).

[Wei09] T. Weise: *Global Optimization Algorithms – Theory and Application*. Germany: self-published, 2009 (cit. on pp. 25, 30).

[Wen10] J. Wenzel: *Mitsuba renderer*. `www.mitsuba-renderer.org`. 2010 (cit. on pp. 70, 102, 163).

[Whi79] T. Whitted: 'An improved illumination model for shaded display'. *Proceedings of ACM SIGGRAPH*. Vol. 13. 2. ACM. 1979: p. 14 (cit. on p. 77).

[Wika] Wikipedia, The Free Encyclopedia: *Airy disk*. `https://en.wikipedia.org/wiki/Airy_disk`. [Online, accessed 02-August-2018] (cit. on p. 87).

[Wikb] Wikipedia, The Free Encyclopedia: *Bayer filter*. `https://en.wikipedia.org/wiki/Bayer_filter`. [Online, accessed 15-August-2018] (cit. on p. 99).

[Yan13] X.-S. Yang and M. Karamanoglu: 'Swarm Intelligence and Bio-Inspired Computation'. Elsevier, 2013: pp. 3–23 (cit. on p. 28).

[Zha17] Y. Zhang, S. Song, E. Yumer, M. Savva, J.-Y. Lee, H. Jin, and T. Funkhouser: 'Physically-based rendering for indoor scene understanding using convolutional neural networks'. *Proceedings of IEEE Conference on Computer Vision and Pattern Recognition (CVPR)*. IEEE. 2017: pp. 5057–5065 (cit. on p. 65).

List of Figures

List of Tables

A Laser Detection Algorithm

The laser peak detection algorithm used in this thesis in based on the publication by Steger [Ste98] in 1998. This publication proposes a robust method to score the image locations which potentially include a ridge. A ridge is defined as a line or a curve in an image with some thickness. Let's assume the function $z(x)$ defines the intensity profile of the curve perpendicular to its direction. This function takes its peak value around the middle of the ridge profile x_{m} and the intensity drops approaching to the edges. As the intensity is maximum at $z(x_{\mathrm{m}})$, one criterion for detecting it is that the first derivative must vanish at x_{m}, i.e. $z'(x_{\mathrm{m}}) = 0$. However, this criterion alone is not robust enough to detect only the salient curves in the image. Another characterization of a salient ridge profile is the magnitude of the second derivative, which must be $z''(x_{\mathrm{m}}) \ll 0$.

To apply this idea, one needs to solve two issues. First of all, the first and second order derivatives of an image must be calculated, and secondly, the curve detection criteria must be applied in the direction of the ridge profile. The latter is because the ridge detection criteria discussed above are only valid when considering the profile perpendicular to the ridge direction.

A.1 Partial Derivatives of an Image

The first and second order derivatives of an image can be estimated by convolving the image with the corresponding derivatives of a Gaussian kernel. Under general assumptions, this kernel is the only alternative which makes the ill-posed problem of calculating derivatives of a noisy function well-posed [Ste98][Flo92]. The first order kernels are given as

$$g_x(x,y) = \frac{-x}{2\pi\sigma^4} \exp\left(-\frac{x^2+y^2}{2\sigma^2}\right), \tag{A.1}$$

$$g_y(x,y) = \frac{-y}{2\pi\sigma^4} \exp\left(-\frac{x^2+y^2}{2\sigma^2}\right). \tag{A.2}$$

And the second order derivatives are defined as

$$g_{xy}(x,y) = \frac{xy}{2\pi\sigma^6} \exp\left(-\frac{x^2+y^2}{2\sigma^2}\right), \tag{A.3}$$

$$g_{xx}(x,y) = \frac{x^2-\sigma^2}{2\pi\sigma^6} \exp\left(-\frac{x^2+y^2}{2\sigma^2}\right), \tag{A.4}$$

$$g_{yy}(x,y) = \frac{y^2-\sigma^2}{2\pi\sigma^6} \exp\left(-\frac{x^2+y^2}{2\sigma^2}\right). \tag{A.5}$$

Given an image $I(x,y)$, the first and second order derivatives I_x, I_y, I_{xy}, I_{xx}, and I_{yy} can be calculated by convolving the image with the derivative kernels above.

A.1.1 Ridge Direction

Steger proposes a method to detect the direction of a ridge by building the Hessian matrix

$$H(x,y) = \begin{bmatrix} I_{xx}(x,y) & I_{xy}(x,y) \\ I_{xy}(x,y) & I_{yy}(x,y) \end{bmatrix}, \tag{A.6}$$

and calculating its eigenvalues and eigenvectors for each (x,y) position on the image. The eigenvector corresponding to the eigenvalue of maximum absolute value indicates the perpendicular direction over the ridge, and its value scores the saliency of the ridge.

A.2 Detection of the Laser Profile

The laser detection algorithm in this thesis applies the Hessian matrix approach, to score the positions on the image with high chances of containing the laser profile. Image positions with high scores are then detected and the surrounding intensities of this point in the corresponding image column are selected for peak localization. Supposing an image column c contains a high ridge score at $I(i_c,c)$, the center of the peak profile i_m in this column with sub-pixel accuracy is estimated as given in the equation below.

$$i_m = \frac{\sum\limits_{k=i_c-N}^{k=i_c+N} k \times I(k,c)}{\sum\limits_{k=i_c-N}^{k=i_c+N} I(k,c)} \tag{A.7}$$

This method, which is commonly used for laser triangulation peak detection, is also known as the center of gravity or center of mass approach [Fis96]. Combination of this method with Steger's ridge detection method makes the laser localization robust to image noise.

Since a red laser line is used for triangulation in this thesis, the red channel of the color camera was always used for laser profile detection.

Publications

Journal and Conference Publications

1. **M. Mohammadikaji**, S. Bergmann, J. Beyerer, J. Burke, and C. Dachsbacher: 'Sensor-Realistic Simulations for Evaluation and Planning of Optical Measurement Systems'. *IEEE Sensor Journal* (2020), vol. TBA: pp. 1–14

2. **M. Mohammadikaji**, S. Bergmann, J. Burke, J. Beyerer, and C. Dachsbacher: 'Sensor-realistic simulation of images in diffraction-limited imaging systems'. *tm-Technisches Messen* (2018), vol. 85(s1): pp. 95–102

3. **M. Mohammadikaji**, S. Bergmann, S. Irgenfried, J. Beyerer, C. Dachsbacher, and H. Worn: 'Inspection planning for optimized coverage of geometrically complex surfaces'. *Proceedings of IEEE Workshop on Metrology for Industry 4.0 and IoT*. IEEE. 2018: pp. 52–67

4. **M. Mohammadikaji**, S. Bergmann, S. Irgenfried, J. Beyerer, C. Dachsbacher, and H. Wörn: 'Probabilistic surface inference for industrial inspection planning'. *Proceedings of IEEE Winter Conference on Applications of Computer Vision (WACV)*. IEEE. 2017: pp. 1008–1016

5. **M. Mohammadikaji**, S. Bergmann, S. Irgenfried, J. Beyerer, C. Dachsbacher, and H. Wörn: 'A framework for uncertainty propagation in 3D shape measurement using laser triangulation'. *Proceedings of IEEE Instrumentation and Measurement Technology Conference*. IEEE. 2016: pp. 1–6

6. **M. Mohammadikaji**, S. Bergmann, S. Irgenfried, J. Beyerer, C. Dachsbacher, and H. Wörn: 'Performance characterization in automated optical inspection using CAD models and graphical simulations'. *XXX Messtechnisches Symposium*. De Gruyter, 2016

7. S. Bergmann, **M., Mohammadikaji**, S. Irgenfried, H. Wörn, J. Beyerer, and C. Dachsbacher: 'A phenomenological approach to integrating Gaussian beam properties and speckle into a physically-based renderer'. *Proceedings of International Workshop on Vision, Modeling, and Visualization*. 2016

8. S. Irgenfried, S. Bergmann, **M., Mohammadikaji**, J. Beyerer, C. Dachsbacher, and H. Wörn: 'Image formation simulation for computer-aided inspection planning of machine vision systems'. *Proceedings of Automated Visual Inspection and Machine Vision II*. vol. 10334. SPIE, 2017

9. S. Irgenfried, H. Wörn, S. Bergmann, **M., Mohammadikaji**, J. Beyerer, and C. Dachsbacher: 'CAD-basierter Workflow für den semi-automatischen Entwurf optischer Inspektionssysteme'. *at - Automatisierungstechnik* (2017), vol. 65(6)

10. S. Irgenfried, H. Wörn, S. Bergmann, **M. Mohammadikaji**, J. Beyerer, and C. Dachsbacher: 'A versatile hardware and software toolset for computer-aided inspection planning of machine vision applications'. *Proceedings of Information Systems Architecture and Technology Conference*. Springer, 2018: pp. 326–335

Technical Reports

1. **M. Mohammadikaji**: 'Surface inspection planning for laser line scanners'. *Proceedings of the 2015 Joint Workshop of Fraunhofer IOSB and Institute for Anthropomatics, Vision and Fusion Laboratory.* KIT Scientific Publishing, 2015
2. **M. Mohammadikaji**: 'Towards surface inference in industrial inspection'. *Proceedings of the 2016 Joint Workshop of Fraunhofer IOSB and Institute for Anthropomatics, Vision and Fusion Laboratory.* KIT Scientific Publishing, 2016
3. **M. Mohammadikaji**: 'Automatic planning for optimizing the surface coverage in industrial inspection'. *Proceedings of the 2017 Joint Workshop of Fraunhofer IOSB and Institute for Anthropomatics, Vision and Fusion Laboratory.* KIT Scientific Publishing, 2017

SCHRIFTENREIHE AUTOMATISCHE SICHTPRÜFUNG UND BILDVERARBEITUNG
(ISSN 1866-5934)

Herausgeber: Prof. Dr.-Ing. habil. Jürgen Beyerer

Band 1 **JONATHAN BALZER**
Regularisierung des Deflektometrieproblems Grundlagen
und Anwendung. 2008
ISBN 978-3-86644-230-6

Band 2 **IOANA GHEŢA**
Fusion multivariater Bildserien am Beispiel eines Kamera-Arrays. 2011
ISBN 978-3-86644-684-7

Band 3 **STEFAN BRUNO WERLING**
Deflektometrie zur automatischen Sichtprüfung
und Rekonstruktion spiegelnder Oberflächen. 2011
ISBN 978-3-86644-687-8

Band 4 **JAN WASSENBERG**
Efficient Algorithms for Large-Scale Image Analysis. 2012
ISBN 978-3-86644-786-8

Band 5 **MARTIN GRAFMÜLLER**
Verfahrensfortschritte in der robusten Echtzeiterkennung
von Schriftzeichen. 2013
ISBN 978-3-86644-979-4

Band 6 **JÜRGEN BRAUER**
Human Pose Estimation with Implicit Shape Models. 2014
ISBN 978-3-7315-0184-8

Band 7 **MARKUS MÜLLER**
Szeneninterpretation unter Verwendung multimodaler Sensorik
und Salienzmaßen. 2017
ISBN 978-3-7315-0240-1

Band 8 **ROBIN GRUNA**
Beleuchtungsverfahren zur problemspezifischen Bildgewinnung
für die automatische Sichtprüfung. 2015
ISBN 978-3-7315-0313-2

Band 9 **THOMAS STEPHAN**
Beitrag zur Unterwasserbildrestauration. 2017
ISBN 978-3-7315-0579-2

Band 10 **JAN-PHILIP JARVIS**
A Contribution to Active Infrared Laser Spectroscopy for Remote Substance Detection. 2017
ISBN 978-3-7315-0725-3

Band 11 **MIRO TAPHANEL**
Chromatisch konfokale Triangulation – Hochgeschwindigkeits 3D-Sensorik auf Basis der Wellenlängenschätzung mit optimierten Filtern. 2018
ISBN 978-3-7315-0646-1

Band 12 **SEBASTIAN HÖFER**
Untersuchung diffus spiegelnder Oberflächen mittels Infrarotdeflektometrie. 2017
ISBN 978-3-7315-0711-6

Band 13 **MATTHIAS RICHTER**
Über lernende optische Inspektion am Beispiel der Schüttgutsortierung. 2018
ISBN 978-3-7315-0842-7

Band 14 **MATHIAS ZIEBARTH**
Wahrnehmungsgrenzen kleiner Verformungen auf spiegelnden Oberflächen. 2019
ISBN 978-3-7315-0890-8

Band 15 **JOHANNES MEYER**
Light Field Methods for the Visual Inspection of Transparent Objects. 2019
ISBN 978-3-7315-0912-7

Band 16 **MASOUD ROSCHANI**
Probabilistische Planungsverfahren für die deflektometrische Oberflächeninspektion. 2019
ISBN 978-3-7315-0907-3

Band 17 **MAHSA MOHAMMADIKAJI**
Simulation-based Planning of Machine Vision Inspection Systems with an Application to Laser Triangulation. 2020
ISBN 978-3-7315-0989-9
